ONE-DIMENSIONAL MARXISM

Althusser and the Politics of Culture

SIMON CLARKE
VICTOR JELENIEWSKI SEIDLER
KEVIN McDONNELL and KEVIN ROBINS
TERRY LOVELL

Allison & Busby
London and New York

First published in 1980
by Allison & Busby Limited
6a Noel Street, London W1V 3RB
and distributed in the USA by
Schocken Books Inc, 200 Madison Avenue, New York, NY 10016

Copyright © 1980 by individual contributors and
Allison & Busby
All rights reserved

Phototypeset in Times by Grainger Typesetters Ltd,
2 Carlton Court, Grainger Road, Southend-on-Sea, Essex
and printed in Great Britain by

British Library Cataloguing in Publication Data
    One Dimensional Marxism.—(Motive).
      1. Althusser, Louis
      I. Clarke, Simon   II. Series
      335.4'092'4   B2430.A474   80-40595
      ISBN 0-85031-367-8
      ISBN 0-85031-368-6 Pbk

Printed and bound in Great Britain by
Biddles Ltd, Guildford and King's Lynn

Contents

Introduction — 5

1 Simon Clarke — **Althusserian Marxism** — 7

2 Victor Jeleniewski Seidler — **Trusting Ourselves: Marxism, Human Needs and Sexual Politics** — 103

3 Kevin McDonnell and Kevin Robins — **Marxist Cultural Theory: The Althusserian Smokescreen** — 157

4 Terry Lovell — **The Social Relations of Cultural Production: Absent Centre of a New Discourse** — 232

For
Herbert Marcuse

Introduction

This book consists of four papers which have emerged from very different contexts and which have very different motivations. What they have in common is a rejection of the Althusserian interpretation of Marx and a reassertion of those elements of the marxist tradition that have been suppressed by Althusserianism.

These elements can be summed up by the three terms used by Althusser to describe the major deviations from marxist "orthodoxy": "humanism", or a belief in the creative potential of human beings, a creative potential that is stunted and alienated under capitalism; "empiricism", or the belief that there is no higher basis for knowledge than experience, so that the basis for a critique of capitalist society can only be the experience of the mass of the people oppressed and exploited under capitalism; and "historicism", or the belief that knowledge, being based on socially mediated experience and being validated through social practice, is necessarily the product of social conditions at a particular time and place, conditions which are historically relative and which can be changed by those who live under them. These ideas have always been subversive of dogmatic marxism, which attempts to abstract marxism from the historical experience from which it derives and attempts to give marxism an absolute authority as source of a knowledge of history that is inaccessible to those who live and make that history.

The authors of the papers that make up this collection believe that it is these subversive elements of marxism, dismissed as the unscientific "humanist", "historicist" and "empiricist" residues of "bourgeois" forms of thought, that are fundamental to the politically and intellectually liberating potential of marxism. The papers that make up this collection therefore share a rejection of the most fundamental tenets of Althusserianism. Each paper addresses Althusserianism in its own way, and reaches its own conclusions. None of the papers attempts to provide an alternative dogmatism, a new set of catch phrases, that purports to provide the secret of the universe. Individually and collectively what the papers do insist on is a consideration of the implications of the apparently "scientific" interpretation of marxism being proposed by Althusserians, and reconsideration of those elements of the marxist heritage that have been condemned in the name of "science".

The Althusserian movement is a very recent phenomenon, and yet it has come to dominate the interpretation of marxism, at least in the French- and English-speaking worlds Althusserian concepts have been assimilated into the discourse of many marxists who have never heard of Althusser and are used with such an easy familiarity that many believe they come from Marx himself. For many marxists the adequacy of the Althusserian interpretation of Marx is so self-evident as not to merit examination. And yet it is an interpretation that was formulated within the last two decades on the basis of a total rejection of previous "readings" of Marx, and it is only in the last five years or so that it has acquired a mass following. It seems very strange that a theory which rejects the entire history of marxism as a chronicle of errors, which claims that even Marx was not a self-conscious marxist, which rejects as irrelevant the experience of the working-class movement within which marxism has developed, and which finds the secret of marxism in various avant-garde (and often very esoteric) versions of psychoanalysis and philosophy of science, should be so rapidly accepted as marxist orthodoxy.

The extent to which this orthodoxy is unquestioned is shown by the strong anti-marxist movement now developing among disillusioned Althusserians who so identify Althusserian orthodoxy with marxism that in rejecting the former, often for good reasons, they reject the latter as well. In such a context it is of inestimable importance to dissociate marxism from Althusserianism, to insist that the reactionary elements of Althusserianism express its dogmatism, and to appeal for a serious re-examination of the truly revolutionary elements of the marxist tradition, embodied in the work of marxists vilified by Althusserianism and in the long history of popular struggles against economic, political and cultural oppression.

SIMON CLARKE
Althusserian Marxism

Introductory note

This paper has a long history. The original draft was written in 1970 on the basis of an attempt to relate *Reading Capital* to a reading of *Capital*. This was a task that I began with a certain limited sympathy for Althusser's interpretation, at least to the extent of agreeing that *Capital* is Marx's central work and of agreeing that *Capital* is not simply a work of economics. However it was a task that ended in total frustration as a result of a failure to find any substantial connection between *Reading Capital* (with the exception of Rancière's contribution that was suppressed in the second edition and in the English translation) and *Capital*. Drawing such a negative conclusion, and naïvely imagining that others would reach the same conclusion, I put the draft in my bottom drawer.

As the years went by it became clear that Althusserianism was not the passing fancy of a few avant-garde intellectuals, but that it was rapidly becoming a major intellectual current, indeed the dominant form of marxism among the generation of students and academics who encountered marxism after 1968. After some years of continuing fondly to imagine that it would go away of its own accord, I sat down in 1976 to take up my critique again. The paper that follows is the result.

It turned out that it was not a bad time to sit down to a critique of Althusserian marxism. In 1976 Althusserianism seemed to be at its highest point. Even marxists from non-Althusserian backgrounds were abdicating, either espousing Althusserianism or, tacitly or explicitly, abandoning hope for marxism. However, the tyranny of Althusserianism, expressed in its attempt to proclaim itself the only true faith, had also reached such a pitch that increasing numbers of marxists who had happily ignored Althusserianism began to question the Althusserian claims, diffidently at first, but with growing self-confidence over the last three years. This counter-current was given added strength by the fragmentation of the Althusserian camp into orthodox Althusserians, the followers of Lacan, of Foucault, or of various brands of Hindess and Hirst. The claim to represent the only true faith was weakened, as always, by the schismatic tendencies that offered a rapid proliferation of only-true-faiths, caricatured in its most extreme form by Hindess and Hirst, whose many publishers could not keep up with the succession of doctrinal reversals which they inflicted on their increasingly bemused flock.

The initial reception of this paper was mixed. I was very gratified by the enthusiastically positive response of those comrades with whom I was working and those who shared my rejection of Althusserianism, but at first these were few and far between. The most common response was one of surprise that anyone should reject the Althusserian enterprise *in toto,* as I was doing. This seemed to reflect the effectiveness with which Althusserianism has established its claim to represent the only true, scientific, anti-economist marxism, and to consign all other interpretations of Marx to the dustbin of history. Many who did not follow Althusser, or had little interest in doctrinal questions, still felt that Althusser was asking the right questions, even if his answers were inadequate or incomplete. Many disliked Althusser's own politics, or specific Althusserian claims, while still identifying the Althusserian project with that of Marx. The response from Althusserians was one of outrage, and newcomers to the debate should be warned that my interpretation of Althusser is by no means uncontentious. The paper was described in the following terms by anonymous readers: "almost entirely inadequate ... repetitively stated ... incoherent ... a bald series of assertions ... crude distortions ... misrepresentations ... grotesque misreading ... a form of intellectual dishonesty ... pathetic". A rather less sympathetic Althusserian reader considered it "the worst article I have ever read on Althusser ... the very worst kind of dogmatic, ill-informed polemic ... absolutely appalling ... a sloganising and dogmatic manner ... an absence of analysis . . .a series of totally unsubstantiated attacks ... the article is worthless ... nothing short of scandalous ... nonsense ... the most philistine and philosophically naïve epistemology . . . absolutely breathtaking . . ."

Since 1976 the paper has circulated quite widely in duplicated form, and has elicited increasingly favourable responses that seem to indicate that the ranks of the dishonest sloganising philistines are growing fast, and that more and more people are prepared to reconsider Althusserianism not in minor details but in its foundations. However, despite this groundswell it remains the case that it is Althusserianism that dominates the publishers' lists, and Althusserians who dominate among editorial advisers to those publishers prepared to consider marxist works.

In the last three years there have been considerable developments within Althusserianism, leading to a proliferation of small sects. Although some of these sects reject the divinity of Althusser, I continue to consider them Althusserian because their heresies arise out of the internal development of the faith. Thus the two-volume romp by A. Cutler, B. Hindess, P. Hirst and A. Hussain, *Marx's "Capital" and Capitalism Today,* counterposes the latest heresy to something identified as "marxist orthodoxy" which is nothing other than the Althusserian faith to which the authors originally adhered.

My paper was written before the emergence of the more recent Althusserian heresies, and so considered only the earlier work of Hindess and Hirst, *Precapitalist Modes of Production,* and that only in footnoted asides. In commenting on that work I must now admit that I occasionally caricatured it and attributed to Hindess and Hirst positions that they were not to adopt explicitly until their self-criticism. At the time this was a polemical device, drawing out the implications of their argument to show the absurdities they were led into. The force of this device was weakened when, to my amazement, Hindess and Hirst followed the logic of their arguments through to such absurdities. However, this paper is not concerned with the finer points of Althusserian doctrine, nor is it concerned to provide a complete account of Althusser's political and theoretical development. It is concerned with the foundations of Althusserianism laid out in his most influential works, *Reading Capital* and *For Marx.* For this reason, and because the paper has already been quite widely quoted, I have not made major changes in it for publication here.

Finally, a few words need to be said about the form of this paper. It is an interpretation of Althusser that, at the time it was written, was outrageous. It would be possible to support the interpretation by extensive quotation from Althusser's works, but extensive quotation could equally well be used to refute this interpretation. For this reason the form of the paper is that of a textual commentary on Althusser's major works, and I have made very little use of direct quotation. This means that the reader should easily be able to evaluate my interpretation for him or herself by turning to the original texts that I discuss. It is important to make this point in order to counter the charges of distortion or of falsification. I do not imagine that my readers are incapable of reading Althusser for themselves and making up their own minds, and I hope that the form of presentation that I have adopted will make this as easy as possible for them.

No paper of this length can offer a comprehensive account of Althusserianism, nor a comprehensive account of alternative interpretations of Marx. In this paper I concentrate on offering a critical interpretation of Althusser's two basic and most influential texts. In extensive footnotes, however, I also offer a more sketchy commentary that touches on later developments in the work of Althusser and of his followers, and on wider philosophical and theoretical tendencies to which Althusserianism is related. Those who are interested in the central interpretation and critique of Althusser can read the text without getting bogged down in the more esoteric points elucidated in the footnotes. Those who are interested in trying to situate Althusser's work in a wider perspective, or in relating the work of later Althusserians to the canonical texts, might find some of the footnote commentary suggestive or provocative, even if it does not provide rigorous analysis. The aim of the footnotes is to indicate the ways in which my interpretation of Althusser's central texts can also illuminate the other aspects of Althusserianism not touched on here.

In this paper I concentrate on Althusser's interpretation of Marx's theory of society, and particularly the Althusserian notion of the mode of production. I devote relatively little attention to Althusser's methodological discussions, or to his theory of ideology, both of which have been influential. Althusser's methodology, inconsistent as it is, seems to me to be quite unoriginal, offering banal versions of a range of the more esoteric versions of neo-positivism whose basic position of a separation of thought and reality ("theory" and "observation") leads in both cases to linguistic idealism of one form or another. This methodology has been extensively discussed elsewhere. In this context I would like particularly to recommend Edward Thompson's spirited defence of the empirical idiom in *The Poverty of Theory.* The importance of this work is that it addresses the methodological problems confronted by the practice of historical materialism and so satisfies the Althusserian's own insistence that philosophy cannot legislate for "science", but that each "science" has to define its own methods, an insistence systematically ignored in the ruminations of the Althusserian epistemological censors. I offer only brief footnote comments on the theory of ideology, but I hope that this gap is amply compensated for by the papers by Terry Lovell and by Kevin Robins and Kevin McDonnell in this volume. Finally, I have written elsewhere on the development of the Althusserian model by Poulantzas and by the "vulgar Poulantzians", and on the foundations of structuralism in the work of Lévi-Strauss.[1] Thus this paper is restricted in its scope and should be read not in isolation, but as a part of a growing movement of intellectual and political resistance to Althusserianism that cannot be glibly dismissed as the moralistic droolings of outraged bourgeois humanists to which the

Althusserians (like their political mentors) would reduce all opposition.

The interpretation of Marx that I offer in opposition to the Althusserians is characterised as broadly as possible in the hope that I can avoid counterposing one rigid orthodoxy to another. Marxism has been plagued since its inception by the fact that the leadership of marxist political movements has not trusted its followers to read Marx for themselves, but has insisted on offering predigested versions of Marx. I do not want to offer such a substitute in this paper. Thus the paper is at times very dense, because it is trying to deal concisely with major questions, and at times only suggestive, because it is trying to open up discussion of Marx's work and not to impose a new closure. If at times the tone of the paper is assertive and dogmatic this is because there are some points on which I think it is essential to make a stand, even if they cannot be elaborated in a brief space. However, I have no authority for my views beyond the texts that Marx has left behind and the mass of conflicting interpretations that have been a part of the living reality of the working-class movement. Thus I am more than happy for the reader to disagree, and if my tone stimulates disagreement and induces the reader to make up his or her own mind, then my aim would have been achieved. This paper is a polemic and not an encyclical, the aim of which is to ask people not to take Althusserianism at face value; to ask them to read Marx before *For Marx, Capital* before *Reading Capital,* and to read it not as the fossil form of the Logos but as the product of a lifetime's involvement in political and ideological struggle in which Marx sought to forge a weapon for the proletariat in the battle for socialism, a socialism which for Marx could only have a *human* face.

The argument

The development of capitalist crisis and of working-class militancy in the mid-1960s created the context in which left intellectuals in Britain, as elsewhere, developed an interest in the Marx of the working-class movement, turning away from the various attempts to interpret Marx in terms of a philosophy of the subject. This was the context in which Althusser replaced Sartre and Lukács as the "grid" through which Marx was read. At the time it seemed that Althusserianism was merely a passing phase, a stop on the way to Marx himself. However the Althusserian enthusiasm had lasted just long enough to leave a generation who had come to read Marx through Althusser, to substitute *For Marx* for Marx, *Reading Capital* for reading *Capital*. The legacy of this phase is not an Althusserian movement, as caricatured briefly by

Theoretical Practice, which lacked any political base. The legacy is found in a new orthodoxy in the interpretation of Marx, embodied in a series of concepts and assumptions whose Althusserian origins have been largely effaced. This is the new context in which it seems to me that a renewed critique of Althusserianism is necessary, a critique which focuses on the point which earlier critiques deliberately and specifically omitted, the question of the adequacy of Althusser's interpretation of Marx.[2]

In order to write such a critique it is necessary to find some basis on which the critique may be coherently presented. The most impressive attempt to impose a purely theoretical coherence on Althusser's work is that of Glucksmann, who sees Althusserianism as a variant of bourgeois metaphysical philosophy.[3] One could construct equally convincing accounts of Althusserianism as a variant of the Lacanian interpretation of Freud, in which the economic plays the role of Freudian unconscious, the political the role of the conscious, and the theorist that of the analyst.[4] One could add other structuralist influences to the Lacanian inspiration and see Althusserianism as an "overdetermined" system: the philosophy of the concept derived from Cavaillès,[5] the Lévi-Straussian conception of society as an "order of orders".[6] One could follow Poulantzas in seeing Althusserianism alternatively as an attempt to transcend the opposition between structure and history represented by the opposition between Sartre and Lévi-Strauss, attempting to historise Lévi-Strauss's structures by structuring Sartre's practice. All these constructions could be convincing, but all have to *impose* a coherence on Althusser, and none give him a marxist pedigree.

Examination of theoretical antecedents can reveal a host of contradictory influences on Althusser's work, but cannot reveal its *specific* foundations. However much Althusser may borrow from bourgeois theorists, his *starting* point is marxist, and, specifically, the marxism of the orthodox communist movement. There is no doubt that Althusser's work begins as a reconsideration of stalinist "dogmatism" in the light of developments subsequent to the Twentieth Congress of the CPSU, and represents an attempt to develop a critique of the "economism" of that dogmatism that does not fall into the twin "deviations" of "humanism" and "historicism".[7] These have historically been the terms which have been applied to the opposition to dogmatism from the right and from the left, forms of opposition that re-emerged in the communist movement in the wake of destalinisation. Hence Althusser seeks essentially to perpetuate communist orthodoxy, but to set that orthodoxy on a new foundation, and this explains his readiness to draw on sources which have hitherto been unorthodox for a communist. His entire work is characterised by the tension between the orthodox and the unorthodox, the two being brought together around the supposed focus of Althusser's work, the reinterpretation of marxist theory. This reinterpretation involves the invocation of a real, but hitherto unknown, Marx, who can only be recovered from the marxist texts through the grid of a "reading", which has in fact involved the abandonment of most of Marx's work as non-marxist, and the replacement of most of Marx's own concepts by others introduced by Althusser.

In this paper I want to establish that the interpretation of Marx proposed by Althusser in no sense represents a renewal of marxism. Rather I want to show that Althusser's attempt to refound a dispirited orthodoxy leads him inexorably to the adoption of theoretical and philosophical positions which can be rigorously characterised as "bourgeois". Hence Althusserianism offers familiar, if rather esoteric, bourgeois ideologies wrapped, often insecurely, in marxist rhetoric, which serves to give both bourgeois ideologies and stalinist politics an authentically marxist appearance. It is this duplicity which makes Althusserianism so dangerous, for it induces many sincere marxists to enter a labyrinth in which increasing frustration can lead them to abandon marxism itself.

In the first section I shall try to indicate theoretically the course which led Althusser from an attempt to find a new foundation for the authority of the intellectual within the party, and of the party within the working class, to the adoption of a bourgeois theory of society and associated bourgeois philosophy. I shall then try to establish the bourgeois foundations of Althusser's work by examining his and Balibar's main contributions.

Althusserianism, stalinism and bourgeois sociology
The context of Althusser's project is the period of destalinisation after the Twentieth Congress of the CPSU. For Althusser, as a philosopher, destalinisation meant the end of Zhdanovism, of subordination of philosophy to the party, and so the possibility both of recovering the professional respect of colleagues and of intervening in political activity on an independent basis, as an intellectual. The project which the Althusserians set themselves was the political restoration of the French Communist Party (PCF) through the restoration of the thought of Marx, seeking in the revolutionary experience of the Soviet Union in 1917, and of China in 1937, the lessons which, mediated by theory, could underpin a rational politics in France in the 1960s. This project rested on a belief, also expressed in the introduction to *For Marx*, that the political errors of the PCF were to be explained by its lack

of theory, a lack of theory which made the Party very vulnerable to theoretical and practical "opportunism" in the event of its abandonment of stalinist dogmatism.[8] This project apparently begins, therefore, with an innocent return to the texts of Marx.

The innocence of this return is, however, only superficial. Althusser does not approach the works of Marx, Lenin or Mao as a disinterested student of the texts. These works provide only an authority to which he, as an intellectual, can refer to support an ambition which is already inscribed in his political project. The starting point of Althusser's project is the critique of the crude economism and evolutionism of stalinist dogmatism, while avoiding those interpretations dubbed "humanist", which Althusser sees as being simply the other face of economistic interpretations, the two united in their "historicist" understanding of the marxist dialectic. Althusser's initial project is therefore to purge marxism of all traces of "historicism".

Rancière argues very convincingly that whatever original political ambition the critique of stalinist dogmatism may have had, the project soon became its own justification. Since Althusser was committed to the transformation of the PCF from within, it was necessary for him to find an authority for his theory higher than that of the party, which had hitherto ruled in such matters. His work, therefore, soon comes to be dominated by the need to find in Marx the justification not directly for his politics, but for his project of intellectual subversion. The basis of his "antihistoricism" is therefore the need to establish the autonomy of theory and the authority of the theorist. This underpins the early insistence on the separation of marxist philosophy from historical materialism, the defence of the autonomy of "theoretical practice", the insistence on the priority of dialectical over historical materialism and so of philosophy over politics, as well as the later transformation of the definition of philosophy which altered these relationships, but left the position of theory and the theorist unchanged.

Rancière argues that Althusser's project soon finds itself in a hopelessly contradictory position. In order to subvert the PCF from within on the basis of the authority of theory and in the absence of a significant political base, it is necessary to have the confidence of the leadership of the party. Until theory has achieved the transformation of the party, it is necessary to subordinate oneself to the leadership of the party in order to be able to continue the process of theoretical subversion. The long-term strategy of theoretical subversion of the dogmatism which continued to dominate the PCF demanded a short-term tactic of accommodation to, if not defence of, the theses of the leadership of the PCF. It is this contradiction which, as Rancière shows, illuminates another series of fundamental Althusserian distinctions: the separation of ideology, within which politics is fought out, from science, of an empirical from a theoretical rhetoric.[9] These distinctions make it possible for Althusser to dissociate his theoretically subversive formulations from their apparent political implications, a technique which is apparent in his essay "Marxism and Humanism", in *For Marx,* and which was used to counter the accusation of Maoist tendencies on the appearance of the essay "On the Materialist Dialectic".[10]

Rancière charts the progressive inversion of tactical and strategic considerations in Althusser's work from 1963 onwards. It was in 1963 that Althusser made his only direct political intervention, objectively on behalf of the leadership of the PCF, attacking the nascent student movement for its challenge to the integrity of science. This attack had serious consequences for the subsequent development of the student movement in its creation of an "authoritarian left" current which stood above the revolt of the students and young workers. From this time the attack on "economism" was veiled, all Althusser's polemics being aimed at "humanism" and "historicism", theoretical tendencies which the cognoscenti knew to be complementary to "economism", but which also happened to represent the internal opposition to the PCF leadership from the right and from the left.[11] The subversive elements of Althusserianism became increasingly esoteric, while the attacks on "humanism" and "historicism" strengthened the leadership they were supposed to undermine, providing a means of restoring the authority of that leadership among the intellectuals by attacking its political opponents in the name of the texts of Marx and Lenin and not directly of the authority of the party. The crunch came in 1965, with the publication of *Reading Capital*. This work came under sharp attack from the PCF leadership not for the attack on "historicism", which was the esoteric radical element in the work (but which, as we shall see, can equally have reactionary implications), but for the autonomy which was attributed to theory, precisely Althusser's defence against the subordination of his intellectual project to the dictates of the political leadership of the party. The latter was worried because the left leadership of the Communist students' organisation, the UEC, was using similar arguments to defend its right to political autonomy. It could not therefore tolerate a competing authority in the interpretation of Marx, even if that authority was Marx himself. In response to just criticism, Althusser reissued *Reading Capital* with the omission of the more scandalous texts, and made his self-criticism in *Lenin and Philosophy.*[12]

I do not outline this sordid history as the basis of an *ad hominem* critique, but because it is necessary to an understanding of the origins of Althusserianism. When Althusser undertook the task of regeneration in the early 1960s, to counterpose Marx to the party as an authority was a very radical move. Althusser almost immediately came under pressure from within the party, the result of which was that Althusser's project came to be focused entirely on establishing its own possibility by establishing the autonomy of theory. With Althusser's self-criticism the autonomy of theory in relation to the party, and with it the attempt to put forward an original interpretation of Marx, was effectively abandoned. His serious work is therefore largely confined to his period of independence from 1960 to 1965.

In this period the attempt to establish the autonomy of theory through the reinterpretation of Marx led to the imposition of a particular conception of society on Marx's work. Hence the particular, and rather parochial, ambition of Althusser's reinterpretation acquired a much wider significance. The tragedy of Althusserianism is that the conception of society in question is that which dominates both stalinist dogmatism and bourgeois sociology.

Rancière focuses his critique on the affinity between Althusser's conception of the relation between theory and politics and the mechanical materialist conception which Marx destroyed in his "Theses on Feuerbach". However the affinity between Althusser's work and the dominant forms of bourgeois ideology is both broader and more fundamental than this.

The link between Althusser's particular ambition and his adoption of a bourgeois ideological conception of society is very direct. Althusser's particular ambition is to establish the autonomy and authority of mental over manual labour. This relationship between the mental and the manual is, however, a peculiar characteristic of capitalist production relations. In order to show, therefore, that this peculiar characteristic of capitalism is socially necessary, Althusser has recourse to a theory which establishes the social necessity of capitalist production relations themselves, and this "eternisation" of capitalist relations of production is precisely the defining characteristic of bourgeois ideology. Thus it is that Althusser follows mechanical materialism in confusing the social and technical divisions of labour: in identifying the separation of mental from manual labour, and the subordination of one to the other, with the technical requirements of production with an advanced divison of labour, and not with *the domination of capital over labour and the associated appropriation of the creative powers of labour by capital.* This confusion is the basis of a series of ideologies which serve to justify the subordination of labour: to capital in bourgeois ideology, to the reformer in utopian socialism, to the party and to the state in stalinism. It is the ideological foundation of the eternisation of bourgeois relations of production, constituted in its classical form by the political economy whose definitive critique was made by Marx and whose renunciation is the necessary basis of any authentic marxism.[13] Let us look more closely at this ideology.

Classical political economy bases itself on a distinction between production, which is seen in technical terms as the realm in which labour sets to work means of production to make products, and distribution, in which the product is transformed into revenues which accrue to the various classes in society. Relations of distribution are therefore superimposed on production as the social framework within which material production takes place. In the capitalist mode of production the superimposition of relations of distribution on relations of production is achieved simply by ascribing revenues to factors of production and assigning classes to these factors as "owners". It is therefore ownership of the means of production which provides the foundation for the major distributive classes of which society is composed. This conception of society is based on the "trinity formula", the form of appearance of bourgeois relations of production according to which the "factors of production" are the sources of the revenues of the component classes of society. It is a form of appearance which eternises bourgeois relations of production, because it makes them appear as relations already inscribed in the technical structure of the material production process. It is an *ideology* because it postulates as eternal that which is historically specific, it is a *bourgeois* ideology because what it postulates as eternal is the bourgeois production relation. In so far as such eternisation of bourgeois relations of production is the *sine qua non* of bourgeois ideology, in the rigorous sense of that term, it is this conception of society which is the foundation of all bourgeois ideology.

This conception of society, although it is fundamentally bourgeois, can also be found underlying certain ideologies which have played a major role in the working-class movement. The relation between Ricardianism and utopian socialism is well known. Utopian socialism is characterised by the above bourgeois conception of society, basing itself on a *moral* critique of bourgeois relations of *distribution*, and so aiming at the transformation of relations of distribution without any transformation of bourgeois relations of production, the revolution being introduced from *outside* because of the necessarily *moral* basis of the utopian critique. At a later stage of capitalist development "economism" gave this bourgeois conception a new radical twist. Bourgeois relations of distribution continue to be founded on the technical relations of bourgeois production, but the socialisation of production, conceived as an increasing technical scale of production, leads progressively and naturally from competitive capitalism through monopoly capitalism to state capitalism, which is equated with socialism. Economism has a more scientific appearance than utopianism had. In reality, however, it has no scientific foundation at all, for it is simply not the case that the socialisation of production can be reduced to technical concentration, nor that the latter increases without limit. Hence the adoption of this "economistic" version of socialism, by basing itself on a conception of society which is in turn founded on the eternisation of capitalist relations of production, has the perpetuation of such relations as its practical consequence. This economism entered the Russian working-class movement through Plekhanov and Menshevism, and was criticised, though not unambiguously, by Lenin. In the wake of the revolution and the NEP, this economism crept back into the CPSU in the form of stalinist dogmatism, providing the means within the Soviet Union to establish the identification of development of the productive forces with the development of socialism and to establish the authority of the state, as representative of the social character of the process of production, over the isolated workers who are only its technical agents.

Marx's most fertile years were devoted to the elaboration of the critique of classical political economy. In this critique Marx shows that the errors of political economy derive from its conception of production. For Marx the relations of production are not separated from and contrasted with material production as an externally derived *form* imposed on a pre-existent *content.* Production is seen as a process which is indissolubly social and material, *production both of material products and of social relations.* Moreover this unity is not a harmonious unity, at least in a class society, but is a *contradictory unity:* the *contradictory unity of the forces and relations of production.* In a capitalist society this contradictory unity exists in the specific historical form of the contradiction between production as *the production of value and as the production of use-values.* It is this contradiction which Marx identifies at the beginning of *Capital,* in the "Hegelian" first chapter, where it is located at the heart of the commodity. The clear distinction between value and use-value, located in the "elementary form" of capitalist wealth, makes it possible for Marx to develop *for the first time* the contrast between concrete useful labour and abstract value-creating labour, the point which "is crucial to an understanding of political economy" because it underpins such concepts as "labour power", "constant and variable capital", and "surplus value". The latter concept, is, for example, transformed. It is no longer seen as the revenue which accrues to a distributive class as its share of the material product. It is now seen as the product of the labour process as a process of production of value, of the *compulsion* imposed on the worker within the labour process to work beyond the time necessary to reproduce the value of his or her labour power:

> We now see that the difference between labour, considered on the one hand as producing utilities, and on the other hand as creating value, a difference which we discovered by our analysis of a commodity, resolves itself into a distinction between two aspects of the production process.
>
> The production process, considered as the unity of the labour process and the process of creating value, is the process of production of commodities; considered as the unity of the labour process and the process of valorisation, it is the capitalist process of production, or the capitalist form of the production of commodities.

This understanding of production therefore makes possible a theory which gives exploitation and class relations an *objective* foundation in production instead of a *subjective* foundation in a particular moral evaluation of the justice of relations of distribution.

The *contradictory* foundation of production is the key to the marxist theory of history and to the marxist concept of the totality. First, the *"law of motion" of capitalism,* expressed (perhaps misleadingly) in the tendential "law" of the falling rate of profit and the countervailing tendencies it calls forth, expresses the concrete *historical development* of the fundamental contradiction. Secondly, the relations of production are from the beginning *social* relations, "the relations of production in their totality constitute what are called the social relations, society, and specifically, a society at a definite stage of historical development."[15] There is, therefore, no question of reductionism in taking the relations of production as the starting point for the analysis. The determination of social relations as relations of production is *the specific and determinate historical process by which social relations are subsumed under the dominant relation of production and so are determined as developed forms of that relation.* The basis of this process is the contradictory foundation of production which constantly forces capital beyond the immediate process of production in order to accomplish its valorisation. In *Capital* Marx shows this rigorously for distribution, circulation and even consumption as moments of the total process of social production which are *subsumed historically* in the relations constituted around the immediate process of production, subordinated to the production of value as moments of the process of valorisation of capital. Correspondingly, the social relations of production appear in specific economic, political and ideological forms, and their determination as moments of the "relations of production in their totality" can only be through their historical subsumption under the dominant relation of production in the development of the contradiction on which that relation is based, the analysis of which can establish concretely both the *forms of domination* of social relations by the capital relation and the *specific limits* of that domination.

It is very important to stress the fact that Marx is concerned with the concrete historical development of the fundamental contradiction, with specific and determinate historical processes, and not with the necessary development of the concept, whether this is interpreted in the Hegelian sense of the dialectical development of the Idea or in the positivist sense of the deductive elucidation of the fundamental postulates of the theory. Marx is developing a theory of real human history, he is not attempting to legislate for history, to dictate theoretically what history can and cannot be. It is in this sense that marxism is not a historicism: it does not seek to formulate either analytical or dialectical laws of historical development. Hence the contradictory foundation of production underlies the historical development of a society based on that form of production, but the contradiction cannot determine its own outcome. Thus even the "absolute general law of capitalist accumulation" is immediately qualified: "like all other laws, it is modified in its working by many circumstances."[16] For example, the "law" of the falling rate of profit does not determine that the rate of profit will fall. What it does determine is that an increase in the organic composition of capital, effected by, for example, the concentration or centralisation of capital, will lead to a fall in the rate of profit *unless* it is compensated by an increase in the rate of exploitation. Hence the law tells us to expect that the concentration and centralisation of capital will be associated not with a necessary fall in the rate of profit, but with the most strenuous efforts on the part of capital to increase the rate of exploitation by increasing the productivity of labour, by intensifying labour or by lengthening the working day. This law is not the logical elaboration of the concept, it is the theoretical formulation of a fundamental aspect of the everyday experience of the working class. In exactly the same way social relations are subsumed under the dominant relation of production not in a logical reduction which dissolves the specific characteristics of those relations, but in a specific historical process through which capital, institutionalised (it must be added) in the capitalist enterprise, seeks to overcome the social barriers set to its valorisation and in so doing *tends* to seek to turn the whole of society into a machine for the production of surplus value. This is a specific historical process, it is a tendency that is resisted, and it is a contradictory process in which the barriers are never finally overcome. Hence the domination of capital in any particular society has specific limits, those limits being historical limits that are established through struggle and that cannot be defined in advance. It is *to the extent that* any particular social relation has been historically subsumed under the capital relation that it can be considered as a form of that relation, and only to that extent. This subsumption is never determined in advance, it is always contested, and it has constantly to be reimposed if it is to be maintained. Thus Marx is not trying to develop a predictive theory that can reduce the world to a set of formulae, he is trying to develop a deeper understanding of the forces in play in order to intervene more effectively to change the world: "The philosophers have only *interpreted* the world, the point, however is to *change* it" wrote Marx in the last of his "Theses on Feuerbach", and presumably he meant it.

The errors of economism derive directly from its failure to grasp the significance of Marx's critique of classical political economy, and so from its retention of the bourgeois conception of production which characterises the latter. On the one hand, the *separation* of the forces and relations of production abolishes the dialectical relation between the two aspects of the process of production, so that the primacy of production takes the form of a technological determinism which necessarily rests on the metaphysical foundation of dogmatic claims about the nature of the world. On the other hand, because the "forces and relations of production" are seen as technical relations of production on which are superimposed social relations (of distribution), the *contradictory* foundation of production, and so the basis of the marxist theory of history, is abolished. Instead we have a relation between the "forces and relations of production" which is alternately one of correspondence and dislocation, and the theory of history is replaced by a metaphysical law of history, the "dialectic", seen as a mechanical, extra-historical law which determines history as a succession of modes of production by governing the progressive, and exogenous, development of the forces of production which underlies it, each mode being defined ahistorically by the specific *form of appropriation* of the surplus (rather than form of *production*) appropriate to a particular level of development of the productive forces. The stalinist theory of modes of production, its separation of dialectical from historical materialism, and its evolutionism are all consequences of the adoption of the bourgeois conception of production.[17]

There can surely be no doubt that the starting point of any attempt to restore marxism must be the critique of this dogmatic version of marxism. To this extent Althusser's project does at least begin at the beginning, even if it does not make its true objective explicit. Althusser is also quite right to point out that not every critique of economism is a marxist critique. In particular, even if we might doubt the political motives and the wider theoretical implications of his attack, Althusser is quite right to point out the complementarity of the "humanist" critique to the "economist" deviation it sought to transcend. To this extent Althusser is quite right to attack the "historicism", that is to say the metaphysical philosophy of history, characteristic of both "economism" and "humanism". However the question we have to ask of Althusser is whether he actually gets to the root of these "deviations", whether he offers a fundamental critique which will enable us to restore its authentically revolutionary character to marxism, or whether he rather offers us a renewed version of dogmatism, deprived of its most "scandalous" dimensions, to accompany the elimination of the most "scandalous" aspects of stalinism in the renewal of the revisionism of the PCF.

In his *Reply to John Lewis* Althusser spells out for the first time his understanding of the "stalinist deviation". He sees stalinism as a renewal of the economism of the Second International, "the *posthumous revenge of the Second International*". He also sees this economism as a *bourgeois* deviation, determined as a moment of the economism-humanism couple which is supposedly characteristic of bourgeois ideology. Finally, he notes that this ideology is bourgeois because it eliminates the relations of production and the class struggle. Althusser presents these findings, which have, in one form or another, long been almost a commonplace among marxist critics of stalinism, as an original and tentative discovery ("this is only a hypothesis"). However, we must give Althusser credit for recognising the economism of stalinism, even if he did so rather late. But we now come to the heart of the matter. We have to ask whether Althusser offers us a marxist critique of this ideology.

The answer is that he does not. To see this we must look at the way Althusser appears to understand this couple. Althusser does not provide a *theoretical* critique of the couple at all. He argues that the complementarity of the elements of the couple is based on the complementarity of the "economism" of the capitalist's ideology and the "humanism" of legal ideology, the law being the point at which the two are joined as a pair. The "economism", in the sense of *the concept of the economic on which economism is based,* is not questioned at all by Althusser. As I shall argue in this paper, Althusser retains the bourgeois conception of production at the core of his version of marxism. The implication of Althusser's critique is that his objection is to the *reductionism* of both economism and humanism, and not to the concept of production on which they are based. This is the sense in which he regards "historicism" as the foundation of both "economism" and "humanism". These two deviations are based on the illegitimate generalisation of their specific orientations to society of the lawyer and the capitalist. This is, correspondingly, why the focus of Althusser's interpretation of Marx is the nature of the marxist totality, for he is seeking a non-reductionist concept of the whole as a structured combination of elements which can, in a sense, *reconcile* "humanism" and "economism". The error of stalinism is not, therefore, founded in its conception of production, but in its conception of the totality, not in its understanding of the economic, but in its attempt to reduce the "relative autonomy" of other "instances" of the whole. Althusser is trying to develop a non-metaphysical conception of the whole in which the bourgeois (metaphysical) concept of production can continue to find a place.

It is not surprising that Althusser is unable to provide a theoretical critique of the "economism-humanism couple", for in the course of his critique he rejects as "ideological" precisely the theory which Marx developed to provide this critique, the theory of commodity fetishism. The couple is not constituted at the level of the law, on the basis of the complementarity of the capitalist and the lawyer, but at a much more fundamental level, that of the commodity. The theory of commodity fetishism shows us precisely how, in the exchange of commodities, social relations appear in the form of relations of *subjects* to *things*. To put the point "philosophically":

> Circulation is the movement in which the general alienation appears as general appropriation and general appropriation as general alienation. As much, then, as the whole of this movement appears as a social process, and as much as the individual moments of this movement arise from the conscious will and particular purposes of individuals, so much does the totality of the process appear as an objective interrelation, which arises spontaneously from nature; ... circulation, because a totality of the social process, is also the first form in which the social relation appears as something independent of the individuals, but not only as, say, in a coin or in exchange value, but extending to the whole of the social movement itself. The social

relation of individuals to one another as a power over the individuals which has become autonomous... is a necessary result of the fact that the point of departure is not the free social individual.[18]

It is the theory of commodity fetishism that makes it possible to understand the ideological significance of the law, and it is the theory of commodity fetishism that enables us to penetrate the ideological "humanism-economism couple" and so to criticise it by transforming our conception of social relations, and not by simply rearranging them into a new type of whole.

Rancière's critique of Althusser brings out very clearly the *political* significance of Althusser's approach to stalinist economism. Fundamentally Althusser's theoretical relation to economism reproduced the relation of orthodox communism to the politics of stalinism. From the point of view of the orthodox communist parties in the 1960s destalinisation involved a break with the methods of the stalinist period, without a fundamental break with its politics. The "excesses" of the stalinist period found their justification in arguments which rested on reductionism and evolutionism, which made it possible to defend any policy as necessary means to an inevitable end. Destalinisation involved an abandonment of the reductionist evolutionism of stalinism, so making it legitimate to question the means employed (and this is precisely how Althusser poses the question in his *Reply to John Lewis* — stalinism involved the adoption of unjustified means in pursuit of unquestionable ends). This limited freedom of manoeuvre, however, could not throw into question the authority of the party and the inevitability of socialism. Althusserianism offered the party one means of defending its position, by justifying the authority of the party on the basis of its scientific understanding of the "conjuncture" rather than its privileged relation to an inevitable future, and by basing the inevitability of socialism on political and not "economic" factors and so dissociating the coming revolution from the crisis of capitalism. This latter dissociation of economic from political struggle and of economic from political crisis must prove very attractive for a party which is seeking precisely to retain control of growing working-class militancy on the shop floor and to establish its political moderation in a period of capitalist crisis.[19]

It would be absurd to reduce the appeal of Althusser's work to a narrow concern of the leadership of the French Communist Party. The major appeal of Althusserianism has been to young intellectuals, particularly in academic institutions, most of whom have no affiliation with the Communist Party, and most of whom would no doubt seek to dissociate Althusser's politics from his theoretical "achievements". We therefore have to understand the basis of the appeal of Althusserianism to these intellectuals. Certainly it has a superficial appeal in responding to the most outrageous aspects of stalinist dogmatism, in having a superficially advanced and sophisticated character, in offering a central place in the revolutionary process to the intellectual, while devaluing those ("economic") working-class struggles from which the intellectual is excluded, and in having a rhetorical "ultra-leftist" dimension in asserting the ubiquity of a "class struggle" which is related only in the "last instance" to the "economic struggle". However, it is difficult not to believe that serious marxists would feel distinctly uneasy that the deeper appeal of Althusserianism is not to their political, but to their bourgeois intellectual instincts. On the one hand, Althusserianism rigorously reproduces both the division into academic "disciplines" and the relations of authority of the bourgeois academic institution. On the other hand, Althusserianism rigorously reproduces the familiar doctrines of bourgeois sociology and philosophy, and in particular the dominant forms of each, structural-functionalism and neo-positivism. The reasons for this convergence are not hard to find, for bourgeois sociology is based precisely on the rejection of the "evolutionist economism" of marxism, and so is preoccupied with the articulation of the levels of a complex whole, while bourgeois philosophy is based on the rejection of the "historicism" of marxism, and so is preoccupied with the eternal status of scientific truths. (I am not *reducing* sociology and philosophy to their central ideological preoccupations. It is *in so far as* these are their concerns that they are *bourgeois*.)

Bourgeois sociology follows classical political economy in being based on a conception of production as a technical process which underpins the eternisation of capitalist relations of production and so characterises this sociology rigorously as a form of bourgeois ideology. Contemporary structural functionalism, like Althusserianism, rejects a crude technological determinism. It follows classical political economy in basing itself on the *distinction between the technical relations combining factors in material production and social relations of distribution, constituted by ownership of the means of production, which are mapped on to the relations of production.* The former cannot, however, be reduced to the latter, for they involve the relation of "ownership" which is defined politically and/or ideologically. Social relations cannot therefore be reduced to technical relations. The starting point of sociology cannot therefore be the "economy", the relations of production, for this only exists within society. The starting point can only be the pre-given whole, "society". On this basis structural-functionalism defines a variety of different levels according to the functions they fulfil in relation to the whole. The identity of functions and levels varies from one account to another, but the basic principle is unchanged. The differentiation of functions determines that each level should have its own specificity and its own autonomy relative to other levels. The different functions are hierarchically ordered, the technical requirements of material production normally being primary because of the supposed primary requisite of physical reproduction. The hierarchy takes the form of limits imposed by one level on the variation of other levels. Within these limits of variation the different levels are themselves structured under the dominance of their relative functions in the whole, and not under the dominance of other levels. They are therefore determined as levels of the complex whole, and not as expressions of other levels.[20]

Bourgeois philosophy rests on similar ideological foundations. I have already noted the historical foundation of the subject-object relation in commodity fetishism. More specifically, with its secularisation, philosophy acquires the primary role of defender of the scientific claims of bourgeois ideology (that is to say, of guarantor of those "truths" of bourgeois science which are "held to be self-evident" and so which cannot be established by those sciences themselves). The contemplative character of bourgeois science, which is based on the bourgeois separation of mental from manual labour, becomes the basis on which the authority of science is established ideologically. The historical character of the concepts of science is systematically effaced and they are given an eternal reality of their own. Hence the bourgeois philosophy of science is focused precisely on legitimating the supposedly universal character of historical categories and of giving particular truths an eternal status. This is as much the case with nominalism or conventionalism, for which no reality corresponds to the categories of science, as it is with positivism, for the categories whose validity is relative remain themselves equally, or even *more* securely, absolute. Hence bourgeois philosophy is admirably suited to Althusser's task, which is precisely to establish the authority of his own version of science.[21]

In other disciplines, as I shall indicate in passing in this paper, Althusser reproduces the most avant-garde positions of bourgeois ideology. In this paper I shall concentrate on Althusser's theory of society, since others have discussed his philosophy at length. The importance of Althusser in other fields should not, however, be ignored. In particular, in political science Althusserianism, as interpreted by Poulantzas, offers a marked convergence with the approach of systems theory.[22] In the study of cultural phenomena

Althusserianism legitimates the most avant-garde forms of neo-Freudianism, in terms of the supposed *univeral* function of ideology, the "interpellation of the subject".

This reproduction of the most avant-garde theoretical positions of the contemporary bourgeois social sciences must go a long way to explaining the appeal of Althusserianism to young intellectuals, for many of the latter come to marxism in response to the inability of the bourgeois disciplines to cope with the radicalisation of the intellectuals which has underlain the contemporary "crises" in those disciplines. It is easy for Althusserianism to capture these intellectuals, for it offers an easy familiarity embedded in a radical rhetoric which claims familiar themes for marxism. This is the great danger which Althusserianism poses, for it is also characterised by the same dead-ends, and the same empty circles as the theories that have been rejected. If Althusserianism is taken for marxism, the responses of many will be a rejection of marxism along with bourgeois theories, and a turn to the more congenial familiarity of empiricism. If marxism is to capitalise on the "crises" in the social sciences it is essential that Althusserian marxism be revealed for what it is — a superficially radical rhetoric within which the discredited doctrines of the bourgeoisie find their last (latest?) resting place.[23]

In this paper I shall look at Althusser's most important works, *For Marx* and *Reading Capital*, in order to establish that Althusser's work is consistently underpinned by a conception of the relations of production which is, in the strict sense, bourgeois. As a result of this Althusserianism reproduces the arguments of bourgeois ideology. My critical comments on Althusser will largely be directed to establishing this connection between the conception of production and the reproduction of bourgeois sociological and philosophical positions, and with showing schematically that the marxist concept of production, developed in Marx's critique of classical political economy, has quite different implications for the theory of society and for philosophy. Limitations of space dictate that the latter arguments are necessarily only indicative. In the last analysis it is not my formulation of Marx's critique of political economy that I would like to counterpose to Althusserianism, but that of Marx himself. This critique was the quite self-conscious product of ten years of work in which Marx knew precisely what he was doing. Its recovery does not require a "symptomatic" reading, but a naïve one, a reading which pays attention to what Marx says, *and what Marx says he is saying,* without reading Marx through the grid of bourgeois ideology. If "marxists" would only read Marx, and particularly Marx's critique of political economy in *Capital* and in

Theories of Surplus Value, forgetting about his "absences" and "silences" until they have mastered the clear and insistent arguments that are *present* in his work, Althusserianism would become no more than a bad memory.[24]

In looking at *For Marx* and *Reading Capital* I shall show how the attempt to establish the autonomy of theory leads to a bourgeois interpretation of Marx. *For Marx* reproduces the anti-reductionist arguments of bourgeois sociology, *Reading Capital* reproduces the anti-historicist arguments of bourgeois philosophy, before attempting to "dehistoricise" the stalinist concept of the mode of production. I shall begin with a brief look at the displaced anticipation of future positions in Althusser's essay on Montesquieu.

The project defined

In retrospect we can already see Althusser's project at work in his essay on Montesquieu. This essay broaches the subject of Marx's dialectic obliquely, by attributing to Montesquieu himself the discoveries which are later seen as marking Marx's scientific revolution. In this essay we learn that Montesquieu did not have a circular expressive totality, but a totality in which there was determination in the last instance by the "principle", but in which the reverse effectivity of the "nature" on the "principle" was possible within certain limits.[25] This conception is then compared to that of Marx: "In both cases it is a matter of a unity which may be harmonious or contradictory, in both cases this determination does nevertheless cede to the determined element a whole region of effectivity, but subordinate effectivity." This essay also discovers a way of breaking with historicism that was later adopted by Balibar in *Reading Capital*. The unity of nature and principle of the state may be either adequate or contradictory. In the latter case the state form will change. Hence we have a dynamic but non-teleological totality.[26]

This essay leads us already to question the marxist character of Althusser's most fundamental concepts, when he can find these concepts in the work of the *mechanical materialist* Montesquieu. The concept of determination in the last instance is particularly illuminated by this essay, for it is clearly given a mechanical interpretation here: the last instance limits the free variation of the other instances, but within these limits it has no privileged effectivity. The last instance is therefore seen in essence as an *external* restriction on the range of possible forms, but in no way as determining within this range. Thus the concept of "relative autonomy", as autonomy within limits, is already prefigured in this essay. The essay strikingly confirms Rancière's argument that Althusser assimilates Marx to mechanical materialism.

We can deal very briefly with the first two essays in *For Marx* which mark the tentative and exploratory beginnings of Althusser's return to Marx. The first essay introduces the discussion by noting the Feuerbachian problematic embedded in Marx's early works.[27] The second essay, "On the Young Marx", explicitly attacks the economistic foundation of stalinism for the first time. However, the attack is focused on modes of understanding Marx's work, rather than on Marx's work itself. The essay introduces the concepts of the "problematic" and the "epistemological break".

The essay attacks "historicist" interpretations of Marx's work, introducing a caricature of Hegel as a surrogate for "economism", and affirms the scientific character of Marx's work as well as the political need to return to that work. However, the project is defined in terms of the renunciation of ideological problematics in favour of a return to reality: it is the *idealist* character of the historicist interpretation which is challenged here, in its belief in the coherence of the world of ideology. This idealist historicism is criticised in terms of a materialist historicism, a logic of the irruption of real history in ideology itself: according to Althusser Marx did not change problematics, but broke with ideological problematics as such, to found science directly on an encounter with reality.[28]

This formulation may be closer to Marx than later versions, but it was inadequate for Althusser's purposes for several reasons. First, the historicist conception of ideology will always threaten to swamp a positivist conception of science and so threaten the autonomy and the integrity of theory because there is no way of *guaranteeing* the break with ideology, and so history, in any particular case. Secondly, the conception of science, which comes "within a hairsbreadth of 'positivism'",[29] leaves no place for the philosopher to play an independent role as theoretically (later politically) informed arbiter of scientificity. Thirdly, the mode of attack on stalinism, which is to reduce stalinism to "historicism" and to assimilate "historicism" to "Hegel", dictates that Althusser complete the elimination of "historicism" from his interpretation. These preoccupations soon come to prevail in the Althusserian interpretation of Marx.

In the essay "Contradiction and Overdetermination" Althusser develops his attack on economism, now coming into the open and attacking the vulgar notion of history as the simple expression of the basic contradiction between forces and relations of production. This latter notion is assimilated to Hegel through the concept of inversion, so that the essay focuses on the relations between Marx's and Hegel's dialectics, the problem being that of the specificity of the marxist dialectic. Althusser's basic argument is that if Marx had simply inverted the Hegelian dialectic, he would have remained within the ideological problematic of Hegelian philosophy.[30]

The specific properties of Marx's concept of dialectic are expressed in the concept of overdetermination. The Russian revolution did not take place because in Russia the contradiction between forces and relations of production had reached its highest point of development, but because of an "accumulation of circumstances and currents" which "*fuse* into a ruptural unity", making it possible for the general contradiction...to become *active* in the strongest sense, to become a ruptural principle". The contradiction is therefore very complex, this complexity being expressed in the concept of overdetermination:

> The *unity they* [the accumulation of "contradictions", "circumstances", "currents"] *constitute* in this "fusion" into a revolutionary rupture, *is constituted by their own essence and effectivity,* by what they are, and according to the specific modalities of their action. In *constituting* this *unity,* they *reconstitute* and complete their basic animating unity, but at the same time they also bring out its *nature:* the "contradiction" is inseparable from the total structure of the social body in which it is found, inseparable from its formal *conditions* of existence, and even from the *instances* it governs; it is radically *affected by them,* determining, but also determined in one and the same movement, and determined by the various *levels* and *instances* of the social formation it animates; it might be called *overdetermined in its principle.*[31]

Returning to Marx, Althusser argues that Marx does not simply invert Hegel's dialectic, but changes both its terms and its relations. The terms civil society and state are replaced by the ideas of mode of production, social class and state. Instead of a dialectic in which the superstructure is an expression of the structure, Althusser introduces the notions of "determination in the last instance by the (economic) mode of production" and "the relative autonomy of the superstructures and their specific effectivity."

This essay is of central importance in establishing the framework within which discussion of the marxist dialectic will take place. It is therefore essential to isolate the basis of the critique of stalinism in play here. It is worth pointing out initially that it is not based on any examination of the works of Marx or of Lenin. It is rather based on the observation that many different "circumstances" and "currents", sometimes referred to as "contradictions", were in play in the Russian revolution, and that these currents and circumstances cannot be *reduced* to the status of *expressions* of a basic contradiction. The problem is therefore that of the relation of the "contradictions" in play in a "current situation" to the basic contradiction. Economism is unable to explain the object with which Althusser has confronted it, so an alternative conception of the dialectic is called for.

The power of Althusser's argument hangs on the appropriateness of the problem he poses. This problem is not a theoretical problem: the series of currents each with its own essence and effectivity is presented to theory as a given, not itself subject to a critical examination which is reserved for the concept of the dialectic. The explanation of the revolution is already given. Russia was the weakest link because "it had accumulated the largest sum of historical contradictions then possible." This sum is explained by the fundamental contradiction of being "the most backward and the most advanced nation", which in turn alludes to the fact that Russia was "pregnant with two revolutions."[33] Russia's revolutionary situation is therefore explained ultimately by her revolutionary situation — the perfect circle of empiricism.

The explanation of the Russian revolution is not in question. We already know all the complex factors which act as "effective determinations". As marxists we also know that "of course the basic contradiction dominating the period...is active in all these 'contradictions' and even in their 'fusion'".[34] The problem is to reconcile the two theoretically. But if the "effective determinations" are known independently of the dialectic, this dialectic can be no more than an empty rhetoric, a declaration of faith in the universal, but invisible, power of the marxist dialectic. For Althusser the account of the "effective determinations" is the given to which the dialectic must be moulded. The concept of overdetermination is therefore counterposed to the concept of expression on the basis of the principle of the irreducibility of the "real" (i.e. the world of appearances). Where does this principle come from? Far from being a marxist principle, it is the cardinal principle of bourgeois empiricism. In effect this principle asserts that the world is as it appears in bourgeois ideology, so that the object is already given in that ideology. Marx asserts that *the world cannot be identified with this appearance, and so to understand the world is to offer a critique of its forms of appearance, forms expressed in the categories of bourgeois ideology.* Althusser's objection to economism reproduces the objection of bourgeois empiricism and not that of marxism.

In view of Althusser's arguments that marxism is not an empiricism it is important to be very clear what is meant here by *bourgeois* empiricism. The error of bourgeois empiricism is not, as Althusser would have us believe, that it seeks knowledge of reality. For most people this is not "empiricism", for it is virtually a tautology: the concept of knowledge implies a reality that is known (even if that reality is spiritual). The error of bourgeois empiricism is that it mistakes its own ideological preconceptions for reality, thus it gives us knowledge only of its ideological preconceptions: instead of taking reality for its object, it takes its given object for the real. For Marx, therefore, what appears at first as the "real" is reducible, not because Marx is a metaphysician who wants to find ideal essences beneath reality, that are in some sense more real than reality, but because the appearances must be subjected to critical examination to discover whether or not they accord with reality. Thus the error of bourgeois empiricism is that it is insufficiently critical of its own preconceptions. Marx does not counterpose his own privileged vision of reality to the mystical illusions of bougeois ideology, he counterposes the concept of the critique to the concept of the given, so it is through a critique of the preconceptions of bourgeois ideology that Marx arrives at a more adequate basis for knowledge, and more adequate can only mean more adequate *to reality*. Bourgeois ideology is not merely a particular point of view, it is a point of view that is *false*.[35]

Althusser does not question the fundamental concepts of stalinism, and in particular the economist conception of production which underlies its conception of the contradiction between forces and relations of production as the *precondition* of history. He rather seeks to develop an alternative concept of the whole which will relate the economistic "relations of production" to history in a *non-reductionist* manner. Thus this critique focuses not on the concept of production, but on the question of the *"complexity"* of a whole which both is and is not subject to determination by the economic. The "complexity" of this whole expresses the contradictory requirements imposed on it.

Althusser's critique of economism calls to mind the alternative approaches to Ricardianism of Marx and of vulgar economy. Ricardo's theory of value led him into a contradiction, for he sought to identify the forms of surplus value (profit and rent) immediately with surplus value itself, despite the fact that the two contradicted one another. Vulgar economy responded to Ricardo's "reductionism" by abandoning any attempt to develop the critique of immediate appearances, and so abandoned Ricardo's theory of value. Marx, on the other hand, offered a *critique* of Ricardianism's metaphysical concept of value, making value a social, historical, phenomenon, and rigorously relating the forms of appearance of surplus value to surplus value as *transformed forms,* founding the contradictory relation between the two in the development of the contradiction inherent in the commodity itself. Althusser, faced with the contradictions of economism, follows vulgar economy in making the appearance the measure of all things, and so in effectively abandoning the law of value, which is the specifically capitalist form of the contradiction between forces and relations of production, by abandoning it to the last instance which never comes, instead of subjecting the metaphysical dogmatist formulation of the law to a marxist critique.[36]

The point can be made by looking not at a superficial account of 1917, but looking at the specific features of leninism in that context. Lenin did not have the problem of discovering a formulation of the dialectic sufficiently "sophisticated" to relate an accumulation of already given "contradictions" to a fundamental contradiction. Lenin's problem was precisely the opposite, it was the problem of locating, in all their complexity, the conflicting social forces in play in Russia in 1917. The essential conflicts and their interrelations were not immediately apparent, but were only located on the basis of a rigorous marxist analysis which started from the fundamental contradiction introduced by the mode of domination of capital over Russian society. It was this analysis which enabled Lenin to locate the fundamental class divisions in Russia, most notably in *The Development of Capitalism in Russia* and in *Imperialism,* and to locate the relation between the resulting conflicts, expressed in the objective (because founded in the relations of production) unity of the slogan "Bread, Peace and Land". Far from taking the "currents" and "circumstances" as given, Lenin subjected them to a rigorous examination. It was only *to the extent that* the Bolshevik Party located the fundamental cleavages in Russian society as *different forms* of the same fundamental contradictiton that the "ruptural unity" created by the Bolsheviks was an objective rather than an opportunistic unity. Lenin's marxism consists not only in his faith in an ability to *create* a unity from the given currents and circumstances, but also in his understanding that a successful socialist revolution depends on the *objective foundation* of such a unity.

The next essay, "On the Materialist Dialectic", seeks to give some substance to the claims of "Contradiction and Overdetermination" while at the same time responding to criticism by seeking to establish the autonomy of theory. This dual aim makes the essay confusing.

The essay starts with a conception of the "social formation" as being composed of a series of levels, the levels being defined as practices. The determinant practice is "material production". Practice itself is defined as "any process of *transformation* of a determinate given raw material into a determinate *product,* a transformation effected by a determinate human labour, using determinate means (of 'production'). In any practice thus conceived, the *determinant* moment (or element) is neither the raw material nor the product, but the practice in the narrow sense: the moment of the *labour of transformation* itself, which sets to work, in a specific structure, men, means and a technical method of utilising the means".[37]

The discussion of this conception of the social formation is actually centred on one pivotal practice, namely theoretical practice. Within theoretical practice "Theory" is central: the "Theory of practice in general", "in which is theoretically expressed the essence of theoretical practice in general, through it the essence of practice, and through it the essence of transformations, of the 'development' of things in general". Theory is the guardian of orthodoxy in both theoretical and political practice.[38]

Having established the centrality of Theory, Althusser proceeds to establish its autonomy. This is achieved by insisting that the determinant moment of theoretical practice is the means of theoretical labour — "'theory' and method", so that theoretical practice is not dominated by either its raw material or its product.[39] Altusser further insists that the structure of practices within which theoretical practice is inserted is complex, bringing us back to the overdetermined complex whole. Althusser tells us no more about this whole, beyond the denial that his is a pluralist conception since the unity of the whole is not sacrificed. It is simply that the unity is "the *unity of the complexity itself*", which sounds very like the contingent unity of the world of appearances. This unity also, we are assured, implies domination: *"the complex whole has the unity of a structure articulated in dominance"*.[40]

The originality of this essay lies in its introduction of a particular concept of "practice" as a central concept of marxism. The concept is not, however, introduced on the basis on a reading of Marx, *but quite explicitly in order to establish the autonomy of "theoretical practice"*. The reason for this is also clear — the essay in question is a response to criticism from within the PCF. The response to criticism is not a defence of positions taken, but a defence of the autonomy of theory.

This small fact is of enormous significance for understanding Althusser's marxism, for it is from this pragmatic origin that a completely new version of Marx is developed to provide the outer defences of the autonomy of theory. This version of Marx does not derive from a *"reading"* of Marx at all, but from the need to invent a Marx who can defend the isolation, autonomy, and authority, of theoretical activity. The link between the two is provided by the concept of *practice,* and the link is plain in this essay, for the interpretation of Marx is proposed very clearly on the basis of a discussion of "theoretical practice". In order to establish the autonomy of theory Althusser introduces a conception of practice in which practice is defined as *concrete practical activity,* which involves the *abstraction of this practical activity from the social relations in which it is inserted,* so that it becomes trivially the case that any and every practice in Althusser's sense is autonomous, for the connection between practices has been dissolved. Hence the apparently very concrete concept of practice offered by Althusser is in fact an ideological abstraction, for it abstracts from the social relations within which any practice must exist. In generalising this result to all other practices, Althusser generalises the ideological conception of production, and the associated conception of society, which is implicit within it: the conception of production as a concrete practical activity independent of the social relations within which it is inserted. In adopting the liberal defence of the autonomy of science, Althusser adopts the liberal view of society which accompanies it.[41]

The obviousness of the centrality in marxism of the concept of practice, as defined by Althusser, does not bear very close examination. This can be brought out most clearly if we look at what Althusser calls "material" production. The application of the general concept of practice to the practice of material production gives us a definition of the labour process in which men work up nature with means of production. In this process the labour of transformation is first said to be the determinant moment, but we soon find that we have to "abstract from men in the means of production", so that it is the means of labour which are determinant.[42] This claim is asserted with respect to theoretical practice, and generalised to other practices. The term "determinant" is given no content, for we are never told *what* is determined by the means of labour. Far from being obvious that the labour process is determined by the means of labour, this is in general not the case, but is rather *a specific historical achievement of the capitalist mode of production.* In other modes the labour process is "determined" by labour, and not by the means of labour. In capitalist society the labour process is determined by capital and the domination of the means of labour is one form of this determination.[43]

It is impossible to conceptualise this in the Althusserian framework, for the reduction of production to the labour process as a process of production of use-values *implies the exclusion from society of the capitalist,* who is conspicuous by his absence from the labour process, *and so of the fundamental relation of production of capitalist society.* In the obviousness of the bourgeois concept of practice there is no room for the relations of production, so that the process of production comes to be seen as a purely technical process. The identification of the dominance of capital with some supposedly natural domination by the means of production, inscribed in the "essence of practice in general", implies the eternisation of capitalist relations of production, which is precisely why this conception of production is at the base of bourgeois social science.

The domination of Althusser's "marxism" by this bourgeois conception of society extends to his conception of the relation between the various practices which makes up the whole. The social whole comprises four fundamental practices: material production which transforms nature, political practice which transforms social relations, ideological practice which transforms consciousness, and scientific practice which transforms notions into knowledge. The latter three practices are related through their their objects: they represent different modes of appropriation of the "current situation", which can make their differentiation rather difficult at times. Theoretical practice grasps the social whole in thought in order to inform political practice, which can then transform that whole in action. The product of theoretical practice therefore acts as means of production of political practice, whose product in turn provides raw material for theoretical practice. Political practice is therefore the "real *condensation*, the nodal strategic point, in which *is reflected the complex whole* (economic, political and ideological)".[44]

In this whole material production is said to be determinant in the last instance. This is, as least initially, conceived in the mechanical way already identified in the essay on Montesquieu. The ("economic") mode of production dictates, with the force of natural necessity, certain modes of distribution, consumption and exchange, and certain relations between the economic, political and ideological. In other words the (economic) mode of production determines the *limits* of the autonomy of the political and the ideological by imposing certain constraints on the "political and ideological social relations", and by assigning certain functions indispensable to economic production to the political and ideological levels.[45]

In this conception the political and theoretical (whether scientific or ideological) represent the concrete acts in which the social world is practically and mentally appropriated.[46] It is the world of the social actor of sociology. The economic, by contrast, represents the appropriation of nature, the world of material production of the bourgeois economist.[47]

The "determination in the last instance by the economic" turns out to represent simply the bourgeois theory of functional prerequisites, with the pre-requisites hierarchically ordered, material production and reproduction being the most fundamental. The Althusserian critique of the supposedly planar quality of the Hegelian theoretical space certainly leads us to a structural conception, but it is the conception of the bourgeois social sciences. Althusser's "practice" is simply the desocialised production of the classical political economists, or the ahistorical social action of contemporary sociology. Althusser follows bourgeois social science in divorcing capitalist social relations from their historical foundation and seeks instead to found them in an ahistorical concept of practice, just as political economy gave them an eternal foundation in the nature of production, and sociology in the nature of social action. It is the similarity of *The Structure of Social Action* to the structure of practice that explains the uncanny resemblance of the complex whole structured in dominance to *The Social System*.[48]

The Althusserian conception of the social whole has important political implications. The separation of production, as the realm of necessity, from the "political" and "ideological", or distribution and exchange, as the social realm immediately implies that political intervention in the former is fruitless, while in the latter it is proper and possible. In exactly the same way bourgeois sociology regards production as non-problematic, confining its attention to "reproduction", itself seen in exclusively "social" terms. The "economic" struggle is necessarily defensive, confined by relations of production which it cannot challenge, concerning only the rate of exploitation.[49]

While the capital relation, according to this ideology, cannot be challenged directly, political action can act on and transform the whole. This "over-politicisation" of the theory means that it is always ultimately "historicist", in the sense that in the explanation of history it always has ultimate recourse to the consciousness of a historical subject.[50] This is not a return to the left historicism of the self-conscious class subject. Class consciousness cannot be revolutionary for Althusser since ideology necessarily obscures the character of the social relations which a revolutionary practice must transform.[51] Only a revolutionary scientific theory can guide revolutionary politics, the Party being the means by which theory takes command of proletarian politics. Guided by this theory, the Party can establish the political significance of a particular "current" or "circumstance", can identify it as a "displacement", a "condensation" or a "global condensation" of the fundamental contradiction (rather than a petty-bourgeois adventure). The revolution must therefore be entrusted to the immense theoretical labour of the scholar-hero, not to the supporting cast of millions, and must wait on the specific "temporality" of theoretical practice. This is precisely the bourgeois materialist conception, characteristic of utopian socialism, which Marx criticised in the third thesis on Feuerbach.

Althusser's "self-criticism", which removes Theory from its pedestal and gives it to the "proletariat", doesn't improve matters for the philosopher alone can extract it from the normal state in which it is contaminated by bourgeois ideology. Thus Althusser argues, against Vico, that history is "even more difficult to understand" than nature "because 'the masses' do not have the same *direct practical* relation with history as they have with nature (in productive work), because they are always separated from history by *the illusion that they understand it . . . between* real history and man there is always a screen, a separation, a *class ideology of history*". Hence marxist science can only be discovered by the philosopher who brings the class struggle into theory, and grasps the class struggle through theory. This is the "contribution of communists to science" (and to the "masses"), and it sounds very like a renewed form of Zhdanovism.[52]

It is fundamentally because Althusser does not question the bourgeois conception of the "economic" that he does not break with economistic politics, for the marxist critique of the bourgeois conception of production transforms the associated conception of politics. If bourgeois relations of production are treated as technical relations, they cannot be challenged politically. The struggle of the working class at the level of production cannot affect the social relations within which production takes place, but can only limit the rate of exploitation. The political struggle is therefore dissociated from the struggle at the point of production, and concerns political and legal measures to transform class relations, which are supposedly constituted by "ownership" of the means of production. The marxist concept of production, by contrast, leads to a quite different understanding of politics. On the one hand, it sees *in social production* the foundation of the reproduction of the capital relation, and so the foundation of resistance to the capital relation. On the other hand, it sees the bourgeois state as a developed form of the capital relation, in the sense that the bourgeois state is seen as a mediated expression of the domination of capital, whose effectiveness is therefore subordinate to the dominant relation of production. A *revolutionary,* as opposed to a purely insurrectionary, politics has therefore to combine the struggle at the point of production with the struggle for state power in such a way that the domination of capital in all its forms can be overcome. Thus a marxist politics has to overcome in practice the separation of "economics" and "politics" which Marx overcame in theory. And it should go without saying that Marx could only overcome it in theory because the working class was *already* overcoming it in practice.[53]

Marx rediscovered: Reading Capital
Reading Capital seeks to realise the project mapped out in *For Marx* of establishing an "anti- historicist" interpretation of Marx. The project is dominated by the need to defend the autonomy of scientific theoretical practice. It is therefore essential to show that the autonomy of theory was the cornerstone of Marx's work. This is attempted in the first essay of the book.

According to Althusser Marx's epistemological break consisted in his breaking with the empiricist conception of knowledge, defined as the identification of the "real object" and the "object of knowledge", which is also the foundation of "historicism".[54] Once the object of knowledge and the real object have been radically distinguished from one another, of course, it is a simple matter to keep historicism at bay. Althusser's argument is based on the trivial and insignificant observation that theoretical practice is an empirically distinct practice. Hence it is based once again on the principle of the "irreducibility of appearances". Althusser seeks to demonstrate that this radical distinction is found in Marx by distorting quotations from the 1857 Introduction and by insisting that Marx's own theoretical revolution took place entirely within thought. I shall deal with the latter point first.

Marx's epistemological break entailed a transformation of the "problematic" of classical political economy. What was the basis of this transformation, if it was effected purely within thought? The answer is that the new problematic is a mutation of the old, which is already implicit within the latter. The new problematic is produced, therefore, not by Marx, but by the old problematic itself.[55] The Hegelian autogenesis of the concept is replaced by the autogenesis of the problematic as subject of theoretical practice. Instead of the dialectical *development* of the contradiction we have its analytical *elimination*, giving a ruptural, rather than continuous, but no less teleological account of the history of theory.[56] Real and rational are divorced, the former only intervening in the latter in so far as scientific practice is subverted by the intrusion of extra-scientific "interests".[57] Marx freed the problematic of political economy from the intrusion of bourgeois interests, so making possible the autodevelopment of the problematic which had hitherto been blocked. The political implication is clear and intentional: preserve the autonomy of science.[58]

The specific argument is absurd. While it is true that classical political economy is inconsistent, it is not true that this inconsistency determines a particular direction of theoretical development: the same inconsistency led to the replacement of classical political economy not only by marxism, but also by neoclassical economics. There is no sense whatever in which the concept "labour power", nor any of the other fundamental concepts which Marx introduced, is implicit within the classical discourse. The specificity of Marx's concepts in relation to those of the classics *is defined by the transformation of the concept of production* from one in which social relations between classes were superimposed on technical relations between factors to one in which the two constitute a contradictory unity. In the classical conception exploitation concerns the *distribution* of a given product. In Marx's conception exploitation dominates the *production* of that product. In the classical conception there is no contradiction between the technical relations of production and the social relations of distribution, nor is there conflict within production, for production and distribution are separated from one another. In Marx's conception production of use-values is subordinated to the production of social relations, in the capitalist mode of production to the production of *value,* so that there is a contradiction within production, and the forces and relations of production constitute a *contradictory* unity, in the capitalist mode of production the contradictory unity of production as production of *value* and as production of *use-values*. There is no way in which Marx could have arrived at this conception of production had he been confined to speculative thinking, to the world of theory.

Althusser's argument is based on the separation of thought and reality. This leads him to accept without question the basic formulation of the classical problem of knowledge, a formulation in terms of the confrontation of a knowing subject with the object to be known.[59] In the Althusserian variant the subject and object are known as "theoretical practice" and the "concrete-real". The fact that Althusser dissociates his "subject" from the empirical human subject which is its "support" in humanist philosophy does not prevent him from reproducing the bourgeois philosophy of the subject: the history of bourgeois philosophy for the last hundred years has been dominated by the attempt to achieve precisely this dissociation. The fundamental problem which Althusser's philosophy has to face is that of bourgeois philosophy, that of reuniting subject and object, real-concrete and concrete-in-thought. Within such a theoretical field the reunion can only be achieved metaphysically, by God, Nature or the Party. It makes no difference whether this metaphysical philosophy of guarantees is its own justification (original definition of philosophy) or is endorsed by the Party (revised definition).[60]

This philosophy of knowledge is bourgeois in the strict sense because of its connection with the eternisation of the bourgeois relations of production, which is the defining feature of bourgeois ideology. This eternisation is based on the extraction of these relations of production from historical reality and their fixation as the given presupposition of history. Relations of production are turned into a fixed metaphysical category whose objective foundation is no longer historical but must be established by philosophy as eternal. The bourgeois ideological conception of society therefore calls forth a philosophy whose task is to provide the *a priori* foundation for the fixed, eternal, and so ideal, categories of that ideology, a philosophy which must be analytical rather than dialectical, and based on the radical separation of thought and reality. It is in this sense that we can call such a philosophy a *bourgeois* philosophy. This philosophy will have its variants. A crude reductionism will call forth a crude positivism to justify its claims that the absolute, the technical relations of production, is also real. A more sophisticated theory which takes the "mode of production" of "society" for its starting point must reject such a crude positivism, for the starting point, "society" or the "mode of production" is an abstraction to which no reality corresponds. In either case the relation between the abstract determinations and the concrete as the "concentration of many determinations" is not seen, as it is for Marx, as the *historical* relation between fundamental relations and their historically developed forms, but as the *epistemological* relation between theory and reality. The question of the materialist dialectic in this version of "marxism" has to be settled by philosophical and not by historical investigation because the basic concept of marxism has been plucked out of history and transformed into an eternal category of thought.

Marx rejected the "theoretical field" of the classical philosophy of knowledge, the conception of the relation of men and women to the world in terms of a universal subject-object opposition. Hegel had first shown the way to overcome this opposition, but he did so only formalistically, identifying the two immediately and seeing the objective as the "immanentisation" of the subjective. In putting the Hegelian dialectic on a materialist foundation Marx overcame this opposition in a historical and a materialist way, not dissolving it in thought, but rather establishing the foundation of the opposition in a real historical process in which the subjective and objective moments are dissociated from one another. Specifically, the philosophical opposition of subject and object is the expression in philosophy of the contrast between the two moments of exchange which develops with the development of commodity relations (cf the quotation from the *Grundrisse* on page 25 above). The theory of commodity fetishism provides the means by which the essential unity of subject and object can be recovered, while at the same time grasping the opposition between the two categories as a specific historical form of appearance of social relations. Marx's conception of the commodity as a "sensuous-supersensuous"[61] unity perfectly captures this characteristic of the social, providing the means to reveal the ideological character of "the problem of knowledge". It is an idealist fiction to imagine that the world can be the direct object of the *contemplation* of some subject, and it is correspondingly an idealist fiction to conceive of ideology or knowledge in terms of a *vision* of the world, whether that of the empirical subject or of the "problematic" which possesses him or her. *The world can only be the direct object of practical engagement in the world, just as the subject can only exist in such engagement. Contemplation can only be the one-sided appropriation of a part of the social practice of a sensuous-supersensuous person,* and so is marked by the character of that social practice. Thus the difference between bourgeois and marxist political economy is essentially a difference between two class practices. However, it is not fundamentally the difference between the criteria of science applied by different classes, nor the difference in class "interests". The difference is between the different practices in which different classes are engaged and from which the notions that form the starting point of theoretical reflection are abstracted. Bourgeois political economy takes as its starting point the notions in which the bourgeoisie thinks its own practice, which are the notions embedded in that practice. Its apologetic character is founded in the trinity formula on which it is based. Marxist political economy, by contrast, reflects on the practical activity of the proletariat under capitalism.[62] Its superiority over bourgeois political economy does not lie in a claim to truth as against falsity, nor in its identification with the "negative moment" of the dialectic of history, nor in its renunciation of the intrusion of class interest, but in its ability to comprehend the class practice of the bourgeoisie as well as that of the proletariat, expressed in its ability to comprehend bourgeois political economy. These are the terms in which Marx conducted his critique of political economy.

In order to establish that Marx renounced Hegelianism in separating the order of reality from the order of knowledge, Althusser takes the unusual step of looking at Marx's work, specifically the 1857 Introduction. This is a strange choice of text, since it is overwhelmingly, and quite self-consciously, Hegelian in inspiration.[63] Marx is here trying to locate the implications of the materialist critique of the Hegelian dialectic before setting out on the project that would culminate in *Capital*. The text is therefore of exceptional interest, but can hardly be used if one wants to *distance* Marx from Hegel. The importance of the text must be qualified by the observation that it does not represent a reflection on the accomplished marxist dialectic, but rather an "anticipation of results", whose achievement would take another ten years.[64] We should not, therefore, regard this text as a substitute for the actual operation of the marxist dialectic in *Capital*.

Althusser concentrates on the third section of the Introduction. In this section Marx is looking at the consequences of the abandonment of the Hegelian proposition that the real is the product of thought, a proposition based on the *conflation of* thought and reality. In the course of his argument Marx notes that it is a *"tautology"* to say that "the concrete totality is a totality of thoughts, concrete in thought, in fact a product of thinking and comprehending". Hegel's error lies not in this tautological observation, but in his seeing the "concrete in thought" as a "product of the concept which thinks and generates itself outside or above observation and conception" instead of seeing it as a "product, rather, of the working up of observation and conception into concepts". Since Marx has only just noted that the "real concrete" is the point of departure for observation and conception, it is quite clear that Marx does not intend to separate thought and the real, but taxes Hegel with effecting this separation on the basis of a tautology. In the same vein Marx notes that even for speculative thought which does not engage with the real world the subject, society, *rather than the concept*, remains the presupposition. Althusser defends his separation of "thought" and "reality" by picking up these Hegelian "tautologies" and attributing them to Marx.

Althusser also picks up on Marx's discussion of the relationship between the order of categories in the development of the analysis and the order in which they appear historically in order to establish the "anti-historicist" character of Marx's conception of theory. Marx points out Hegel's confusion of "the way in which thought appropriates the concrete" with "the process by which the concrete itself comes into being". This confusion leads Hegel to seek to analyse the relations between the elements of contemporary society in terms of "the historic position of the economic relations in the succession of different forms of society". This identification of the order of appearance of categories with their contemporary relationship is a double error. First, the order of *historic appearance* of the categories does not correspond to the order of their "*historic position*" (i.e. in which they were "historically decisive"). It is only retrospectively that we can use the abstract categories to understand previous forms of society. Secondly, the development of new relations is not necessarily subordinate to existing relations, but may subordinate the latter and so *transform* the structure of the totality and not simply *develop* it. For example money exists before capital, expressing the "dominant relations of a less developed whole", whereas it subsequently expresses "those subordinate relations of a more developed whole which already had a historic existence before this whole developed in the direction expressed by a more concrete category".

Althusser concludes from this section that "the production process of knowledge takes place entirely within knowledge", despite the fact that the whole section is quite explicitly concerned with the "historical existence" of the categories and not with their theoretical production, arguing not that their order is determined within knowledge, but that it is "determined, rather, by their relation to one another in modern bourgeois society".[65]

What Marx criticises in this passage is not Hegel's "historicism", his search for a relation between the historical and theoretical development of the categories. It is the *ideological* character of Hegel's solution, which projects on to history the dialectic of contemporary society, to which he objects because it makes contemporary society into the pinnacle of history: "the so-called historical presentation of development is founded, as a rule, on the fact that the latest form regards the previous ones as steps leading up to itself, and, since it is only rarely and under quite specific conditions able to criticise itself . . . it always conceives them one-sidedly". It is *because the dialectic is located solely in thought* that Hegel can project the order of categories of contemporary society, which express their relation in contemporary society, on to history.[66]

Hegel's errors which Marx locates in the 1857 Introduction do not derive from his identification of real and ideal, but from the *specifically idealist form* of this identification which leads him to see the dialectic as being located entirely in thought. The form of the dialectic cannot be constructed in theory, but requires a prodigious labour of historical investigation to uncover it. *What Althusser identifies as Marx's breakthrough is precisely what Marx identifies as Hegel's error!* The implictions of the simple "inversion" of Hegel's dialectic, which Althusser derides, are far-reaching. Thus, while the mystical side of Hegel's dialectic was easily identified in principle, its practical criticism was "no trifle".

The extraction of the rational kernel did not consist in discovering a new "abstract and idealist" form, but in divesting the "real content" of any such form, for the materialist dialectic is the "real course of history itself".[67] The form of the dialectic could not be discovered in theory, nor in "history" as the realisation, manifestation or representation (*Darstellung*) of a dialectic which lies *outside* it. It is the elimination of the *idealist foundation* of the Hegelian dialectic that is the immediate basis of the complexity of the marxist dialectic. The first part of the 1857 Introduction makes this clear, arguing that the Hegelian dialectic tends to reduce the complexity of the totality of moments of the process of social production, seeing these moments as unmediated identities. The materialist foundation of the marxist dialectic means that there is no possibility of discovering beneath the mediations of the process a more fundamental identity of its moments.[68] Marxist dialectic thus differs from the Hegelian in that its mediations are real, reality offering a *resistance* to the development of real contradictions which cannot be dissolved in thought but which must be overcome in reality. The Marxian dialectic is thus dissimulated, not in the form of the *presentation* of the Lacanian unconscious, but in the mediated form of *the historical development* of the materialist dialectic.

Elimination of the idealist foundation of the Hegelian dialectic implies the renunciation of the temptation to accomplish purely formal reductions of the complexity of the real. Because Althusser does not understand this, he does not understand the significance of Marx's critique of Ricardo. Ricardo did not simply forget to mention the word "surplus value", he insisted on seeing the forms of surplus value as simple manifestations of surplus value, without realising that these forms contradict the essence they are supposed to express. Marx's response was not to invoke some "relative autonomy" to accommodate this contradiction, but to develop the *concrete mediations through which surplus value makes its appearance* in the forms of profit, interest and rent.

It is precisely to the extent that Hegel's dialectic remains entirely within knowledge that it is a simple, unmediated, idealist dialectic. In setting the dialectic on a materialist foundation *Marx did not simply carry out a formal operation within knowledge, but transformed the relation between knowledge and the real by locating the dialectic in history.* In *Capital,* as the result of intensive historical investigation as well as theoretical elaboration, Marx arrives at the materialist dialectic. In the development of the basic contradiction in the heart of the commodity between use value and value Marx is not describing a formal mechanism occurring within thought. As Engels noted: "As we are not considering here an abstract process of thought taking place solely in our heads, but a real process which actually took place at some particular time or is still taking place, these contradictions, too, will have developed in practice and will probably have found their solution. We shall trace the nature of this solution and shall discover that it has been brought about by the establishment of a new relation whose two opposite sides we shall now have to develop, and so on". The relation between thought and the real is clear to Marx: "the ideal is nothing else than the material world reflected by the human mind, and translated into forms of thought". Marx even warns us against Althusser: "If the life of the subject matter is ideally reflected as in a mirror, then it may appear as if we had before us a mere *a priori* construction".[69] Although rigorously empiricist in Althusser's sense, this couldn't be further from bourgeois empiricism, from the treatment of reality as a planar world of irreducible appearances. It is this bourgeois empiricism which dictates that the categories which are mobilised to explain these appearances can only be located in thought, on the basis that only the appearance is real. The radical separation of thought and reality is therefore the epistemological basis of the doctrine which seeks to translate the appearances of bourgeois society into absolutes, to dehistoricise bourgeois social relations and so give them an eternal character.[70]

Althusser's adoption of this philosophy has more than a hint of *déjà vu*. If the dialectic is torn from its materialist foundation and is relocated in theory, it reverts to the "wholly abstract, 'speculative' form in which Hegel had bequeathed it". In this form "the entire heritage of Hegel was limited to a sheer pattern by the help of which every theme was devised, and to a compilation of words and turns of speech which had no other purpose than to be at hand at the right time where thought and positive knowledge were lacking". This is precisely the dialectic of stalinist diamat. But Althusser does not follow Marx in setting this mystified dialectic on its feet, in reversing the stalinist subordination of "historical" to "dialectical" materialism. He rather sweeps away the dialectic altogether. Engels noted the consequence of this reaction to Hegelianism: "Only when Feuerbach declared speculative conceptions untenable did Hegelianism gradually fall asleep; and it seemed as if the reign of the old metaphysics, with its fixed categories, had begun anew in science.... Hegel fell into oblivion; and there developed the new natural-scientific materialism which is almost indistinguishable theoretically from that of the eighteenth century. . . . The lumbering cart-horse of bourgeois workaday understanding naturally stops dead in confusion before the ditch which separates essence from appearance, cause from effect; but if one goes gaily hunting over such badly broken ground as that of abstract thinking, one must not ride cart-horses."[71] It is its domination by such a metaphysical materialism, expressed in its articulation in terms of fixed categories, that explains the failure of classical economics. It is only the application of the dialectic taken from Hegel, but set on its feet, that enables Marx and Engels to see these categories not as fixed but as *expressions of processes interacting in a contradictory, historical, totality.* This is the revolutionary *theoretical* significance of Marx's "historicism", it comes from Hegel, and it is suppressed by Althusser.[72] It is not surprising, then, that Althusser cannot understand Marx's true break, that with the *metaphysical materialism* of classical political economy.

Althusser's critique of the Hegelian dialectic is not original. It reproduces that of the revisionism of the Second International, and its ambition is the same: to divorce marxist science from marxist politics. For both, the revolutionary side of the marxist dialectic is eliminated by the separation of science and ideology, of fact and value, on the basis of the Kantian separation of thought and reality, resulting in the claim that marxism is not a "moral" theory. In both cases politics is taken out of the hands of the working class and put into those of the party. It is no coincidence that the neo-positivist philosophy of knowledge espoused by Althusser, whether in "theoreticist" or "politicist" variants, is precisely the modern version of the positivism employed by the earlier revisionists. "The Hegelian dialectic constitutes the perfidious element in the Marxian doctrine, the snare, the obstacle which bars the path to every logical appreciation of things . . . What Marx and Engels achieved that was great was not achieved thanks to the Hegelian dialectic, but against it."[73] Marx was undoubtedly right to revise one of Hegel's laws of the dialectic: "Hegel remarks somewhere that all facts and personages of great importance in world history occur, as it were, twice. He forgot to add: the first time as tragedy, the second as farce."[74]

In the second essay of *Reading Capital* Althusser turns back to the specificity of Marx's theoretical discovery. Since many of the main points anticipate Balibar's fuller discussion, I shall deal only briefly with this essay.

Althusser starts with a very lengthy discussion of different conceptions of historical time, reducing "historicism" to the supposedly Hegelian conception of historical time characterised by a homogeneous continuity and contemporaneity. Althusser's conclusions can be briefly stated: the principle of the "irreducibility of the real" dictates that each level of the complex whole should have its own time, while the conception of knowledge as an autonomous practice dictates that the times cannot be related to a "single continuous reference time" because the complex whole is not a *real object* but *an object of knowledge* in which the relations between the levels are therefore *functional* and not temporal. The final conclusion is that "there is no history in general, but only specific structures of historicity". The argument is trivial and irrelevant, the conclusion depending on the double insulation of the real as irreducible and unknowable. Since there is no way of leaving theory, which knows nothing of time, it is difficult to see how a theory of history of any kind is possible. There is no way of getting from "the 'development of forms' of the concept in knowledge" to "the development of the real categories in concrete history" without encountering a single continuous reference time which readmits the possibility of "history in general".[75]

After much polemicising against "historicism" Althusser eventually comes to pose the central question of his text: "what is the object of *Capital*?" This is discussed in terms of Marx's originality with respect to classical political economy. Althusser takes the definition of political economy found in Lalande's *Dictionnaire Philosophique* as the basis of his discussion.[76] Since this relates essentially to vulgar and not to classical economy the discussion is very confused. Althusser regards the key features of Marx's critique to be his critique of the anthropological conception of human needs and of the "empiricist-positivist" conception of economic facts as in essence measurable. This leads Althusser to interpret the first part of the 1857 Introduction, which establishes the priority of relations of production over those of consumption, distribution and exchange, as a critique of the supposed anthropological basis of classical political economy.

If Althusser were right about Marx's critique of political economy, then Ricardo would have been a marxist. Althusser concedes that Ricardo's economics was based on production, even believes, wrongly, that he "gave every outward sign of recognising" the relations of production, only lacking the word. While Althusser notes that this absence is crucial, he doesn't seem to have any idea why. Ricardo did not ignore the relations of production because he saw them as being constituted by some anthropologically defined needs, but because he saw production in purely technological terms, so leading him to establish class relations at the level of distribution. Nor was Ricardo so naïve as to ignore the fact that profit receivers own means of production, or that rent receivers own land. His error was to see the social aspect of relations of production as social relations of distribution *superimposed on* an eternal structure of production, and so to see the *production* of surplus value as a natural process, only its *appropriaton* being socially determined. *It is the realisation that production is the production of social relations* and not simply of material products that enables Marx to examine the *form* of value as well as its magnitude, and so to uncover the fundamental contradiction between value and use-value which is the basis of the argument of *Capital.* It is this discovery that capitalist relations are not eternal but *historic,* a discovery which depends on the critique of metaphysical materialism by the dialectic derived from Hegel, that constitutes Marx's "historisation" of classical political economy.[77] In renouncing the Hegelian heritage and returning to metaphysical materialism Althusser proves the point by his inability to separate Marx from Ricardo.

Althusser correctly argues that Marx sees production as being "characterised by two indissociable elements: the *labour process* ... and the *social relations of production* beneath whose determination this labour process is executed". Having noted the indissociable character of the elements, Althusser goes on to discuss them quite separately! The argument is purely Ricardian: the process of production as a technological process determines certain functions. The "relations of production" assign agents to these functions by distributing these agents in relation to the means of production. The relations of production do not therefore determine the *production* of surplus value under capitalism, but only its *appropriation.*

The two essential features of the labour process, for Althusser, are its material nature, and the dominant role of the means of production in that process. Althusser correctly notes that Marx's insistence on the material character of the labour process, on the importance of use-value to political economy, led him to give proper consideration to the necessity for material reproduction. But he also sees this as the key to the discovery of "the concept of the *economic forms of existence* of these material conditions",[78] the distinction between constant and variable capital. Althusser seems blissfully unaware of the fact that the latter distinction is a *value* relation and not a *physical* relation, and so derives from the (social) relations of production and not from the (technical) nature of the labour process. He shares his ignorance with classical political economy, which could not distinguish fixed and circulating from constant and variable capital precisely because it could not understand the dual nature of production. The capacity for capital expended on labour power to vary has nothing whatever to do with the material features of the labour process, but depends on the ability of the capitalist to compel the labourer to work beyond the time of necessary labour.

This is not the only example of Althusser's confusion: it is consistent. Thus we find that such a technologistic interpretation also emerges from Althusser's discussion of the supposed dominance of the means of labour over the labour process. This dominance is simply asserted in the wake of a quotation to the effect that the means of labour can be used to indicate "the degree of development of the labourer" and "the social relations in which he labours". It is similarly asserted that "the means of labour determine the typical form of the labour process considered: by establishing the mode of attack on the external nature subject to transformation in economic production, they determine the *mode of production,* the basic category of marxist analysis (in economics and history); at the same time they establish the level of *productivity* of productive labour".

The asserted dominance of the means of labour is central to Althusserianism both in establishing the autonomy of theoretical practice and in founding the domination of capital. It is used in two senses: firstly that of the dominance of the means of labour over labour. However, this dominance, for Marx, is simply the expression within the labour process of the domination of capital over labour, and as such is specific to the labour process under capitalism. Secondly in the sense of the quote above, that the means of labour determines the labour process. In an empirical sense the assertion is trivial: given certain tools only certain operations can be performed. But in the theoretical structure of marxism this is very far from being true. The basic category of marxist analysis is the (historical) concept of the social form of production and not the (technical) concept of the means of labour.

Given Althusser's Ricardian conception of production, it is inevitable that he should also have a Ricardian conception of the relations of production. These are seen as co-determinant of the mode of production. This is not, however, in the marxist *contradictory* unity of forces and relations of production, but in the classical harmony of the "unity of this double unity", *unity of the technically determined relations of production and the socially determined relations of distribution.* The former represents the *distribution of functions,* the latter the *distribution of agents.*[80]

This conception of the "relations of production" makes it very difficult to give any meaning to "determination in the last instance by the economic". The economic cannot be determinant in the first instance because the "relations of production" are fundamentally political or ideological, and not economic relations. This is because Althusser's "relations of production", like those of classical political economy, are *relations of distribution mapped on to production* by law or custom which assign rights to shares in the product by virtue of the *ownership* of factors. Hence "relations of production" can only be legal or ideological relations, they *"presuppose the existence* of a legal-political and ideological *superstructure* as a condition of their peculiar emphasis". This means that the political or ideological levels are in fact determinant. Althusser tells us that it is the relations of production which establish "the *degree of effectivity* delegated to a certain level of the social totality", but since the "relation of production" is itself constituted by such a level it is difficult to see how this could establish that the economic is determinant in the last instance. In the end Althusser has recourse to a new concept of causality to escape the dilemma: the idea of structural-causality-in - a - complex - whole - structured - in - dominance - in - the - last - instance-by-the-economic. As part of an interdependent whole the economic is an effect of the structure of the whole itself. The causality is therefore one in which the whole is a cause visible only in its effects. It is this invisible whole that is secretly dominated by the economic.[81]

This idea of the complex pre-given whole structured in dominance is not as original as it may sound. Althusser has managed to reproduce the theoretical structure of contemporary bourgeois sociology. This is not surprising as the theoretical foundation of both is the conception of production also found in classical political economy. It is this "absent presence" in the Althusserian discourse that makes it possible for "sophisticated" readers to find a content for its rhetoric. Although the rhetoric is unfamiliar to the sociologist, the content is very well known.

Althusser asks how we can conceptualise the levels of a social formation and their interrelation. The starting point is the "pre-given" whole, the irreducible appearance with which bourgeois sociology begins. The principle of articulation of this whole must be prior to any of the pre-given levels of this whole and is found, in bourgeois sociology, in the idealist fiction of "society", which is a cause visible only in its effects. Scandal is normally avoided by adopting a "nominalist" interpretation of this fiction, which exists only in theory which, of course, must not be confused with the real. This theoretical fiction determines the differentiation of global social functions, the functions being hierarchised into material, social and ideological reproduction on the basis of an "anthropology of needs".[82] The pre-given whole of bourgeois sociology is thus complex, and it is structured in dominance in the last instance by the "economic", or material production. Corresponding to these functions are specific, relatively autonomous, institutional levels which ensure that the functions in question will be fulfilled. Economic institutions ensure material reproduction by assigning functions to agents through the division of labour. Political institutions assign agents to functions by means of the law of property and contract. Ideological institutions "assure the *bonds* of men with one another in the ensemble of the forms of their existence, the relation of individuals to their tasks fixed by the social structure".[83] The domination of Althusser's "marxism" by the theoretical "problematic" of bourgeois sociology is total. The consequences of ignoring Marx's critique of Ricardo are grave, for Ricardo is not simply a historical figure, he is the very foundation of contemporary bourgeois sociology.

Marx avoids the need to introduce concepts of "overdetermination" and "determination in the last instance" by *transforming the concept of production.* The relations of production are not the expression in production of politically or ideologically constituted relations of distribution. The latter are subordinate to the former. Marx is not so naïve as to believe that relations of production do not presuppose, either empirically or analytically, relations of distribution:

> If it is said that, since production must begin with a certain distribution of the instruments of production, it follows that distribution at least in this sense precedes and forms the presupposition of production, then the reply must be that production does indeed have its determinants and preconditions, which form its moments. At the very beginning these may appear as spontaneous, natural. But by the process of production itself they are transformed from natural into historic determinants. . . . The questions raised above all reduce themselves in the last instance to the role played by general-historical relations in production, and their relation to the movement of history generally. The question evidently belongs within the treatment and investigation of production itself.[84]

The question concerns, therefore, *the primacy of production in the historical development of a differentiated totality.* It has nothing to do with the question of the empirical possibility of production without superstructures, nor with the metaphysical question of the possibility of a concept of production defined without reference to superstructures.[85] *The primacy of production is founded in history and not in the mind, a fact of history, not the condition of its possibility.*

Marx takes production in society as his starting point. In this sense he starts with society as a pre-given whole. But this pre-given whole is the concrete historical anchorage of his analysis, and not its theoretical point of departure. The *theoretical* starting point is production, and the specific differentiation and articulation of "levels" is developed on the basis of the analysis of production. Marx makes the point in a quote which Althusser uses to establish "overdetermination":

> The specific economic form, in which unpaid surplus-labour is pumped out of direct producers, determines the relationship of rulers and ruled, as it grows directly out of production itself, and, in turn reacts upon it as a determining element. Upon this, however, is founded the entire formation of the economic community which grows out of the production relations themselves, thereby simultaneously its specific political form . . .[86]

In his analysis of this quotation Althusser collapses these two sentences into one in arguing that the text proves "that a certain form of combination of the elements present necessarily implied a certain form of domination and servitude indispensible to the survival of this combination, i.e. a certain *political* configuration (*Gestaltung*) of society". But (*aber*) this is not at all what Marx says. The first sentence (*Satz*) makes no reference to political configuration, but refers rather to the "relationship of rulers and ruled, *as it grows directly out of production itself*", and it is this relationship which reacts back on the economic form of surplus labour extraction. The second sentence is separated from the first by the emphatic "however" and argues that the economic community and its specific political form is founded on "this", the "this" referring to the combination of specific economic form and relation of ruler to ruled which grows out of production as forms of the relation of production.

To argue that economic, political and ideological relations have to be analysed as *historically developed forms of the relations of production* is not to offer an "economist" position. It is to argue that the unity of the different forms of social relation as relations of class exploitation is more fundamental than any separation or specification not only of "political" and "ideological" but also of "economic" relations as distinct forms of the relations of production. If the differentiated forms of appearance of these class relations are taken as they present themselves, as pre-given, "relatively autonomous" levels, any attempt to explain one in terms of another, even "in the last instance" is bound to be reductionist. Marx's analysis reveals, however, that class relations whose immediate foundation is the production of surplus value in the process of production, are not purely "economic", but are in class societies multidimensional power relations which are expressed in particular ideological forms. This is why *Capital* is not simply a work of economics. In it Marx does develop rigorously the economic form of the relations of production, but he also develops an analysis of the typical ideological form of the capital relation as the basis of his critique of political economy, and he at least indicates the way to develop the political form, as exemplified in the quote above.[87]

Balibar's contribution to *Reading Capital* brings out clearly the connection between the anti-historicist project of that work and the adoption of the bourgeois concept of production. In order to construct an analytical version of Marx the basic concepts must be purged of historicity and founded entirely "within theory". History will then be a construct of the mode of production and not its starting point. [88] Classical political economy and its ideological heir, functionalist sociology, provide precisely the transhistorical foundation on which to construct the concept "mode of production". Balibar bases his concept of the mode of production on a universal, transhistorical conception of production-in-general as the invariant of history. Each specific mode is then a variant combination of the invariant elements and relations which enter this combination, and history the succession of such modes. The concept "mode of production" is thus the basis of the theory of history (as the basis of comparison), and of the science of society (in specifying each mode as a series of articulated practices whose articulation is the object of the science of society).

The elements of the mode of production are the labourer, the means of production and the non-worker. The relations which combine these elements are the relation of real appropriation and the property relation. In the capitalist mode of production "capital is the owner of all the means of production *and* of labour [*sic*], and therefore it is the owner of the entire product", and this is the specifically capitalist form of the property relation. The relation of real appropriation is that designated by Marx as "*the real material appropriation of the means of production by the producer in the labour process...,* or simply as the appropriation of nature by man". Initially in Balibar's presentation this relation involves only the labourer and the means of production. However we subsequently find the capitalist intervening as well, the capitalist's control being a "technically indispensable moment of the labour process", so that the relation of real appropriation comes to be defined as "*the direct producer's ability to set to work the means of social production*". Although Balibar's exposition is hardly clear, it eventually emerges that *the difference between these relations is previously that between the classic relations of distribution and relations of production.* Hence the difference is assimilated to that between supposedly distinct technical and social divisions of labour: the organisation of production and the organisation of exploitation. The mode of production is the combination of these relations, *"the relationship between these two connections and their interdependence"*.[89]

Balibar develops the obvious anti-historicist implications of the concept at some length in his second chapter.[90] Textual support is given for this position, the texts in question being those of Freud seen through the eyes of Lacan. Unfortunately, however, Balibar has little more of substance to say about the concept itself, and gives us no reason to believe that it is Marx's concept at all. In a section which did not appear in the first edition of *Reading Capital* Balibar informs us, without evidence, that "Marx constantly defines the 'relations of production' . . . by its *kind of ownership* of the means of production, and therefore by the mode of appropriation of the social product which depends on it". This "property" connection must be sharply distinguished from the law of property, we have to look for "the relations of production *behind* the legal forms, or better: behind the secondary unity of production and law". We are not, however, told either how to do this, or what we will find.[91]

The section on the productive forces is no more illuminating. Balibar describes the respective labour processes characteristic of manufacture and modern industry, noting that the former can be characterised by the *"unity of labour-power [sic] and the means of labour"*, the latter by *"the unity of the means of labour and the object of labour"*.[92] Balibar then concludes that "*as a consequence* of the relationship between the elements of the combination, the natures of those elements themselves are transformed" (my emphasis), although he has merely noted that the two change concomitantly and hasn't even discussed the causation of the change.

Although Balibar adds very little to Althusser's brief comments on the concept of "mode of production", he does raise the question of "determination in the last instance" which Althusser essentially ignored. The argument is terminologically confused. It begins with an extraordinary discussion of fetishism, which even Balibar has subsequently recognised is "*bad*", which I shall charitably ignore.[93]

Balibar develops the concept of determination in the last instance in relation to the feudal mode of production, basing himself on a quotation from *Capital,* vol. III, in which Marx considers labour rent. In this passage Marx notes that the non-coincidence of necessary and surplus labour in time and space implies that the surplus labour of the direct producer must be extorted by "other than economic pressure". Balibar argues that this is the "characteristic difference between the feudal mode of production and the capitalist mode of production". This difference in turn derives from "the form of *combination* of the factors of the production process" in the two modes of production. Hence in the capitalist mode of production " the coincidence of *the labour process and the process of producing value*" implies that the "corresponding 'transformed forms' in this social structure, i.e. the forms of the relations between classes, are then *directly economic forms* (profit, rent, wages, interest), which implies notably that *the state does not intervene in them* at this level". (This is the theory of "revenue sources".) On the other hand "in the feudal mode of production there is a *disjunction* between the two processes. . . . Surplus-labour cannot then be extorted by 'other than economic pressure'. . . . Even before we have analysed the 'transformed forms' for themselves, we can conclude that in the feudal mode of production they will not be the transformed forms of the economic base alone, . . . *not directly economic but directly and indissolubly political and economic*". Finally, Balibar reaches a definition of determination in the last instance: *"The economy is determinant in that it determines which of the instances of the structure occupies the determinant place."*[94]

The fundamental error which underlies this account is located in its initial premises, the belief that the defining feature of the feudal mode of production is its domination by the political. A number of points in Balibar's analysis lead us to seek an alternative basis for the differentiation of the social forms of production. Firstly, the passage from *Capital* on which it is based concerns labour rent, the *simplest form* of feudal *ground rent*, and not the feudal "mode of production". In the continuation of the passage Marx discusses other forms of feudal rent in which labour and surplus labour *are* coincident in time and space. None of the passage makes any reference to determination by the political level, but merely to the use of "other than economic pressure". Hence the attempt to explain the supposed domination by the political by reference to the "form of *combination* of the factors of the production process" does not even get off the ground.[95] Secondly, it is worth noting that in the very quotation with which Balibar introduces the discussion Marx refers not to politics but to Catholicism as appearing to play the chief part in the middle ages.[96] Thirdly, as he realises in his "Self-Criticism", Balibar's claim that capitalist relations are directly economic gives the economic an autonomy which would undermine the whole theory of overdetermination.[97] Fourthly, if the economic is not determinant in the first instance, it is difficult to see how a theoretical argument can establish that it is determinant in the last instance without relying on an anthropology of needs which would assert that material reproduction is the prime function of society, an assertion which is not only theoretically unacceptable, but which is also demonstrably false: in the capitalist mode of production mass starvation is a far less significant barrier to reproduction than the threat of a declining rate of profit.

The belief that the political is dominant/determinant in feudal society is not a marxist belief, but one which bourgeois historians counterpose to marxism. It is a conception which derives very directly from the ideology in which the bourgeois revolution was conducted, an ideology whose most systematic expression is to be found in classical political economy. Although the latter was ahistorical, regarding bourgeois relations of *production* as eternal, it was not so naïve as to believe that capitalism had no prehistory. Its ahistorical character lies precisely in seeing this prehistory as no more than the prehistory *of capitalism*. It does this by contrasting the eternal bourgeois relations of *production* with historically given relations of *distribution*, the latter only coming into harmony with the former with the triumph of capitalism. Hence the pre-capitalist modes are all characterised by political intervention which distorts relations of distribution that would otherwise have arisen spontaneously as capitalist relations on the basis of the eternal structure of production. Political intervention is required because in non-capitalist modes the surplus does not accrue "naturally" to the exploiting classes. The feudal lord is therefore seen as a disfigured capitalist landowner, using his political power to secure not only his land rent, but also the "profit" of the capitalist or "self-employed" petty producer, and even to depress the "wages" of the direct producers.[98] Classical political economy is a very revolutionary doctrine, expressing the alliance between capital, artisan and peasant in its critique of feudal relations of production. The problem with Althusserianism is that it is mixed up with the wrong revolution.[99]

There is no more basis for the claim that the political is determinant in feudal society than for the claim that it is determinant in capitalist society. There is no difference in principle between the two. In every class society relations of exploitation are not simply economic relations between particular individuals, they are class relations in which those individuals relate as members of social classes. Thus the existence and the perpetuation of a class relation is the historical presupposition of particular relations of exploitation, and the perpetuation of class relations in any class society requires a state that will act politically in an attempt to confine members of the exploited class within the boundaries of the dominant class relation. The state is as much a class state in capitalist society as it is in feudal society, and capitalist society, as much as feudal society, requires a class state. Within capitalist society the state is necessary to preserve the commodity character of labour power, and it has to do this not only in the period of "primitive accumulation", when capitalist social relations are being formed, but also as the fundamental aspect of its everyday operation in capitalist society.[100] It is the commodity character of labour power that defines the class character of the capital relation, and the subordination of the labourers to the wage form involves the intervention of the state. Within feudal society the state is necessary to preserve the dependent character of the labourer, a necessity which is all the more pressing to the extent that land has not been entirely engrossed by the dominant class. Thus the characteristic feudal class relation, the relation of personal dependence, presupposes historically the existence of an authority that is able to impose and to preserve that relation of dependence.[101] Thus neither feudal nor capitalist class relations can be considered in isolation from the class state that is one aspect of those relations.

In order to construct a transhistorical concept of the mode of production Balibar takes as his starting point Marx's definition of the labour process, found in *Capital* but as likely to be encountered in any engineering textbook. From this Balibar derives the elements which enter his concept of the mode of production, although the elements do not exist outside the mode of production, their content being specified by the two relations of the mode of production. Although marxist terms are applied to these relations they are, as I have noted, essentially the classical conceptions of the relations of production determined by the technical requirements of the labour process, and relations of distribution which receive a politico-legal or ideological definition in terms of the distribution of (relation of ownership to) the means of production. If these two relations are to be superimposed on one another as relations which define a single combination they must connect the same elements with one another. This is awkward, since the non-worker who appropriates surplus labour and figures in the relations of distribution does not play any role, as a non-worker, in production itself. Various expedients are adopted to avoid embarrassment: in the capitalist mode of production the capitalist is insinuated into the process of production as a technically indispensable element of the labour process, the element of co-ordination and control. In the Asiatic mode of production the non-worker *appears* to play a part in the labour process as personification of the "higher unity", "the communal conditions of real appropriation".[102] The non-worker is therefore implicitly assigned a place in the labour process as expression of a general requirement of co-operation. This, however, raises further difficulties, for the non-worker is not a feature of all societies, but only of *class* societies.[103] He cannot therefore appear as a transhistorical element of the invariant *without eternising exploitative social relations.*

Further problems arise in the treatment of the "*labourer* (labour power)",[104] for it is not the same element which enters the forces and relations of production, as is indicated by the parenthesis. *It is precisely its attempt to root relations of distribution in technical features of the labour process that explains the classical failure to distinguish the concept of labour from that of labour power,* and the two are systematically confused in Balibar's treatment. If we define the relation of production in terms of property, then the non-worker owns the means of production and the *labourer* in the slave mode of production, and the means of production and *labour power* (in one phase of the circuit of capital) in the capitalist mode of production. On the other hand, the forces of production implicate neither labourer nor labour power, *but concrete labour. The distinction between these totally different concepts is the basis of Marx's critique of political enonomy.* It is only because he saw the capitalist mode of production as a historical phenomenon that he could unravel the confusion of the physical aspect of labour as concrete useful labour and its social aspect, under capital, of value-creating abstract labour. It is no use arguing lamely that the elements have no content until specified in a mode, because this argument is circular and so vacuous. *There is no sense whatever in which labour, labourer and labour power are the same thing,* just as there is no sense in which the non-worker and the form of co-operation are the same thing.

If the two relations of Balibar's combination can only be brought together by eternising exploitative relations of production and by confusing the social and the physical, his characterisation of the relations is also faulty. I shall focus on the concept of relations of production. The relation of production is conceived as a relation of distribution mapped on to the general structure of production, hence as a relation of distribution of means of production, hence as a property relation. This is the orthodox stalinist definition.

"The economic relation of production appears . . . as a relation between three functionally defined terms: owner class/means of production/class of exploited producers."[105] This relation is consistently defined in terms of the legal relation of ownership. The immediate problem this poses is that of disentangling the relation of production from the legal forms in which it appears.[106] This is doubly difficult for the Althusserians. First, because their epistemology demands that the extraction of the non-legal relation should be effected in theory, hence analytically. If "we are obliged ...to describe it in the peculiar terminology of legal categories" it is difficult to see how this can be done.[107] Secondly, and more fundamentally, because the "relation of production" is simply a relation of distribution mapped on to production by the legal connection of ownership of means of production, it is *only* the latter legal connection that constitutes the relation of production. Hence there is no relation of production other than that defined legally for the Althusserians. This is because they do not ask what is the basis on which the surplus product is *produced*, but rather what is the basis on which the *already produced* surplus product becomes the *property* of the exploiter, a question which is a purely legal question of *title* to shares in the product. Hence Balibar cannot do anything more than to *specify* this legal relation at the level of production. Thus the Althusserians are consistently and necessarily unable to specify any concept of "property relation" that is distinct from the legal relation of ownership.

There is, certainly, a relation between ownership of the means of production and ownership of shares of the product, *but it is the ideological relation constituted, in capitalist society, by the "trinity formula" which ascribes revenues to "factors"*: the capitalist is *entitled to* the surplus product because he has *title to* one of the factors of production. That this formula is indeed ideological can be established even at the level of the isolated process of production. The capitalist cannot own the surplus product *because* he owns the means of production, for the latter are soon used up in production. He owns the surplus because he owns the *whole* product. He owns the whole product because he owns means of production *and* labour power. However, so long as the proletariat is dominated by "bourgeois romantic illusions" about their "human" rights and dignities,[108] it is ideologically more sound that they think of the wage as their share in the product than as the price of their substance.

Marx goes beneath the level of appearances to ask not what is the basis of the property of the exploiter in the surplus product of the direct producer, but rather what is the basis of the *production* of the surplus product by the direct producer? This question *leads us directly to relations of production* and is prior to any questions of relations of distribution and so of legal relations. Having established the basis in production of the expenditure of surplus labour, the question of the appropriation of that surplus labour is relatively trivial. Hence the relation of production is more fundamental than the property relations which express it. To see this it is worth working back from the "trinity formula".

The capitalist owns the surplus product because he owns the

means of production and labour power. But he owns means of production and labour power because he is a capitalist, because he can constantly replace means of production and labour power as they are used up. He is therefore a capitalist *before* he is owner of the means of production. As an *owner* the capitalist is in a *formally symmetrical* position to the labourer, for it is in the market that labourer and capitalist meet as *owners*. The question we have to ask concerns the basis of the *substantive asymmetry* of this encounter: why can the capitalist buy the worker's labour power, while the worker cannot buy the means of production? Why can the labourer be united with the objective conditions of labour only under the domination of capital? The answer lies in the circumstances in which capitalist and labourer enter not production but circulation, the capitalist as owner of *money capital* (not means of production), the worker as owner of nothing but his or her labour power. The capitalist relation of production is, correspondingly, not founded on the relation between labourer and owner of means of production, but on that between free labour and capital, and this is why it cannot be seen as an interpersonal relation. *The relation with which we are concerned is not fundamentally a property relation, but a relation between classes.* This relation is not *defined* by the legal connection of the members of these classes to the elements of the labour process, but by the *modes of participation of the different classes in the total process of social production* (which includes not only production, but also circulation, distribution and consumption).[109]

The basis of this relation in the capitalist mode of production must be sought in the conditions which determine that the capitalist as owner of money confronts the labourer as owner of no more than his labour power. This is not the question of the historical conditions of the capitalist mode of production, but rather of the process within the capitalist mode of production by which the latter *reproduces* its own conditions of existence. In other words the key to the capital relation is not to be found in the isolated process of production, but in the process of *total social reproduction*. Although Balibar recognises that the analysis of reproduction is important, he fails to understand that it is fundamental to the definition of the mode of production itself.[110]

Balibar's separation of production and reproduction is a common one, based on an over hasty reading of *Capital*. In *Capital* Marx does consider the different moments of the circuit of capital independently of one another, in turn, before he looks at the circuit of capital as a whole. It is only when he turns to reproduction in volume one and to the circuit of capital in volume two that Marx ties the argument together and situates the previous discussion. It is only when he does this that the social form of the capitalist mode of production is revealed, because it is only in the circuit as a whole that the production and reproduction of capital has its rationale. This should be clear if we consider the moments of the circuit separately, for if we do so we are unable to find the fundamental class relation of capitalist society. In the consideration of the commodity form, the moment of circulation considered in isolation, Marx cannot find any class relations, but only relations between free and equal owners of commodities. In the consideration of the production process Marx cannot find class relations either, for here we have only relations between individual capitalists and individual workers. The capitalist process of production is a process of production of capital, only to the extent that it is a process of production of surplus value. Surplus value is the difference between the value expended in variable capital and the value realised in the sale of the product, after deduction of constant capital, and neither of these sums exist if production is considered in isolation. Thus the production of surplus value presupposes the commodity form of the product and of labour power, while the capitalist form of circulation presupposes the production of surplus value: capitalist production and circulation presuppose one another in the unity of the circuit of capital. The circuit of capital describes the series of economic forms taken by capital and labour in the subordination of labour to the production of capital. This series cannot be reduced to one of its forms: the class relation is the unity of forms expressed in the circuit of the reproduction of the capital relation. This unity is expressed in the confrontation of capital with free labour, and the persistence of the capital relation depends on preserving the "free" character of labour, i.e. the commodity form of labour power. In parts VII and VIII of volume one Marx shows how this commodity form is preserved through the permanent dispossession of the worker in the circuit of capital, through the expansion and contraction of the reserve army of labour, and through the use of the law and of force. It is this class relation, i.e. a total social relation, that is the presupposition of the production and accumulation of capital, whose forms are described in the metamorphoses of the circuit of capital. This relation cannot be reduced to the economic forms in which it appears (this is precisely the fetishism of the commodity that inverts the relationship between social relation and economic category), let alone to one of those forms. The basis of capitalist social relations is the commodity form of labour power, and not the capitalist's ownership of the means of production. The latter is only one aspect of one form of capital within its circuit, an aspect which is, moreover, *technically*, rather than *socially*, necessary for the capitalist to be able to set in motion the labour power which he has purchased, and as such the foundation for the illusions about the technical necessity of capital expressed in the "trinity formula" and destroyed by *Capital*.[111]

Having discussed the relations of production at some length there is little to be said about the Althusserian conception of the forces of production, for it is simply the other side of the coin. It is because the technical division of labour is seen as a set of positions determined by the technology of production, because relations of production are eternised, that the forces/relations distinction is seen in terms of a distinction between technical relations of production and social relations of distribution, expressed in terms of the technical and social division of labour or of the supposedly distinct relations of real appropriation and relations of production. It is because Marx sees the relations of distribution as moments of the relations of production, and sees the latter as indissolubly technical and social, that he had "difficulty" in "clearly thinking the distinction between the two connections".[112] *Anlalytically* we can argue that the technical characteristics of the forces of production impose constraints on the relations within which production takes place, just as *analytically* we can argue that the relations of production impose constraints on the forces which can be brought into play. But this does not mean that we can isolate two sets of relations of production, two divisions of labour, one technical and one social. The distinction between the two is not "a real distinction but simply a *modal distinction*, corresponding to two ways of conceptualising the same process. Technical and social division are two aspects of the *same division*. The functions which ensure the technical reproduction of the process are the same as those which determine its social reproduction".[113] The analysis of *Capital* is founded on the *contradictory unity* of use value and value, not on the harmonious "unity of this double unity". It is small wonder that Balibar's concept of the relation of real appropriation is difficult to decipher. Either he is unable to separate technical and social divisions of labour, or he reduces the relation to a technical characteristic of the labour process.[114]

Having specified the inadequacy of the Althusserian concept of mode of production in relation to the capitalist mode of production, I shall turn briefly to indicate its weakness in relation to pre-capitalist modes. I have already noted in relation to the feudal mode of production the classical bourgeois terms in which Balibar poses the question. We are now able to see the significance of the Ricardian definition of relations of production in terms of ownership of means of production for the analysis of pre-capitalist modes. This definition is in essence the imposition of the ideological form of the "trinity formula" on pre-capitalist modes of production. Pre-capitalist "relations of production" are, as I have noted, seen as politically imposed relations of distribution. To define these relations of distribution theoretically, in accordance with the trinity formula, it is necessary to seek "factors" to which to attribute the "revenues" of the various classes, revenues which fall to the class by virtue of its "ownership" of the factors. Hence it is necessary to transpose capitalist legal forms, most notably capitalist "ownership", into pre-capitalist modes of production to understand the relations of production of those modes as debased forms of the ideological interpretation of capitalist relations of production.

The application of this analysis to pre-capitalist modes produces (bourgeois) revolutionary conceptions. I have discussed the feudal mode above. The view of other modes also reflects the relation of capital to such modes. Thus the slave-owner of the ancient world is seen as a capitalist farmer-landowner, free of the burden of rent, but whose idyllic world was destroyed by the Barbarian hordes who brought, precisely, feudalism. In Asia the despot exploited his control of governmental functions to divert the surplus to himself by force, a conception which could legitimate colonial exploitation of the more "backward" peoples, and serve as an awful warning to the civilised world of the dangers of absolutism.[116] The development of capitalism, in this conception, can be identified with the march of reason and universality, sweeping away these various artificial barriers so that the social relations already inscribed in the "relation of real appropriation" can assert themselves. The development of capitalism is then seen as an essentially political development.[117]

Marx did not study any but the capitalist mode of production systematically. He has, however, offered us a schematic account in the section of the *Grundrisse* on the "forms which precede capitalist production". While it is true that this section is primarily concerned to distinguish these forms from the capitalist form, it is sufficiently clear that it does not need to be transformed by a "symptomatic" reading.

At first sight this text appears eminently suited to an Althusserian reading since it is centred on the concept of property. However, the term is not used in any juridical sense in this text, but refers to the specific way in which "the worker relates to the objective conditions of his labour". The term "property" is therefore essentially a synonym for the term "mode of production",[118] referring to specific forms of co-operation in total social production. The property relation in this text is therefore the form of that co-operation which is essential both technically and socially as form of relation to the objective conditions of labour, co-operation which expresses the fact that "the human being is in the most literal sense *zoon politikhon*".[119] It is difficult to distinguish the property relation from the relation of real appropriation, because the two are essentially the same thing, the juridical property relation being simply an expression of the relation of real appropriation.[120] Relations of exploitation emerge on the basis of the latter not as superimposed relations of distribution, but as exploitative forms of co-operation.

Marx's discussion of the pre-capitalist forms of property is aimed precisely at the attempt to establish an "extra-economic" origin of property. In a passage which a symptomatic reading reveals as being aimed at Althusser himself Marx notes:

> What Mr Proudhon calls the *extra-economic* origin of property . . . is the *pre-bourgeois* relation of the individual to the objective conditions of labour . . . Before we analyse this further, one more point: the worthy Proudhon would not only be able to, but would have to, accuse *capital* and *wage labour* — as forms of property — of having an *extra-economic* origin. . . . But the fact that pre-bourgeois history, and each of its phases, also has its own *economy* and an *economic foundation* for its movement, is at bottom only the tautology that human life has since time immemorial rested on production, and, in one way or another, on *social* production, whose relations we call, precisely, economic relations.[121]

The "determination by the economic" which is expressed in Marx's concept of the mode of production does not therefore consist in the attempt to erect pre-bourgeois modes of production on the basis of a bourgeois "economic" foundation. It consists rather in specifying *the forms of the social relations within which production takes place,* in different forms of society. The relations of production on which these various modes of production are based will articulate different forms of exploitation, and correspondingly different relations of distribution. They will be manifested in specific and interdependent economic, ideological and political forms, which must be understood as *historically developed* forms of the relation of production. This emerges very clearly from Marx's notes on the various pre-capitalist forms.[122]

The first form is that in which the individual only relates to the objective conditions through the community. The basis of this mode of production is a particular form of "property" defined, without any reference to its ideological "appearance" or its political "expression", by the mediation of the relation of the individual to the objective conditions of his or her life by the community. This form of relation "can realise itself in very different ways", from the clan community to various forms of Asiatic, Slavonic and pre-Colombian societies. In the clan community the community *appears* natural or divine presupposition, and each individual conducts himself as co-proprietor. In the Asiatic realisation the community *appears* as a part of a more comprehensive unity embodied in a higher proprietor, so that real communities *appear* only as hereditary possessors.[123] The political *expression* of the community may take a more democratic or despotic form. "In so far as it actually realises itself in labour," this may be through independent family labour or through communal labour. These various ideological, political and economic forms are quite explicitly conceived as the forms in which the communal relation of production is articulated. Of course the analysis is rudimentary, and in particular Marx doesn't pose the question of the relation between the various forms in which the relation of production is expressed and the different forms of that relation. The account provides the starting point, however, which is not the relation of distribution, not the physical labour process, nor the articulated combination of the two, but the social form of production, which is prior to both.

Marx's discussion of the other forms of property is more fragmented, but follows the same lines. The ancient form is seen as a product of the modification of the communal form. Communal and private "property" now coexist. The community is based on the need for collective organisation to defend the land against encroachment by others, and so has a warlike organisation and is based in the town. This means that "membership in the commune remains the presupposition for the appropriation of land and soil . . . a *presupposition* regarded as divine etc." The third, Germanic, form has only vestigial communal property, as "a unification made up of independent subjects, landed proprietors, and not as a unity". The commune does not in fact exist as a state or political body.[124]

In these sketches Marx offers the starting point, if no more, for a marxist theory of modes of production. The starting point, the transhistorical absolute, is not provided by an abstract and empty structure of unspecified elements, but by the "tautology that human life has since time immemorial rested on production, and, in one way or another, on *social* production". The task of the theory of pre-capitalist modes of production is to take this as the starting point and to do what Marx has done for the capitalist mode of production, to specify the "one way or another".[125]

Two points might be raised in immediate objection to this approach, however. The account has made no reference to exploitation, nor has it made any reference to the forces of production. The former objection is misguided. To start with forms of appropriation of the surplus is to risk implying a teleology in which modes of production are instituted *in order to* effect exploitation.[126] Such an approach is inadequate, for exploitation can only take place within a constituted mode of production, so that modes of production cannot be theorised simply as modes of exploitation. We have already seen that in the case of the capitalist mode of production the condition for capitalist *exploitation* is a specific form of organisation of total social production in which *co-operation* is effected through commodity circulation. The forms of exploitation characteristic of the modes of production discussed here can be analysed in a parallel way. Thus in the Asiatic form exploitation of the community by the despot and/or the priest depends on communal relations of production and on specific forms of ideological and political expression of these relations. Slavery and serfdom, likewise, are "only further developments of the form of property resting on the clan system". Here the worker is excluded from the community, and so "stands in no relation whatsoever to the objective conditions of his labour" but rather "himself appears among the natural conditions of production for a third individual or community". Hence "slavery, bondage, etc. . . . is always secondary, derived, never original, although (it is) a necessary and logical result of property founded on the community and labour in the community".[127]

The question of the forces of production is one which Marx does not adequately cover in these notes. It is clear that the "form of property" is underlain by particular forms of the forces of production. In one sense the form of property corresponds to, "depends partly on . . . the economic conditions in which it [the commune — *S.C.*] relates as proprietor to the land and soil in reality". Thus the differences in forms of property depend on differences in the extent to which "the individual's property can in fact be realised solely through communal labour" (aqueducts in the Asiatic mode, warfare in the ancient).[128] However the extent to which communal labour is possible depends in turn on the presence of communal forms of social organisation. We cannot therefore derive the form of property from the form of the forces of production. Perhaps at last we have come upon the need for structural causality. Perhaps the complexity of Marx's totality lies, as Balibar indeed argues, in "*the relation between these two connections and their interdependence*",[129] even if Balibar misidentifies the connections.

The question of the relationship between forces and relations of production is intimately connected with the question of history, which brings us back to Balibar's text. Having established a structuralist definition of the mode of production in terms of the combination of forces and relations of production the classic structuralist problem of the reconciliation of structure and history appears. The mode of production has to establish some temporal mode of existence.

The concept of reproduction provides an initial means of deriving a temporality from the synchronic structure of the mode of production. But since the forces and relations of production form a harmonious unity, this *dynamics* of the mode of production simply projects the structure into its "eternity" as a constant and unchanging structure.[130] This is illustrated by Balibar's treatment of the concept of contradiction.

The concept of contradiction defines the dynamics of the structure in the sense of the existence of the structure in time. But it is inscribed within the structure, and so cannot be the means by which the suppression of the structure is effected. Contradiction is not, therefore, fundamental, and its resolution does not take the form of transformation of the structure, but of renewed structural equilibrium. The concept of contradiction is therefore the basis of the understanding of the dynamics of the mode of production, which takes the form of stasis, but cannot help to understand its *diachrony,* the transition from one mode of production to another.[131] To explain this Balibar introduces a different sort of mode of production, a "transitional mode", whose dynamic is also a diachrony.

In the capitalist mode of production, according to Balibar, the forces and relations of production "correspond" to one another. The relationship between them is one in which there is a "*reciprocal limitation* of one connection by the other", so that the contradiction between them is non-antagonistic, in the sense just discussed. On the other hand, there are modes such as the manufacturing mode in which the forces and relations are in a state of "non-correspondence" so that we see a *"transformation of one by the effect of the other",* in this case of the forces by the relations, to bring the two back into correspondence in the capitalist mode of production. Reproduction in a transitional mode therefore takes the form of supersession, but as the product of the effect of the relations of production on the forces, and not of the development of contradictions. This sounds suspiciously like a new variant of "historicism", and Balibar seems aware of the danger, suddenly dissolving his transitional mode and announcing it as a combination of modes of production, bringing the analysis back into the purity of the synchronic but leaving diachrony once more unexplained.[132]

The transitional mode of production brings us back to the concept of the "conjuncture", the current situation, in which it is political practice which takes the whole social formation as its object, and so to the historicism of the class subject which keeps creeping back. In a transitional mode of production the relations of production transform the forces of production. They are able to do this because the "non-economic" levels of the mode of production are no longer limited by the "economic". Their autonomy is unambiguously absolute, for it is political practice "whose result is to *transform* and *fix* the limits of the mode of production".[133] This theory of displacement, drafted in to fill gaping theoretical holes, is given no content. We are simply told that when forces and relations do not "correspond" the political will be dominant and transformation will be possible, but the concept of "correspondence" remains empty. It seems that for Balibar, or for Classical Political Economy, it is only the capitalist and primitive communist modes which are characterised by correspondence, and so are non-transitional.[134]

The concept of the transitional mode does not even formally solve the problem which gave rise to it, for it is still necessary to explain how the transition to the transitional mode is effected. Balibar's "Self-Criticism" provides the means of dealing with diachrony without relapsing into teleology. In his self-criticism Balibar makes three related points. First, he notes that reproduction is not automatic in the capitalist mode of production since it is not, as he had thought, a purely economic matter, but also involves the "superstructure", at least in the reproduction of labour power. This makes it possible for the reproduction of the capitalist mode of production to be interrupted.[135] Secondly, he notes that the combination of forces and relations of production cannot be seen simply as a combination of independently constituted sets of relations, as they are in *Reading Capital,* but must be seen as a combination made "*in the* (social) *form and under the influence of the relations of production themselves*".[136] This means that the mode of production can be transformed by a transformation of the relations of production, by political practice. Thirdly, Balibar points out that the object of his text was the concept of the "mode of production", whereas it is social formations which change.[137] This undermines the attempt to offer a general theory of modes of production or a theory of history.

The net result of these three points is that it becomes possible for any mode of production to change, the class struggle taking the relations of production as its object and so transforming the mode of production. Hence teleology is eliminated only at the expense of reintroducing the class subject of history, and seeing modes of production as creations of such class subjects. We are thus back with a structuralist version of that "left historicism" which is the butt of so much criticism in *Reading Capital*.[138] But the ambition has been achieved, marxist science has been divorced from marxist politics, and so this version of "left historicism" can, paradoxically, be put at the service of revisionism:

> If the effects within the structure of production do not by themselves constitute any challenge to the limits . . . there may be *one of the conditions* (the "material base") of a *different result,* outside the structure of production: it is this other result which Marx suggests marginally in his exposition when he shows that the movement of production produces, by the concentration of production and the growth of the proletariat, one of the conditions of the particular form which the class struggle takes in capitalist society. *But the analysis of this struggle and of the political social relations which it implies is not part of the study of the structure of production.* (Last emphasis is mine.)[139]

The theoretical recourse to a class subject is dictated by the absence of any principle *internal* to the mode of production which can be the basis of an explanation of transition. The concept of class is then introduced as the transcendent principle which, guided by the scientifically attested programme of The Proletarian Party, will create an entirely new structure from the debris of the old.[140] The absence of an internal principle of transition depends on the interpretation of the relationship between forces and relations of production as one of correspondence or non-antagonistic contradiction. Let us examine this thesis a little more closely.

It should not be necessary to point out that such a conception derives from classical political economy and can find no support in Marx's work. It is embarrassing to have to point out to "marxists" that the contradiction between forces and relations of production is antagonistic, since production both reproduces *and suspends* the general conditions of production. The *Preface to the Critique* is not ambiguous: "At a certain stage of their development, the material productive forces come into conflict with the existing relations of production . . . From forms of development of the productive forces these relations turn into fetters. Then begins an epoch of social revolution . . ."[141] This is not simply a rash, crude, hasty, misguided, "Hegelian" formulation, but rather is the way in which Marx constantly conceptualises the relation between the forces and relations of production. The whole of *Capital* is no more than an elaboration of this contradiction in the capitalist mode of production.

In the text on pre-capitalist forms Marx notes, in discussing the ancient mode, that "the presupposition of the survival of the community is the preservation of equality among its free self-sustaining peasants, and their own labour as the condition of the survival of their property".[142] However, reproduction does not simply represent the "general form of permanence"[143] of these general conditions of production, for "the survival of the commune as such in the old mode requires the reproduction of its members in the presupposed objective conditions. Production itself . . . necessarily suspends these conditions little by little . . . and, with that, the communal system declines and falls, together with the property relations on which it was based".[144] The unity of forces and relations of production is thus a contradictory unity of the form of co-operation and its objective conditions. Since production is simply the action of men and women, through determinate relations of production, on the objective conditions of production, it is a tautology to note that the development of economic conditions, within determinant economic relations, will alter the material foundation of the latter, ultimately to condition their replacement by new economic relations consistent with new economic conditions: "The aim of all these communities is survival; i.e. *reproduction of the individuals who compose it as proprietors . . . This reproduction, however, is at the same time necessarily new production and destruction of the old form* . . . Thus the preservation of the old community includes the destruction of the conditions on which it rests". Marx concludes that "in the last analysis, their community . . . resolves itself into a specific stage in the development of the productive forces of working subjects — to which correspond their specific relations amongst one another and towards nature. Until a certain point, reproduction. Then turns into dissolution".[144]

Marx's own position is clear and consistent. Two objections might be raised to it, however. Firstly, the last quotation might be interpreted as the basis of a *philosophy of history* in which the productive forces are seen as the autonomous motor of history acting on history from outside. It might be argued that, just as Hegel projected his own society into the past as the end already inscribed in the beginning of history, and Ricardo, more mundanely, founded the eternity of his own society in the technical features of production in general, so Marx inscribes the communist future in both the present and the past through an alternative mechnical materialist philosophy of history. This is not the case for two reasons. First, it is true that Marx appears to regard it as the historical tendency of every mode of production to develop the forces of production, and he appears to regard modes of production as succeeding one another according to the level of development of the forces of production. However, he does insist on analysing each mode of production as a specific historical phenomenon, characterised by its own particular form of conditions and relations of production. Marx only established the progressive character of the capitalist mode of production so, until and unless this is done for other modes as well, Marx's tentative suggestions must be taken to be speculative and hypothetical. Secondly, this speculative suggestion that history is progressive is not a suggestion that the history of any particular society is progressive. In Hegel's philosophy of history world history, as the progressive self-realisation of the Idea, is dissociated sharply from the history of particular societies, which go into decline once they have played their world-historical role. Marx takes this idea from Hegel, but sets it on a materialist foundation, recognising that it is only with capitalism that world-history makes its appearance, so that it is the expansion of capitalism on a world scale which first defines the historical position of non-capitalist modes of production, and so defines the progressive development of the productive forces as a world-historical phenomenon.

The second objection which might be raised is less serious: it is the objection that Marx's conception of the dialectic of forces and relations of production yields an idealist *theory of history,* because forces and relations of production are seen as generating history of themselves, without any reference to the class struggle, "motor of history". This objection depends on the conception of society in which forces and relations of production are purely economic phenomena, while class struggle, and the history it produces, are purely political. As we have seen, this is far from Marx's conception of the relations of production, according to which these social relations are not technical relations but are the social basis of *both* the "economic community" and "its specific political form". The development of the relations of production, under the impact of changes in the conditions of production, is therefore a development of these relations in their economic, political and ideological forms. In a class society these relations are differentiated class relations, and their development, under the impact of changes in economic conditions, and subject to the constraint of those conditions, is the development of a multi-faceted class struggle. This struggle is not, however, something divorced from production, located in some relatively autonomous political instance, taking the whole social formation as its object. *The class struggle is the form of development of the developed forms* of the relation of production, an omnipresent economic, political and ideological struggle.¹⁴⁵

Conclusion: Althusserianism as intellectual counter-insurgency
Althusserianism is based on a polemical technique which can only be described as intellectual terrorism. Three terms, "historicism", "empiricism" and "humanism" are drafted in to sweep away all possible opposition. To be labelled by such a term is to be labelled a class enemy, an intellectual saboteur. The power of the terms, however, depends on the claim that marxism represents a radical break with all forms of "historicism", "empiricism" and "humanism" in the name of science. In this paper I have argued that far from defining marxism, Althusser uses his triple banner to expunge the revolutionary theoretical, philosophical and political content of marxism in favour of bourgeois sociology, idealist philosophy and stalinist politics.

The most fundamental aspect of Althusserianism is its antihistoricism. I have dealt with this question at considerable length in discussing *Reading Capital*. I have argued that Marx rejects not "historicism" but the idealist philosophy of history, found in Hegel and in classical political economy. This philosophy is based on the eternisation of the present and the projection of this eternity into both the future and the past. In this sense such a philosophy of history is ahistorical, for it dissolves real history in favour of the ideal play of concepts. Marx's historicism is a materialist, but dialectical, historicism which counterposes real history to these idealist fantasies, and so which historises the present. Althusserianism takes up not Marx's critique of Hegel but that offered by mechanical materialism, criticising the speculative aspect of Hegelianism, but not its idealism. Althusserianism does this by adopting the position of classical political economy, which offers the mechanical materialist variant of Hegel's philosophy of history, emulating the unfortunate Proudhon. It does not abolish the ideological implications of this conception, but ignores them. They are concealed by the foundering of the Althusserians as they seek to come to terms with history. Having rejected Proudhonism to discover the capitalist mode of production as the terminus of history, they have to choose between the dominance of the forces of production, giving the economism of Meillassoux or Terray, or that of the relations of production, giving the historicism of Balibar (revised), Cutler, or Hindess and Hirst (mark one), or else to abandon all marxist pretensions by abandoning reality altogether (Cutler, Hindess, Hirst and Hussain).¹⁴⁶

Their opposition to Marx's "historicism" leads the Althusserians to reject the method of historical materialism which sees the dialectic in thought as the retracing, in thought, of the dialectic in operation in history. This leads them to separate "dialectical" from historical materialism, and to replace the marxist dialectic by the most avant-garde versions of absolute idealism, denying the reality of either subject or object of knowledge in favour of the unique reality of knowledge itself. The abolition of its material foundation returns the dialectic to its mystical form, and so leads to its rejection in favour of an analytical logic. Such a logic is *metaphysical,* in the Hegelian and marxist sense that it takes moments of processes for absolute categories, and so eternises the historic. This analytical philosophy of knowledge is therefore the epistemological foundation for the adoption of the bourgeois conception of capitalist society. "Theory" is content to take bourgeois society as it presents itself, and so to present the forms of bourgeois society as eternal conditions of existence of society. Thus the critique of "empiricism" conceals the truly empiricist foundations of Althusserianism. Its adoption of the most banal forms of appearance of bourgeois society is presented as a process which takes place entirely in theory. When the concepts of that ideology generate in thought the world of appearances we live in from day to day the relation between concrete-in-thought and concrete-real becomes unproblematic. The concepts on which the edifice is based have the obviousness of bourgeois ideology, and so their origin is never questioned. When they generate the ideology from which they were plucked, their adequacy is not questioned either. It is in Althusserianism itself that we find the reflexive structure of ideology, it is Althusserianism which produces the "effect of recognition-misrecognition in a mirror connection".[147]

The third sin in the Althusserian canon is "humanism". In *For Marx* theoretical humanism was a prime target, although ideological humanism could be tolerated. Since *Reading Capital* (or is it since "Prague Spring"?) even ideological humanism has come under attack. The critique of "humanism" is not of major theoretical significance. There can be few marxists who believe that Marx takes the "free social individual"[148] as his point of departure, and few who would disagree that in this sense marxism is based on the idea of the "process without a subject" derived from Hegel.[149] Althusser's attack on humanism is of primarily ideological significance. It is clear that humanism has become a serious political threat to the dominance of orthodox party marxism in the period of the "historic compromise" and the "alliance of the left". Although in this political confrontation humanism could hardly be accused of adopting proletarian political positions, it is not so clear in the *ideological* confrontation of humanism and orthodox marxism that the former is the bearer of bourgeois, the latter of proletarian, ideology. Indeed Rancière argues at some length that the reverse is the case.

On the one hand, argues Rancière, although there have been bourgeois humanist ideologies, such as that of Feuerbach, humanism is only a peripheral bourgeois ideology.[150] The conception of "man" embodied in the dominant bourgeois ideology is not at all man the subject, but the man whose human nature must be moulded to fit society, the man of eighteenth-century mechanical materialism, "the man of philanthropy, of the humanities and of anthropometry: the man one moulds, helps, surveys, measures". This is precisely the man of classical political economy, the man who must be planned, regulated, governed, instructed by a superior class, the man who underpins the functional interpretation of the class division of society. This bourgeois conception of man persists in the ideologies of Owenism, of radical philanthropy, and even of Marx in *The German Ideology* (and, it might be added, in his and other marxists' conception of women). It is also precisely this bourgeois conception of man which dominates the revisionism of the orthodox communist parties, the conception of the proletariat who must continue to be led, planned, co-ordinated, disciplined and instructed by the superior class of apparatchiks. It is the conception which Althusser adopts, but with which Marx broke definitively in the third thesis on Feuerbach when he asked who educates the educators.

On the other hand, Rancière continues, the same word, "man", whose nature in bourgeois ideology condemns him to servitude, is appropriated by the proletariat as the means of articulating its rejection of this servitude. It is a word which emerges spontaneously time after time, in the practical struggles of the proletariat, as the expression of a revolutionary aspiration, as the locus of the possibility of a different society than that in which bourgeois man is encased. In the context of these struggles the concept of man the subject (and increasingly of woman the subject too) is the practical expression of the revolutionary philosophical concept, the negation of the negation, for it is only in that concept that the aspirations of the oppressed can be given a revolutionary form, looking forward to a possibility which transcends the negation of humanity rather than back to a past which was its precondition. It is not surprising that having followed Stalin's lead in eliminating the negation of the negation from marxism, Althusser can see no need to retain the concept of "man".

It is not only because his own thought is dominated by the *bourgeois* concept of man that Althusser is unable to understand that the same word can have very different meanings in different practices. It also follows directly from his conception of ideology. For Althusser a word does not derive its meaning from its insertion in a social practice, but rather conceals a concept whose meaning derives from its position in a set of concepts. The word "man" conceals the bourgeois concept of man, and so its intrusion into a proletarian discourse must represent the intrusion of bourgeois ideology (and not simply of sexism). Ideology is embodied in a word, and is to be fought by the theorist who can sift the good from the bad words, draw the "theoretical dividing line between true ideas and false ideas" (cf. note 60). Althusser cannot see that the revolutionary concept of humanity emerges as the expression of a political struggle not against the *word* of bourgeois humanism, but against its *practice,* against the practical tyranny of domination in every institution of bourgeois society of which the bourgeois concept of man is but the ideological expression. He cannot see this because he cannot divorce himself from the sociological conception of ideology as a representation, a distorted vision, an imaginary interpellation of the subject, divorced from the practice of bourgeois domination which is, for Althusser, simply an expression of the technical division of labour.

Althusserian politics is summed up in his reply to John Lewis. The meaning Althusser gives to the slogan "the masses make history" which he counterposes to Lewis's slogan "men make history" is quite the opposite of the Maoist emphasis on the impotence of the bourgeoisie confronted with the collective power of the masses. For Althusser the proletariat must be taught the *omnipotence* of the bourgeoisie:

> When one says to the proletarians that it is men who make history, one doesn't need to be a scholar to understand that sooner or later one will contribute to their disorientation and disarming. One leads them to believe that they are all powerful as men, while disarming them as proletarians in the face of the real omnipotence, that of the bourgeoisie which controls the material (means of production) and political (state) conditions which direct history. When one sings the humanist song to them, one distracts them from the class struggle, one prevents them from giving themselves and using the only power they have: that of *organisation in a class* and of the *organisation of the class,* the unions and the party.[151]

Notes

1. Edward Thompson, *The Poverty of Theory,* London, 1978. S. Clarke, "Marxism, Sociology and Poulantzas's Theory of the State", *Capital and Class,* 2, 1977. S. Clarke, "Capital, Fractions of Capital and the State", *Capital and Class,* 5, 1978. S. Clarke, *The Foundation of Structuralism,* Hassocks, 1980. I should stress that in

writing all these papers I have benefited enormously from discussion with many comrades in Coventry and in various groups of the Conference of Socialist Economists. This work is very much a collective product, even though written by one individual. Thus I am ready to accept full responsibility for its content, but am loathe to accept individually any credit that may be due.

2. N. Geras, "Althusser's Marxism", *New Left Review*, 71, 1972, p. 77n; A. Glucksmann, "A Ventriloquist Structuralism", *New Left Review*, 72, 1972, p. 69. J. Rancière, *La leçon d'Althusser*, Paris, 1974, p. 9.

3. A. Glucksmann, op. cit. Spinoza is Althusser's philosophical inspiration, from whom many central formulations are drawn. Cf. L. Althusser, *Essays in Self-Criticism* (hereafter ESC), London, 1976, pp. 132-41, 187-92. P. Anderson, *Considerations on Western Marxism*, London, 1976, pp. 64-5. Anderson also notes the remarkable similarity of many of Althusser's themes to those of Adorno's *Negative Dialectic*, which is based on lectures delivered in Paris in 1961 (ibid., pp. 72-3).

4. Cf. N. Poulantzas, "Vers une théorie marxiste", *Temps Modernes*, May 1966, p. 1978. This penetrating critique precedes Poulantzas's conversion to Althusserianism.

5. M. Dufrenne, "La philosophie du néo-positivisme", *Esprit*, 1967.

6. Cl. Lévi-Strauss, *Structural Anthropology*, London, 1968, pp. 312-14.

7. The terms "humanism" and "historicism" are used very loosely by Althusserians. This looseness is fundamental to Althusserianism, whose principal critical weapon is the identification of an opponent as "humanist", "historicist" or both. The terms "empiricist" and "economist" are used more rarely. Brewster offers attested definitions of the terms in his glossary in L. Althusser and E. Balibar, *Reading Capital* (hereafter RC), London, 1970, p. 314.

The polemical use of these terms is based on establishing the (almost trivially) non-marxist character of certain simplistic formulations which are characterised as "historicist", "humanist", "economist" or "empiricist" and then generalising the application of the terms so that they cover totally different theories. Thus it is not very contentious to argue that marxism is not a historicism in the Hegelian sense of seeing history as the product of the development of the concept, and so seeing knowledge as the self-realisation of history (although it is not clear that some versions of Althusserianism do not come very close to this). The early work of Lukács certainly tended in this direction, with history being interpreted as the product of the development of the class consciousness of the proletariat, and marxism as the self-realisation of that history. This kind of historicism is developed in the stalinist identification of proletarian class consciousness with the party so that the party is both the subject of history and history's self-realisation. The result is the stalinist identification of the political authority of the party with the scientific authority of marxism. Thus for Stalin the strength of marxism is its scientific character that enables it to predict the course of history and so to guide the party. The authority of the party is therefore based on the scientifically attested truth of its proclamations, a truth that is necessary because history speaks through the party (even where the truth is reversed from year to year). When I refer to stalinist politics in this paper I refer to this attempt to legitimate the authority of the party over its members, and ultimately over the working class, by reference to its superior access to historical truth given to it by the science of which it is the custodian.

The Althusserian polemical technique is to condemn all forms of historicism by condemning one example of historicism. For Althusser the fault of stalinism is its historicism, therefore it is essential to introduce an anti-historicist conception of science, so that the scientist rather than the party becomes the judge of truth. (After the party slapped his wrists Althusser recognised that science could not be insulated in this way and that it was therefore necessary for the party to intervene, through philosophy, to protect the scientist from subversive bourgeois influences: thus Althusser adopts a historicist theory of error but an anti-historicist theory of truth!) Thus Althusser identifies anti-stalinism with anti-historicism. However it is not stalinism's *historicism* that underlies its politics, for a consistent historicism is subversive of stalinism, which is why Lukács was forced to recant. If knowledge is a historical product, rooted in the real world, then neither the party nor science can claim a monopoly of historical truth. Historical truth has to be found in history and in the lives of those who make history, it has to be distilled from the experience of the mass of the working class and is not to be discovered by theoretical practitioners or political manipulators of the concept. It is the *idealism* of stalinist historicism that is at fault, the idealist identification of truth with the party as the ideal expression of history, and it is the mechanical materialist conception of theory as detachable from its history, as having its own authority, and so as being the party's guide, that underlies this idealist historicism. This aspect of stalinism is reinforced by Althusserianism, whether it is the scientist or the party who decides the truth. Thus the Althusserian identification of stalinism with "historicism" and the condemnation of all forms of historicism in fact serves to strengthen the defences of stalinist politics while launching a vicious assault on any attempt to challenge the party's (Theory's) monopoly of truth.

The terms "humanism", "empiricism" and "economism" are submitted to similar polemical distortions. If history cannot provide a basis for opposition to the authority of science and of the party it embodies, nor can the individual, for the individual is also a bourgeois illusion. This radical "anti-humanism" is obtained by generalising the trivial observation that Marx is not a crude utilitarian and justified by reference to Marx's observations about the dehumanisation wrought by capital. In exactly the same way experience, whether of the individual or of the class, is devalued in the name of "anti-empiricism": the claim that knowledge has nothing to do with experience, but is based on a renunciation of experience as necessarily ideological. This claim is obtained by generalising the trivial observation that Marx was not a Humean empiricist who believed that knowledge could be obtained by mechanical procedures of induction. In this way all possible sources of opposition to the authority of the party's writ are anticipated and denounced as expressions of bourgeois ideology: neither history, not the individual, nor experience, can undermine the authority of knowledge, for the validity of knowledge is guaranteed by its procedures, and its purity is protected by philosophy, the intervention of the class struggle in theory. Needless to add that in the course of this paper I shall stress the "historicist", "humanist" and "empiricist" foundations of marxism.

The last term whose meaning needs to be clarified in this note is "economism". The term "economism" is used by Althusserians in a narrower sense than usual, to refer to tendencies that regard the "economy" as playing a dominant or determinant role. However, in the marxist tradition "economism" has generally referred to a separation of the economic from the political, such as is centrally characteristic of Althusserianism. Thus the economism of the Second International that was challenged by Lenin involved the separation of trade union and political struggle so that the party concerned itself only with "political" matters, while the struggle for the mass of the workers was "purely economic". This separation was based on a particular technicist conception of the economy which saw no need to contest the domination of capital at the point of production and no continuity between "economic" and "political" struggle. It is in this sense that I use the term here.

It should finally be noted that when I use the terms such as "stalinism", "dogmatism", "bourgeois ideology" I try to use them in a precise technical sense and do not use them as terms of abuse (many are still proud to be bourgeois or stalinist). "Stalinism" refers to the interpretation of Marx which became the orthodoxy of the Third International, which has deep roots in the working-class movement but was codified in Stalin's *Dialectical and Historical Materialism,* written for the *History of the CPSU (Revised),* and which served as the standard of orthodoxy from its publication in 1937. This text is too often ignored by latter-day marxists. It is by no means as unsophisticated as many might think, and it was not transcended by the revelations of the consequences of the kind of politics that flowed from it. It is my argument in this paper that Althusser only manages to break with this interpretation of Marx by abandoning Marx altogether in favour of pluralism. "Dogmatism" refers to a tendency, of which stalinism is one version, that treats marxism as a cosmology and

80 SIMON CLARKE

regards a particular interpretation of that cosmology as canonical. Thus dogmatism leads very directly into what I have already defined as stalinist politics. By "bourgeois ideology" I intend to refer to theories that are based on the denial of the historical, and so relative and mutable, character of bourgeois social relations. This is the *defining* feature of bourgeois ideology.

8. Rancière, op. cit., pp. 58-60. L. Althusser, *For Marx* (hereafter FM), London, 1969, Introduction.
9. FM, pp. 11-13, 233. cf. p. 199 where we find a clear expression of Althusserian opportunism: ideological notions are acceptable in ideological struggle, but must be expunged from science.
10. Rancière, op. cit., pp. 71-4, 78-9. The essay in question referred approvingly to Mao Tse-tung's *On Contradiction.* According to Rancière the concept of the *bévue,* the "oversight", has its pragmatic origin in this encounter. ibid., p. 79.
11. ibid., Ch. 2. It is only much later (1972-3) that Althusser actually spelled out the relationship between humanism, economism and historicism and revealed that he had really been attacking economism (ESC, pp. 86-90). P. Anderson, op. cit., p. 39, sees Althusser's anti-humanism as subversive of the humanist rhetoric of the PCF in the 1960s. However the subversive character of Althusser's argument was selective, aimed only at the right opposition within the party, and not the leadership itself. The distinction between science and ideology enables Althusser to oppose "theoretical humanism", and so to oppose "Italianism" within the party, while recognising that it may be "necessary" for socialism to adopt a humanist ideology (cf. "Marxism and Humanism" in *For Marx*).
12. Rancière, op. cit., pp. 74-7, 94-102. Rancière dates the positive interest of the PCF leadership in Althusser's work from 1965. ibid., p. 77. Althusser presents this reversal in ESC as the result of cosy discussion with the party leadership about Spinoza.
13. Cf. K. Marx, *Capital*, vol. 1 (Penguin edition), London, 1976, pp. 96, 173-4 and footnotes. L. Colletti, "Bernstein and the Marxism of the Second International", in *From Rousseau to Lenin.* London, 1972, defines revisionism by its conception of the economy, tracing this conception to later marxism and to bourgeois sociology.
14. *Capital,* vol. 1, pp. 125, 132, 304.
15. Marx and Engels, *Selected Works,* vol. 1, Moscow, 1962, p. 90.
16. Marx, *Capital,* vol. 1, p. 798.
17. J. Banaji,"Modes of Production in a Materialist Conception of History", *Capital and Class,* 2, 1977, offers an excellent critique of this theory of modes of production, even if his alternative is rather idiosyncratic. J. Stalin, *Dialectical and Historical Materialism* is the standard statement of it.
18. Marx, *Grundrisse,* Harmondsworth, 1973, pp. 196-7. Althusser's *Reply to John Lewis* originally appeared in *Marxism Today* and is reproduced in ESC, see especially pp. 86-90. E. B. Pashukanis,

Law and Marxism, London, 1978, offers the classic analysis of the foundations of the legal form and its connection with commodity fetishism. Such a marxist critique of bourgeois ideology reveals also the basis of the complexity of the bourgeois category of the subject which Althusser reduces to the term "man" and identifies with any form of humanism: "The net result of abstracting these definitions from the actual social relation they express, and attempting to develop them as categories in their own right (by purely speculative means) is a confused jumble of contradictions and mutually exclusive propositions"(ibid., p. 152). Althusser's tangle of contradictions derives from the theory of ideology he takes from Lacan. This is one of the more esoteric areas of Althusserianism that I shall not look at in detail. Very roughly "ideology" in Althusser's later work is any theory that posits a subject of society. Ideology is necessary for everyday life, because the individual must imagine him or herself to be a subject to function properly in society, but ideology is also always distorted because society is a complex reality that outflanks the subject. Thus science has to understand society as the complex reality beyond subjects, the complex whole that is partially misrepresented in particular ideologies. Clearly this theory of science and ideology raises problems of the relation between the two, for how can there be a knowledge of the whole that is not partial? This has led Hindess and Hirst to reject the distinction between science and ideology and to follow Foucault in seeing society as consisting in no more than the sum of "discourses" through which individual subjects live their relation to society, thus leaping from positivism to pragmatism in one mighty bound. The problem arises because of the radical discontinuity introduced between experience and reality which makes it impossible to reconcile the two. The result is to propose that we must renounce one or the other. Hindess and Hirst make a speciality of disproving their own theories by a *reductio ad absurdum* and then espousing the absurd instead of abandoning their theories. Such are the perils of the life of the mind.

19. I am concerned here only with Althusser's relation to the Communist Party in the mid-1960s. Subsequent developments have seen the leadership espousing the "Italian" deviation that has come to be known as Eurocommunism, leaving Althusser out on a limb. He has subsequently become mildly critical of the party leadership on occasion.

20. Althusser would call this an "expressive totality" because every aspect expresses the functional determination by the whole. He counterposes this to the "structure-in-dominance". Since, however, the "dominance" of a particular level is itself determined functionally, this seems to be no less an "expressive totality".

21. Cf. the programme of the collection "Théorie" (edited by Althusser) which was printed on the cover of its early volumes, including FM and RC: "The 'Théorie' series aspires to take heed of

the *de facto* encounter that is happening before our eyes between, on the one hand, the conceptual development of the philosophical principles contained in Marx's discovery, and on the other hand, certain works in the fields of epistemology, the history of ideologies and of knowledge and in scientific research." Quoted by G. Therborn, *Science, Class and Society*, London, 1976, p. 57n.

22. I have discussed Poulantzas's work at length elsewhere: S. Clarke, "Marxism, Sociology and Poulantzas's Theory of the State", *Capital and Class*, 3, 1977, and " Capital, Fractions of Capital and the State", *Capital and Class*, 5, 1978.

23. Stripped of its radical rhetoric this convergence between "radicalising" sociology and PCF revisionism may be seen as an expression of a political convergence. Lebowitz, *Science and Society*, 37, 1973, pp. 385-403, has argued that the debate between neo-classical and neo-Ricardian economics expresses the struggle between the bourgeoisie and a technocracy which is radicalised by the experience of the growing contradiction between capital and labour expressed in terms of the irrationality of capitalism and not of the class struggle. It therefore underpins a utopian socialism based on a moral critique of capitalism which counterposes the rationality of the eternal relations of production to the irrationality introduced by bourgeois relations of distribution, and so seeks to overthrow the latter while preserving the former. This replacement of a class critique by a moral critique, itself based on a distributional view of classes, is also found in radical sociology. It is, moreover, the basis on which the European communist parties are seeking to widen their appeal.

24. This assertion has particularly incensed Althusserian readers, for it implies the self-evidently absurd proposition that "knowledge is a process with a subject", for which absurdity I do not apologise. I do not imply that Marx's work it "transparent", complete and without ambiguity. Precisely because it is the work of subject, not the mechanical product of a "problematic", it is very incomplete and often ambiguous. This should not detract from the fact that the *central thrust* of Marx's work is clear and insistent, and it should not distract attention from what Marx actually wrote to what he might have written.

25. L. Althusser, *Politics and History*, London, 1972, pp. 52-3. For Montesquieu the "nature" of government refers to the form of sovereignty (monarchy, despotism, republic), the "principle" to the "human passions" which underlie the different forms.

26. ibid., pp. 49-50, 53. Montesquieu also anticipates Althusser's Marx in linking ideology to class via interests. ibid., p. 93.

27. As Rancière points out, Althusser systematically obliterates the young Marx's originality with respect to Feuerbach by seeing Marx's *historisation* of the Feuerbachian problematic as a simple application, op. cit. pp. 24-6. This historisation already transforms the Feuerbachian "problematic" by transforming the status of the Feuerbachian categories from natural categories to forms of

historical existence. I shall not discuss Althusser's exposure of the idealist character of Marx's early works in this paper. In so far as Althusser's schematic comments have any value they derive largely from A. Cornu (*Karl Marx et F. Engels,* Paris, 1955). The idea of the epistemological break depends not on an interpretation of Marx's work but on Althusser's philosophy of knowledge.

28. FM, pp. 57, 77-8, 82. It is ominous that Althusser believes that the French political scientists and English economists gave Marx "his decisive experience of the *direct discovery* of reality via those who had *lived* it directly and *thought it with the least possible deformation*". The English economists had already described the "actual mechanism" of exploitation "as they saw it in action in English reality" FM, p. 78. (Original emphasis unless stated otherwise.) Althusser has considerably modified his interpretation of the break. He now believes that the philosophical break, which is based on Marx's adoption of a proletarian political position, preceded the scientific ("epistemological") break. Moreover the latter did not replace error (ideology) by truth (science), but rather was a break with *bourgeois* ideology on the basis of *proletarian* ideology. It was still an epistemological break, however, because it introduced the (scientific) opposition between truth and error (ESC, pp. 65-8, 121).

29. FM, p. 187n.

30. FM, p. 91. The discussion of Marx's relation to Hegel is centred on the extremely vague notion of the "problematic" whose function is to give scientific status to caricatures. The discussion really has nothing to do with Hegel at all. The term "Hegel" is clearly used to refer to the unmentionable Stalin, but even Stalin's dialectic is more complex than Althusser's caricature allows. In particular Stalin does not have a concept of an "expressive totality". For Stalin the contradiction between forces and relations of production arises precisely because of historical lags that mean that the relations of production have a different "temporality" from that of the forces of production. The forces of production develop continuously, the relations of production discontinuously. This could be called the "ratchet" theory of history, the ratchet being the device by which continuous motion is transformed into discontinuous motion (cf. Stalin, *Dialectical and Historical Materialism,* and the orreries in Edward Thompson, *The Poverty of Theory*).

31. FM, pp. 99,101.

32. FM, p. 111.

33. FM, p. 97.

34. FM, pp. 113, 100.

35. This is the sense of the famous discussion in the *Grundrisse* of the concept of population: "The population is an abstraction if I leave out, for example, the classes of which it is composed" (ibid, p. 100).

36. Cf. R. Rosdolsky, "Comments on the Method of Marx's Capital", *New German Critique,* 1, *3,* 1974, p. 71, who compares the contradictions into which stalinism is led to those which befell

Ricardianism. Althusser finally abandons any marxist conception of value in his preface to *Capital,* vol. 1, in *Lenin and Philosophy* (hereafter LP), London, 1971, p. 87. A. Cutler, B. Hindess, P. Hirst and A. Hussain have belatedly come to the conclusion that Marx's theory of value is irrelevant to Althusserianism. Their *Marx's "Capital" and Capitalism Today,* London, 1977-8, is essentially a rehash of the standard criticisms of the theory of value.

37. FM, pp. 166-7. This conception replaces the "universal concept of Feuerbachian 'practice'" with a "concrete conception of the specific differences that enables us to situate each particular practice in the specific differences of the social structure" (FM, p. 229). Sociologists call this the principle of "structural differentiation" and it is based on the functional division of labour of a harmonious society.

38. FM, pp. 168-70. Glucksmann, op. cit., discusses at length the metaphysical implications of this conception.

39. FM, p. 173.

40. FM, pp. 201-2.

41. A liberal defence of science that has very reactionary implications when it comes to the defence of the academy. L. Althusser, "Problèmes étudiants", *Nouvelle Critique,* Jan. 1964. Cf. J. Rancière, op.cit., chs. 2 and 6. It is this conception of practice that underlies the systematic confusion of science as a social and science as a mental practice, between the social relations within which science is accomplished and the process of scientific production itself. Theoretical practice is for Althusser *both* a social practice which is part of the complex structured whole, and is *also* a privileged practice in which the unity of the whole is accomplished, in which it achieves its "knowledge effect". RC, pp. 66-7. Cf. A. Callinicos, *Althusser's Marxism,* London, 1976, pp. 113-14. Note that the term "*relative* autonomy" means "autonomous in relation to" and not, as it is sometimes interpreted, the absurd notion of "more of less autonomous".

42. FM, pp. 166, 167, 173, 184. No explanation or defence of this progressive reduction is given.

43. This is the sense of Marx's discussion in *Capital,* volume 1, of the transition from manufacture to modern industry discussed at length by Balibar (RC, pp. 233-41). Marx, *Capital,* vol. 1, pp. 548-9 is unambiguous.

44. FM, pp. 167-9, 175-6, 178-80, 210, 215.

45. An alternative conception of the structure of the marxist totality implicit in this essay is developed in the theory of *Darstellung* in *Reading Capital.* In this conception the economic is permanently present in the political and ideological realms, on the analogy of the presence of the Freudian unconscious in the conscious as the "absent presence of a present absence". The economic, like Lacan's unconscious, exists only in its effects. The philosophical inspiration for this conception is not Marx but Spinoza. It is only by recourse to the Spinozist conception of the relation between God and Substance, with the economic taking the role of God and

the political the role of Substance, that Althusser can find a place for the economic at all. Since it is only an act of faith that can establish the determination, even in the last instance, of the economic once a secular, bourgeois, conception of society is adopted, it is hardly surprising that Althusser's dominant philosophical inspiration is that of metaphysical theology. The theory of *Darstellung* has been devastatingly criticised by Glucksmann, op. cit., pp. 83-8. It was abandoned as part of Althusser's self-criticism since it is an essential foundation of his theoreticism in its implication that the structure is only visible to the Theorist. It cannot therefore survive the subordination of the priesthood to the secular power.

46. Cf. "Lenin wrote that 'politics is economics in a concentrated form'. We can say philosophy is, in the last instance, the *theoretical* concentrate of politics"(ESC, p. 38).

47. This is reflected in Althusser's formulation of the distinction between the technical and social division of labour which is the key to his practical defence of revisionist politics. Rancière, op. cit., pp. 243-8.

48. T. Parsons, *The Structure of Social Action,* NY, 1937; *The Social System,* Glencoe, 1951. Parsons enables us to fill many gaps in Althusser's theory. For example, the theory of functional prerequisites provides us with the means of identifying and delineating the practices which make up the complex social practice in a rather less arbitrary and *ad hoc* manner than that adopted by Althusser (cf. FM, p. 191).

49. This conclusion is very clearly drawn in Althusser's preface to *Capital,* volume I, in which he argues that trade-union struggle is necessarily defensive because it can only concern the rate of exploitation (L. Althusser, *Lenin and Philosophy,* op. cit., pp. 82-3). This inept preface has been tactfully demolished by E. Mandel, in *Contre Althusser,* Paris, 1974. N. Poulantzas, *Political Power and Social Classes,* London, 1973, p. 86 makes the same distinction between trade-union and political struggle.

50. Cf. Poulantzas, "Vers une théorie etc.", op. cit., pp. 1979-81.

51. The idea of ideology as a necessary mystification runs through all of Althusser's work. The theory is developed in an essay published in 1970, "Ideology and the Ideological State Apparatuses" (in *Lenin and Philosophy*). Rancière (op. cit., pp. 140-7) offers a devastating critique of this essay. May 1968 had undermined the Althusserian conception of ideology as an imaginary relation, replacing this with a conception of ideological domination as a system of material power relations embedded in and reproduced by specific institutions. Althusser adopts the rhetoric of the latter conception to reproduce his own, idealist, theory of ideology. The idea of the ideological state apparatus is therefore purged of its radical content, for ideological struggle becomes once more the task of the philosopher. The political condition for this reactionary position was the "stabilisation" of the universities after 1968, in

which the PCF participated with enthusiasm. Althusser maintains the old idea of ideology as imagination, analysed not through an analysis of the functioning of the ideological apparatus, but through an *ahistorical* analysis of ideology as "interpellation" of the subject, the apparatus then being simply the means by which the illusion is foisted on the dominated. Rancière also discusses the *sociological* character of Althusser's conception of ideology, which emerges clearly from an earlier text "Théorie, pratique théorique et formulation théorique. Idéologie et lutte idéologique" (mimeo, n.d.). In this text ideology is given an explicitly *sociological* function, which is to permit agents to perform the tasks determined by the "social structure": "In a class society, as in a classless society, the function of ideology is to guarantee the *bond* between men in the ensemble of the forms of their existence, the relation of the individuals to their tasks fixed by the structure..." Further on the "primary function" of ideology is defined explicitly as its indispensability for "social cohesion", and this latter is referred to something called the "social structure", which is *prior to* the division of society into classes (ibid, pp. 29-31), quoted by Rancière, op. cit., pp. 229-31). (Cf. N. Poulantzas, *Political Power*, pp.206-8.) In the "Ideological State Apparatus" paper this function is fulfilled by the interpellation of the subject, which is the necessary condition for individuals to relate to the real relations within which they live. This in turn is because, it is stressed, the reproduction of the relations of production is secured "for the most part... by the legal-political and ideological superstructure" (*Lenin and Philosophy*, p. 141). Thus Althusser reproduces Durkheimian functionalism to the last detail: the function of the collective conscience is to ensure social reproduction by constituting biological individuals as social actors. Different societies then differ according to their forms of individuality, which is functionally related to the form of the division of labour.

52. ESC, pp. 55-7. Althusser is only able to set Vico against Marx because of this extraordinary assertion that the relations of production are natural relations. Cf. Marx's endorsement of Vico, *Capital,* vol. I, p. 493n.

53. This "sociological" conception of the separation between the economic and the political, that corresponds to a surreptitious contrast between the technical and the historical, between production and reproduction, between the natural and the social, and between the immutable and the mutable, is very different from Lenin's distinction between trade-unionist and revolutionary politics. It is a conception that can be found equally in Stalin's version of the distinction between the forces and relations of production, in the political economists' distinction between the production and distribution of wealth, in the sociologists' distinction between economy and society. It should not be surprising, therefore, that academic marxism should also be very vulnerable to it. The "sociologisation" of marxism as an

alternative to (or an eclectic combination of) both stalinism and bourgeois sociology was pioneered in Britain by the new *New Left Review* which introduced Althusser to the Anglo-Saxons as part of its project of making old-fashioned marxism more "sophisticated" by complementing "economism" with a variety of sociological theories, without ever challenging the economistic conception of the "economy", or coming to grips with anything so mundane as capitalist production. Edward Thompson, in his early polemic against this tendency, hit the nail on the head when he noted the historical, capitalist, category of the "economic", drawing out William Morris's lesson that capitalist society was founded upon forms of exploitation which are *simultaneously* economic, moral and cultural, and concluded that "social and cultural phenomena do not trail after the economic at some remote remove: they are, at their source, immersed in the same nexus of relationship" (E. Thompson, "The Peculiarities of the English", *Socialist Register*, 1965, pp. 254-6).

54. RC, pp. 35-6, 40-1, 130n.
55. RC, pp. 27-8.
56. Several commentators have noted the similarity of Althusser's philosophy of science to that of Thomas Kuhn (e.g. D. Schwatzman, "Althusser, Dialectical Materialism and the Philosophy of Science", *Science and Society*, 39, 1975-6, pp.321-24), in that for Althusser science is based on the transformation and development of problematics, for Kuhn it is based on the transformation and development of paradigms. However there is a major difference: for Kuhn a scientific revolution is an irrational event, while Althusser's theory remains firmly within positivistic rationalism. Althusser's philosophy of science has rather complex origins. Althusserians relate it to the work of the surrealist philosopher Gaston Bachelard, but it extracts only one aspect of Bachelard's work and reinterprets it in the light of the French conventionalist tradition of Poincaré and Duhem as developed by Cavaillès and Granger in the light of Vienna positivism. For all these thinkers the defining feature of science is its separation from reality. Since we have no direct access to reality, realism can only be an ideological illusion. Science can only work on ideas, thus the task of science is to investigate the relations between ideas, not the relation between ideas and some supposedly independent reality. In particular science simply seeks to purify our ideas of the irrational by formalising and systematising the ideas with which it is presented in order to eliminate any contradictions. Science therefore has only one foundation, the principle of non-contradiction. The aim of science is to detach ideas from any subjective considerations that are dominated by the ideology of naïve realism. Thus science seeks not truth, in the sense of correspondence with the world beyond science, but consistency. The locus of scientific activity is therefore transferred from the consciousness of the scientist to the concept, thought becoming the

development of a system of concepts of which the thinker is not conscious.

This philosophy is not as strange as it often appears in Althusserian guise. The basic idea is that of neo-positivism: science starts with a series of observation statements that have to be organised into a deductive system. Thus science involves observation and formalisation as its empirical and theoretical phases, formalisation seeking to develop theoretical statements from which observation statements can be deduced without contradiction. However, the major problem positivism has always faced is that of distinguishing between "theoretical" and "observational" statements by discovering a neutral observation language. Carnap originally proposed the language of physics as the neutral language of a unified science, but this privilege was indefensible, and so Carnap adopted a principle of tolerance so that the language selected was arbitrary. From here it is a short step to Neurath's conventionalism which effectively abolished the separation between theory and observations, an abolition pushed to the limit in the work of Bachelard and Cavaillès.

The history of positivism is long and complex, but this extremely formalistic and rationalistic version proved untenable almost as soon as it was formulated. On the one hand, consistency is only provable for certain incomplete mathematical axiomatisations, so the theory's validity is at best confined to limited mathematical applications (Cavaillès was concerned only with mathematics while Bachelard saw mathematics as the model for all the sciences). On the other hand, studies in the history of science reveal that a toleration of inconsistency is often essential to scientific progress, the best-known example being the coexistence of the corpuscular and wave theories of electromagnetic energy. More generally the neo-positivist philosophy of science has collapsed and is progressively giving way to realist interpretations.

This neo-positivist philosophy of science has been ontologised by Foucault, a former student of Althusser's, and, following Foucault, by Hindess and Hirst and others. In this philosophy of the concept human individuals become simply the instruments of an impersonal thought, the "problematic", "episteme" or "discourse" that they live out. Both reality and the subject become constructs of the concept, having no independent existence, so there is no escape from the tyranny of the concept. If a link to reality is desired it can only be established by some kind of "transcendental correlation", which almost inescapably entails a faith in a supreme being who guarantees the correspondence between thought and the real (Glucksmann, op. cit., p. 74). The source of this ontology is Heidegger, not Marx, the Concept replacing Heidegger's Being (see M. Dufrenne, "La philosophie du néo-positivisme", *Esprit,* 1967; E. Morot-Sir, *La Pensée Française d'aujourd'hui,* Paris, 1971), but it is also strongly reminiscent of Durkheim's collective conscience. If discourses exist prior to those who live within them, then this philosophy calls forth an objectivist theory of meaning that can establish the meaning of the discourse as being immanent within it, and not constituted by a subject. Thus it leads directly into Durkheimian semiology derived from Lévi-Strauss and French neo-Saussureanism. Finally Lacan's psychoanalysis, also inspired by the Durkheimian Lévi-Strauss, provides a theory of the subject as the construct of the discourse, "interpellated" into the discourse, giving the illusion of subjectivity that is the basis of the illusory character of all ideology (cf. S. Clarke, *The Foundations of Structuralism*). Thus from a simple tautology, that words are not the same as the things they denote, Althusserianism develops into an all-embracing metaphysical fog which tries to deny the existence of anything but the Word. The proponents of this metaphysic usually defend it on the grounds that it is materialist, not that it is marxist. It is supposedly materialist because it sees knowledge as the result of "practice" by analogy with material production, the product of the mechanical application of logical precepts to a given raw material requiring no human intervention. Could any materialism be more mechanical, less marxist? Althusserianism has succeeded in extracting the rational kernel from the mystical shell of the Hegelian dialectic, but it throws out the kernel, the concept of contradiction, and retains the shell.

57. This is the only connection specified by Althusser (RC, pp. 53, 58, 141). Although he insists that his theory is not idealist (RC, pp.41-2), his insistence on the radically anti-historicist understanding of science (RC, pp.133-4) seems to imply that science depends on its insulation from reality, and so implies a theory of science which can only be idealist. The task of philosophy on the new definition is to maintain this insulation. Hence the absurd idea that Lenin wrote *Materialism and Empiriocriticism* to defend *science* (cf. Rancière, op. cit., pp. 115-21, Pannekoek, *Lenin as Philosopher*, London, 1975).

58. With his self-criticism this point is clarified and modified. On the one hand, Althusser makes it clear that Marx was simply the name of the place where marxism happened as a mutation of German philosophy, English political economy, and French socialism on the basis of the class struggle (ESC, p. 56). On the other hand, the break was not with ideology in general, but with *bourgeois* ideology, proletarian ideology making the break possible (ESC, p. 121).

59. Almost all commentators see Althusser as a bourgeois philosopher, including many Althusserians in the wake of Althusser's self-criticism: P. Hirst, *Theoretical Practice*, 2, 1971. Cutler and Gane deny that this is the case, but only by arguing that Althusser seeks not guarantees but knowledge of scientificity, which doesn't raise any problem of correspondence with the real because science makes no reference to the real: "*real* modes of production constitute an inexistant (imaginary) object" (A. Cutler and M. Gane, "On the Question of Philosophy", *Theoretical*

Practice, 7/8, 1973, pp. 37-8, 46). Conventionalism is as much a variant of the bourgeois philosophy of science as is agnosticism of theology: it refuses an answer instead of denying the question. Despite its apparent liberalism in denying the scientist privileged access to reality, it simply displaces the privilege of the scientist by locating it in his own domain. B. Hindess and P. Hirst offer a demonstration by *reductio ad absurdum*: the Asiatic mode of production does not exist because the scientist (or Hindess and Hirst) cannot construct it as an imaginary object (*Precapitalist Modes of Production,* RKP, London, 1975, Ch. 4). Conventionalism is only one position implicit in *Reading Capital* (cf. ESC, p. 192, where Althusser recognises the risk of nominalism "and even idealism". He believes that it is sufficient to assert the primacy of the real over thought to escape the difficulty). We also find crude positivist references to one-to-one correspondence (pp. 68,255), and the quasi-logical positivist reliance on the privileged access of theory to the "essence of practice in general" (FM, p.169, cf. RC, p. 216, Glucksmann, op. cit., pp. 73-5). I shall not discuss the contortions of Althusser as bourgeois philosopher, but see note 56 above and compare the definition of the problematic of bourgeois philosophy given in RC, p. 35, and the idea of bourgeois philosophy as handmaid of science, remedial response to scientific crisis (or even condition of an epistemological break), rather than as an ideological response to a scientific advance.

60. The new definition of philosophy subordinates philosophy to the class struggle, abandoning the autonomy of theory (ESC, *passim.*). However, the role of the philosopher, representative now of the proletariat instead of Theory, is unchanged. The main difference is a political one: the philosopher has no basis on which to challenge the authority of the party in matters of theory. (Althusser argues that "marxism affirms the primacy of politics over philosophy" but indicates that philosophy is not the "servant of politics" because of its "relative autonomy" (ESC, p. 58n). However he has now deprived himself of any basis on which to contest the authority of the party, and so "relative autonomy" becomes quite abstract). The philosopher is still guardian of revolutionary purity, now defending a spontaneous materialist against the intrusion of the dominant bourgeois ideology, instead of defending a higher rationality against the false ideas which come from social practice. Although the sources of truth and error are inverted, it is still the philosopher alone who can distinguish them. Thus the new definition retains the key features of Althusserianism: the neutrality of science and the necessity of philosophy. Philosophy now joins the class struggle in science, the object of which is not the opposition of mental to manual labour, the appropriation of the creativity of the worker by capital, but the struggle between spontaneous materialism and intruding idealism! The task of philosophy is to identify the class enemy within, the insidious presence of words (rather than problematics — Cutler and Gane, op. cit., pp. 38-40) which contaminate the innocence of the

spontaneous materialist, to draw a "theoretical dividing line between true ideas and false ideas, a political dividing line between the people (the proletariat and its allies) and the people's enemies. Philosophy represents the class struggle in theory. In return it helps the people to distinguish in *theory* and in all *ideas* (political, ethical, aesthetic, etc.) between true ideas and false ideas" (L. Althusser, "Philosophy as a Revolutionary Weapon", *NLR,* 64, 1970, p. 10. Rancière offers a penetrating critique of the new definition, op. cit., ch. 3. Cutler and Gane, op. cit., show its philosophical incoherence). This is precisely dogmatism: scientific truths are elevated to the status of eternal truths as philosophical theses which become the indubitable foundation of science itself (cf. Althusser's argument against Lewis in exactly these terms, ESC, pp. 61-2). Is it just coincidence that the new definition emerges as the challenge to the PCF moves out of the universities, and becomes precisely the attempt to subvert the "innocent materialism" of the workers with seditious words? Althusser, the PCF, and the management of Renault can unite in defence of the innocence of the honest worker.

61. The term *sinnlich-übersinnlich* is applied by Marx to the commodity. *Kapital* I, Berlin, 1952, p. 84.

62. These are the terms in which Marx and Engels conceived their work in the *Communist Manifesto*: "The theoretical conclusions of the communists are in no way based on ideas or principles that have been invented, or discovered, by this or that would-be universal reformer. They merely express, in general terms, actual relations springing from an existing class struggle, from a historical movement going on under our very eyes." (*Selected Works,* Vol. I, p. 46.) Cf. J. Rancière, "Mode d'emploi pour une réédition de *Lire 'le Capital'*, Temps Modernes,* 1973. Althusser appears to have moved towards such a conception in ESC, but he does not spell it out, nor does he develop its implications for his earlier arguments.

63. As Brohm argues, Marx clearly retains the basic laws of the Hegelian dialectic: the idea of the "process of theoretical abstraction as dialectical concretisation", the idea of "the dialectical relation between law and phenomenon, essence and appearance" and the idea of the negation of the negation (suppressed by Stalin for his own good reasons). J.-M. Brohm, "Louis Althusser et la dialectique matérialiste", in *Contre Althusser,* pp. 62-82. Cf. Nicolaus's foreword to his translation of the *Grundrisse,* London, 1973. It should be remembered that "Hegel" in Althusser's discourse is only a straw-man, standing in for the "historicist" humanism-economism couple. Hence Althusser's presentation of Hegel is, to say the least, schematic and misleading.

64. For which reason Marx didn't publish it, as he notes in the Preface to the *Critique of Political Economy* (*Selected Works,* vol. I, p. 361).

65. RC, p. 41, *Grundrisse,* pp. 101-7. Cf. p. 94: "production and consumption . . . appear as moments of one process, in which

production is the real point of departure and hence also the predominant moment."
66. "These categories therefore express the forms of being, the characteristics of existence, and often only individual sides of this specific society." ibid., p. 106.
67. Engels, "Review of Marx's *Critique of Political Economy*", *Selected Works*, vol. I, pp. 372-3. This review is important because, although it tries to popularise, it relates the accomplished Critique back to the unpublished 1857 Introduction. That the work was no trifle is best shown by the development of Marx's analysis between 1857 and 1867. The chapter on Money, written one month after the 1857 Introduction, continues to apply the dialectical method in an idealist manner, so that, for example, the contradiction between the commodity as value and as use-value is constituted in thought (*Grundrisse*, p. 145). In this chapter Marx is straining to get beyond such formulations (p. 151) and does succeed elsewhere in the text (cf. p. 204). But he does not establish an adequate formulation of the materialist dialectic in the analysis of the commodity and of money until the *Critique* and, more completely, *Capital* itself.
68. *Grundrisse*, pp. 93, 99-100. It seems likely that *in a formalistic sense* the latter passage provides the inspiration for the Althusserian conceptualisation of the relation between the various "instances" ("A definite production thus determines a definite consumption, distribution and exchange, as well as *definite relations between these different moments.*" ibid., p. 99).
69. Marx, Engels, *Selected Works*, vol. I, p. 374. Marx, Afterword to Second German Edition of *Capital*, ibid., p. 456.
70. It requires the critical power of the rational, materialist, dialectic to overthrow this empiricism. "In its mystified form, dialectic became the fashion in Germany, because it seemed to transfigure and glorify the existing state of things. In its rational form it is a scandal and abomination to bourgeoisdom and its doctrinaire professors, because it includes in its comprehension and affirmative recognition of the existing state of things, at the same time, also, the recognition of the negation of that state, of its inevitable breaking up; because it regards every historically developed social form as in fluid movement, and therefore takes into account its transient nature not less than its momentary existence; because it lets nothing impose upon it, and is in its essence critical and revolutionary." ibid., pp. 456-7.
71. Engels, ibid., pp. 370-1. It is interesting to note that Althusser's earliest published work was a translation of Feuerbach.
72. Hegel is the theoretical source. As Rancière notes ("Mode d'emploi") the historical source is the slogans of the developing working class movement, slogans whose echo reverberates through all of Marx's works.
73. E. Bernstein, *Voraussetzungen des Sozialismus*, 1899, p. 42, quoted by Brohm, op. cit., p. 85.
74. Marx, *Eighteenth Brumaire*, *Selected Works*, vol. I, p. 247.

75. RC, p. 108. The only coherent theory of history within this framework would be an idealist one in which the structures are inserted in the real as essence of the real. It is difficult to see how else the relation between such pure concepts as the "mode of production" and reality can be conceived than in the "ideal type" relation which Althusserianism constantly insists is idealist (A. Badiou, *Le Concept de Modèle,* Paris, 1969. Cf. RC, pp. 117-18; N. Poulantzas, *Political Power* etc., pp. 145-7). It is common for Althusserianism to reserve its most coherent criticism for the errors into which it falls itself. Poulantzas consistently formulates the relation between modes of production and social formations as the relation between theory and reality (ibid., pp. 15-16; *Classes in Contemporary Capitalism,* London, 1975, p. 22. Cf. Balibar, "Self-Criticism", *Theoretical Practice,* 7/8, 1973, p. 68). The only way to avoid this is to abandon the attempt to relate the "ideal type" to reality at all, and follow the logic of neo-Kantianism by abandoning reality altogether (Cutler and Gane, op. cit., pp. 37-8. 46; Hirst and Hindess, op. cit., *ad nauseam*). This structuralism is renounced by Balibar in his self-criticism (op. cit., pp. 60-61). B. Hindess and P. Hirst (op. cit., pp. 5-9) follow Balibar's self-criticism in concluding that there can be no general theory of modes of production, and so no theory of history. All we can have are general concepts which we then use to develop specific concepts which in turn produce an analysis of the current situation, the latter being a theoretical construct and not something given to theory (ibid., p. 4). The reason for this is familiar: "The reproduction of the transformation of a determinate structure of social relations is the outcome of specific class struggles . . . conducted under certain definite conditions" (ibid., p. 9). What a paradox: anti-historicism is pushed to the limit only to end up, having expelled history definitively from theory, handing history over to the class subject and its study to the empiricism of bourgeois historians. This is the paradox of bourgeois philosophy — history can only be *either* "real" *or* "ideal". In their later work Hindess and Hirst resolve the paradox by abandoning the antinomy of theory and reality in favour of a realistic pragmatism. Note that Stalin does not fall into the "historicist" deviation as defined here by Althusser. For Stalin, the relations of production always *lag behind* the development of the forces of production and this is the source of the *conflict* that for Stalin (as for Althusser) replaces Marx's concept of *contradiction.* Thus Stalin, in *Dialectical and Historical Materialism,* offers precisely the complex structural whole that Althusser espouses.

76. RC, pp. 157, 160. Cf. C. Colliot-Thélène, "Relire 'le Capital' ". *Critiques de l'économie politique,* 9, 1972.

77. Hence "this epoch-making conception of history was the direct theoretical premise for the new materialist outlook." Engels, op. cit., p. 372.

78. This error is not just a slip. Further down the same page we find even more explicitly: "The economic concepts of constant and

variable capital, of Department I and Department II, are merely the economic determinations, in the field of economic analysis itself, of the concept of the *material* conditions of the labour process." Compare his Ricardian definition of wages (*Lenin and Philosophy,* p. 126), and above all his rejection of Marx's theory of value as Hegelian in his Preface to *Capital.* This law is reduced to "a special case of . . . the law of the distribution of the available labour power [*sic*] between the various branches of production", ibid., p. 87. "Vulgar economists commit two kinds of errors: (1) either they assign the 'economic definiteness of form' to an 'objective property' of things (Marx, *Capital,* vol. II, p. 164) . . . (2) or they assign 'certain properties materially inherent in instruments of labour' to the social form of the instruments of labour (ibid.) . . . These two mistakes, which at first glance seem contradictory, can actually be reduced to the same basic methodological defect; the identification of the material process of production with its social form, and the identification of the *technical* functions of things with their *social* functions" (I. Rubin, op. cit., p. 28. The definitive stalinist verdict on Rubin's interpretation was delivered at the so-called "Menshevik trial" of March 1931).

79. RC, p. 173. The quote could have come straight from Stalin.
80. The concept "mode of production" is rapidly increasing its scope as the essay progresses, from being a concept of the labour process expressing the mode of attack of the means of labour on nature to becoming the concept of the social whole itself. RC, pp. 173-8. Marx himself never used the concept consistently or systematically.
81. RC, pp. 177, 180, cf. ESC p. 125, where this is "recognised to be structuralist".
82. As Glucksmann notes, op. cit., p. 80, this anthropological foundation is implicit in *Reading Capital.* Cf. B. Hindess and P. Hirst, op. cit., pp. 14-15.
83. L. Althusser, "Théorie, pratique théorique", op. cit., p. 29, quoted by Rancière, *La leçon* etc., op. cit., pp. 229-30. This conception of ideology is identical to that of Talcott Parsons. Others have noted the remarkable similarity of Althusser's and Parsons's conceptions of theory (P. Walton and A. Gamble, *From Alienation to Surplus Value,* London, 1972), and of politics (Poulantzas, *Vers une théorie,* p. 1979, quotes T. Parsons, *The Social System,* pp. 126-7). Of course the bourgeois analysis of the whole leads immediately to bourgeois analyses of the functionally differentiated "relatively autonomous" levels. Hence "all the levels of the social structure . . . imply specific social relations" (Balibar, RC, p. 220). These levels conventionally implicate classes, status groups and parties. A "marxist" analysis uses the same term, class, for each level but this is no more than a rhetorical device, for the content of the term is identical to the sociological concept at each level. Hence Althusserianism legitimates Poulantzas's attempt to pass bourgeois political sociology off as marxism by wrapping it in the

84. Marx, *Grundrisse,* p. 97.
85. It is because Althusser's "anti-historicism" involves the abandonment of a dialectical, historical materialist, method in favour of an analytical one that Althusserianism is compelled to pose the question in the latter terms. These are precisely the terms of analytical philosophy's critique of marxism: cf. G. A. Cohen, "On some criticisms of historical materialism", *Aristotelian Society Supplement,* 44, 1970, pp. 121-42. Hindess and Hirst, op. cit., p. 19, see determination in the last instance by the economic as something to be founded "in the concept of the economy itself".

    The entire project of these authors is based on the attempt to establish *analytically* the conditions of possibility of society, or of particular modes of production. They have successively reached the predictable conclusions firstly, that one cannot establish *analytically* the conditions of existence of a given historical society, for one can only establish the logical precondition of a *concept.* Thus "theory" can only study the concept of the "mode of production" and has no purchase on the concrete reality of the "social formation". They have then discovered that it is not possible to establish *analytically* the relations of determination postulated by marxism between different forms of social relations, nor the relations of succession between different modes of production, and have therefore concluded that marxism is arbitrary, based on hypotheses that are analytically gratuitous. This conclusion should come as a great comfort to marxists, for the implication is that marxism is not simply a series of tautologies. It is a theory with a real historical content. Edward Thompson deals with this aspect of Althusserianism in his critique, *The Poverty of Theory,* bringing out the political implications of this sort of sociological arrogance. Marx criticises Hegelianism for exactly this sort of idealism, that believes that the features of capitalism can be discovered in the concept of "capitalism", in the Introduction to the *Grundrisse.*
86. RC, pp. 175-6. The quote is from *Capital,* volume III. Cf. E. Laclau, "The Specificity of the Political", *Economy and Society,* 4, *1,*1975, pp. 104-6.
87. Before *Reading Capital* Althusser regarded the latter work as a "positive study" rather than a "systematic exposition of Marx's theoretical position" (FM, p. 47)! Cf. Pashukanis, op. cit., J. Holloway and S. Picciotto, "Capital, Crisis and the State", *Capital and Class,* 2, 1977.
88. This argument occupies a considerable proportion of the text of *Reading Capital.* It is based on the radical separation of thought and the real, the claim that a concept cannot be historical because it

is founded in theory, and so falls with this separation. It is worth noting that if the concept of mode of production is purely in thought it is difficult to see how history can be either its starting point or its product. The belief that it can be is what constitutes Balibar's project as a structuralism. Hirst and Hindess solve the problem in their parody of Althusserianism by abolishing history altogether, op. cit. (conclusion).

89. RC, pp. 201-15.
90. The theory has an "anti-evolutionist" character, breaking with any idea of a "progressive *movement of differentiation* of the forms" or "*a line of progress* with a logic akin to a destiny". RC, p. 225. It is "historicist" as soon as it tries to explain history as projection of structures, though. Cf. note (15).
91. RC, pp. 226-7, 229. A thoroughly Ricardian definition — what is this "mode of appropriation of the social product" if not a relation of distribution? In this passage Balibar systematically adopts Adam Smith's definition of productive labour in terms of the "material nature of the labour and its objects" (p. 232).
92. RC, pp. 236-9. Balibar presumably means unity of *labourer* and means of labour in this passage. In the quote above he presumably means that the capitalist owns means of production and *labour power*. Symptomatic slips! Hindess and Hirst, op. cit., reproduce such slips, e.g. p. 11. Cf. L. Althusser, *Lenin and Philosophy*, p. 87. N. Poulantzas, *Political Power*, p. 32. As Glucksmann, op. cit., p. 81, points out, this contrast is only sufficient to distinguish capitalist from non-capitalist modes of production, as indeed is the definition of modes of production itself. It might seem that this distinction introduces a break with the *eternisation* of capitalist social relations. This is not the case, for the small producer is simply the "self-employed" capitalist who has always featured prominently in bourgeois ideology. Balibar merely seeks the technical conditions which make "self-employment" possible. Hirst and Hindess take up Glucksmann's criticism, mistaking Balibar's position for that of Marx, op. cit., pp. 227-9.
93. "Self-Criticism", op. cit., p. 56. Balibar appears to have transposed Althusser's terminology, so that Balibar's "deter-minant in the last instance" signifies Althusser's "dominant instance". It is also not clear whether "dominance" refers to the really or the apparently dominant "level". In the quote from Marx on p. 217 of RC, Marx makes it quite clear that he is concerned with the appearance, for in Rome "its secret history is the history of its landed property". Cf. *Grundrisse*, p. 97. In all the confusion we get the impression that Balibar has actually explained determination in the last instance! This illusion is fostered by the ambiguous use of the term "mode of production". Mutual functional interdependence in the whole is determination by the "mode of production" if the term refers to the whole, but not if it refers to the "economic". Cf. note (80).
94. RC, pp. 222-4. The instances are now completely autonomous, if it is determined that they be determinant. Determination in the last

instance now simply means that the economic will determine that it doesn't determine anything.

95. *Capital,* vol. III, Moscow, 1962, pp. 770-2. RC, p. 233.
96. RC, p. 217. Poulantzas cannot make up his mind either: *Political Power,* pp. 15, 32, 70.
97. "Self-criticism", op. cit., pp. 65-6.
98. Hindess and Hirst, op. cit., ch. 5, offer a development of this approach. They follow the implications of Balibar's self-criticism in criticising the arbitrary character of the assumed political intervention, realising that forces and relations of production are not independent. They therefore ask what are the technical conditions for given relations of "surplus-product appropriation", i.e. relations of distribution, by asking what are the technical conditions which enable the feudal landowner to intervene politically to separate the direct producer from his means of production. They then locate the power of the landowner in the reproduction of this separation, so denying that relations of personal domination are essential to the feudal mode of production. They don't seem to realise that this is because they have described a disfigured capitalist mode of production, a feudal Robinsonade, in which "self-employed" small producers are exploited by a class of capitalist landowners and merchant capitalists who lease means of production to them. Hindess and Hirst can abolish relations of *personal* dependence only because they implicitly assume the prevalence of generalised commodity relations to impose *class* domination through the operation of the market. This is only implicit because they see the state as a market substitute, imposing "competition" on the peasantry. It is fortunate that their theory is not meant to have any relation to reality. The idea that feudal rent is based on the effective right of *exclusion* of the peasant would have surprised many a feudal lord.
99. The theory of "state monopoly capitalism" reproduces the critique of feudal society expressed by classical political economy. It is now the monopolies which are using political intervention to modify relations of distribution artificially, and the communist party which criticises them on the basis of the eternal character of capitalist relations of production, seeing in "market socialism" the resolution of the contradictions of capitalism. Cf. Poulantzas, *Political Power,* pp. 55-6, for which both pre-capitalist modes and monopoly capitalism require state intervention.
100. Cf. A. Aumeeruddy, B. Lautier and R. Tortajada, "Labour Power and the State". *Capital and Class,* 6, 1978.
101. For Marx this relation of dependence is clearly a *class* relation and not as Hindess and Hirst imagine, an intersubjective relation between particular individuals. It is only the attempt to impose feudal relations of distribution on a capitalist mode of production that leads to the belief that feudalism is contrasted with capitalism by the necessary role of the political in the former. Within this framework political intervention is explained not as an aspect of

98   SIMON CLARKE

the imposition of a class relation on the members of the society, something central to every class society, but because "relations" do not correspond to "forces" of production, as they supposedly do in a capitalist society.

102. RC, pp. 214, 219. In the feudal mode the landlord is "agent of co-ordination . . . agency of combination"(Hirst and Hindess, op. cit., pp. 238-9). Cf. Poulantzas, *Political Power,* p. 25.

103. Because "surplus labour" is primarily a *functional* concept for Althusserians, only the mode of *appropriation* determines whether or not it is inserted in exploitative social relations. This makes it very difficult to identify class societies non-arbitrarily, cf. Hindess and Hirst, op. cit., pp. 24-8, 67-8. L. Althusser, Preface to *Capital,* p. 88.

104. RC, p. 212.

105. RC, p. 233. Paradoxically this definition can give rise to "humanist" temptations, for only *subjects* can own things.

106. This is especially difficult in the capitalist mode of production since it doesn't appear directly in legal form.

107. RC, p. 232. According to Balibar this is Marx's position. As P. P. Rey (*Les Alliances de Classes,* Paris, 1973, pp. 93-111) points out, in *Capital* it is only exceptionally and metaphorically that the relation of production is described as a property relation. Marx is not concerned with this analytical question, but with the question of historical primacy. Cf. *Grundrisse,* p. 98; Preface to the *Critique, Selected Works* I, op. cit., p. 363.

108. "To the extent to which their ideology is freed from bourgeois and petit-bourgeois conceptions, the masses will not recognise one another as 'men' nor seek to claim their 'human dignity'." S. Karez, *Théorie et Politique: Louis Althusser,* Paris, 1974, quoted by Rancière, *La leçon,* op. cit., p. 161.

109. Marx's analysis of the "circuit" of social capital is clear and unambiguous: *Capital,* vol. 1, ch. 23 and vol. 2, chs. 1-4. Too often a "symptomatic" reading is a substitute for the harder, but more rewarding, work of an actual reading.

110. Balibar inverts the relation between production and reproduction, so that analysis of the latter introduces no "new conditions" (RC, p. 263) but is rather simply an account of "the relation between the *totality* of social production and its particular forms (branches) in a given synchrony". (RC, p. 264). Balibar doesn't understand that analysis of production *presupposes* that of reproduction (Glucksmann, op. cit., p. 82). Cf. the amazing contortions of Hindess and Hirst, op. cit., p. 270, where the revolutionary theoretical distinction between capitalism "in form" and capitalism "in the strict sense" is introduced to get to Sraffa's neo-Ricardian definition of capitalism as "commodity production by means of commodities".

111. Cf. on this point S. Clarke, "'Socialist Humanism' and the critique of economism", *History Workshop Journal,* 8, 1979.

112. RC, p. 213.

113. Rancière, *La leçon,* p. 244.
114. RC, p. 174.
115. RC, pp. 214, 238-9.
116. The concept of Asiatic society has had the most chequered career subsequently, buffeted by changes in the role of the state in capitalist society, by the development of the "socialist" state, and by the anti-colonial struggle.
117. This follows ultimately from the failure to root "relations of production" in production, and so the belief that the transformation of relations of production is conditioned by the political rather than by the level of development of the forces of production. This essentially "sociological" view of the development of capitalism, most clearly expressed in Barrington Moore, *The Social Origins of Dictatorship and Democracy,* Allen Lane, London, 1967, is also found in marxist work: cf. P. Anderson, *Lineages of the Absolutist State,* London, 1974; Hindess and Hirst, op. cit.; and my own *The Development of Capitalism,* London, 1974.
118. "The original unity between a particular form of community (clan) and the corresponding property in nature..., which appears in one respect as the particular form of property — has its living reality in a specific *mode of production*". *Grundrisse,* p. 495. Cf. pp. 471, 485-6, 489-93.
119. ibid., p. 84.
120. RC, p. 213. "Property, in so far as it is only the conscious relation ... is only realised by production itself. The real appropriation takes place not in the mental but in the real, active relation to these conditions." *Grundrisse,* p. 493.
121. ibid., p. 489. This is why Marx uses the rather misleading term "property" throughout this text. He is seeking to show that bourgeois property is simply an expression of a "naturally arisen ... historically developed" relation. ibid., p. 485.
122. Poulantzas, *Political Power,* pp. 30-1, 126, offers a confused analysis of this text based on the definition of relations of production as purely economic relations. But the distinction between political and economic cannot be *prior to* the definition of the relations of production. (Cf. Laclau, op. cit., pp. 104-6.)
123. These appearances must be sharply distinguished from the real presupposition, the real relation of the individual to the objective conditions of his or her life. The concept of the Asiatic mode of production does not stand or fall on the presence or absence of particular forms of legal property nor, for that matter, of communal forms of labour. The concept allows for variation in the forms of labour, the legal and ideological forms, and the political forms. Hence much of Perry Anderson's criticism (op. cit., appendix) of the concept is beside the point. It need hardly be added that Hindess and Hirst's "proof" of the impossibility of the Asiatic mode is as incoherent as the rest of their book (op. cit., ch. 4).
124. *Grundrisse,* op. cit., 415, 483-4.

125. "'As long as the labour process,' we read in *Capital,* 'is only a mere process between persons and nature, its simple elements remain common to all social forms of development.' But every particular historical stage of this process 'further develops its material foundations and social forms.' And precisely these social *forms,* in contrast to the naturally given 'content', are what is important" (Rosdolsky, op. cit., p. 66).
126. This is the logical implication of Althusserianism, implicit in *Reading Capital* and developed by Hindess and Hirst, op. cit. "Historicism" comes back in since the class subject is the only agent capable of transcending the existing mode of production and introducing a new one. J. Banaji, op. cit., offers a devastating critique of the approach to modes of production which takes the form of exploitation as its starting point. See also S. Clarke, "'Socialist Humanism' and the critique of economism", op. cit.
127. *Grundrisse,* op. cit., pp. 493, 489, 495-6.
128. ibid., pp. 486, 475.
129. RC, p. 215.
130. RC, pp. 239, 272. It is because the relations are purely formal that they can only be *changed* by being *transformed.* Hence we find Althusserianism taking up the structuralist opposition of reproduction — stasis and revolution-transformation. This gives the rhetoric a radical appearance — "no change without revolution", but in fact represents a repetition of old conservative positions — "no change without revolution, so no change". It is interesting that the Althusserian opposition of structure and practice, and of structure and history, reproduce those of functionalist sociology, and most specifically of Lévi-Strauss. In each case the only way of avoiding that stasis which results from seeing the process as a simple expression of the structure is to introduce a transcendent subject of history. For both Althusser and Lévi-Strauss this subject can only be the scientist. Cf. my *The Structuralism of C. Lévi-Strauss* (Ph.D. thesis, University of Essex, 1975, chs. 4 and 5).
131. RC, pp. 284-91.
132. RC, pp. 304-7. We have at last reached the break with stalinism. The stalinist dialectic is inverted so that it is the relations of production that dominate the forces of production. This means that there is no longer any evolutionism, since the development of the relations of production is indeterminate, to be resolved by the contingent outcome of particular political struggles.
133. RC, p. 306. Cf. Poulantzas, *Political Power,* pp. 87-9, who criticises this conception, only to hand the same function to the state: "The function of the absolutist state is . . . to produce *not-yet-given relations* of production (i.e. capitalist relations) and to put an end to feudal relations: its function is to *transform* and to *fix* the limits of the mode of production" (ibid., pp. 160-1).
134. RC, pp. 215-16. Only in these two modes do the forces and relations divide up their "supports" in the same way. RC, p. 303. The feudal

mode cannot be characterised by correspondence, since the political is there dominant. Poulantzas tries to get around this difficulty by distinguishing between homology and correspondence, *Political Power*, p. 27n, without specifying what distinguishes the concepts from one another.
135. Balibar, "Self-criticism", op. cit., pp. 66, 63.
136. ibid., p. 63. This doesn't mean that he abandons Ricardianism, merely that he now sees the relations of distribution as dominant in the combination. The capitalist mode of production is still "a mode of appropriation of the unpaid labour of others which is only distinguished by a 'different way' of extorting it" (ibid., p. 68). Even after Hindess and Hirst, it is not clear what is meant by "dominance" in this context.
137. ibid., p. 60. These three points sum up the "originality" of Hindess and Hirst with respect to Balibar, mark I.
138. The other alternative is the economism of E. Terray, *Marxism and "Primitive" Societies*, MRP, 1972.
139. Hence the class struggle in production has nothing to do with the revolution, which must be left to the political programme of the proletarian party, which alone can create the revolutionary conjuncture.
140. It is not clear whether the new social formation is to be created by a real class or by the concept of class. Balibar's argument depends heavily on his claim that the new structure cannot develop out of the old because its elements are constituted independently of one another, and so are debris of the destruction of the old, not developments out of it (RC, pp. 276-83). This claim is nonsensical. If the separation of labourers from their means of production is not *at the same time* concentration of these means of production in the hands of capitalists, then production would cease. "The same process which placed the mass face to face with the *objective conditions of labour* as free workers also placed these conditions, as *capital*, face to face with the free workers", K. Marx, *Grundrisse*, p. 503.
141. *Selected Works*, vol. I, op. cit., p. 363.
142. *Grundrisse*, op. cit., p. 476.
143. RC, p. 359.
144. *Grundrisse*, op. cit., pp. 486, 493-5.
145. For marxism, therefore, class struggle is not a dynamic practice counterposed to a static structure. This opposition of structure and process is characteristic of metaphysical materialism which finds the fixity of its categories compromised by the flux of history. For marxism the structure is itself a structure of processes, the fixed points are moments of a developing totality. Cf. Poulantzas, *Political Power*, pp. 64-5, who separates relations of production from social relations of production and opposes them as structures to practice.
146. C. Meillassoux, *Anthropologie économique des Gouro*, Hague, 1964; Terray, op. cit.; Balibar, "Self-criticism", op. cit.; A. Cutler,

"Response", *Theoretical Practice* 7/8, 1973; Hindess and Hirst, op. cit.; Cutler, Hindess, Hirst and Hussain, op. cit.

147. RC, p. 67. This is exactly the same phenomenon as we find in bourgeois sociology, where the division between high theory and empiricist research, both slaves to the same banal bourgeois ideology, guarantees both by leaving the ideology itself unquestioned as debate centres on the "opposition" between empiricism and theoreticism. In the case of Talcott Parsons this is not immediately obvious, since he presents a very familiar ideology in a particularly systematic way. When we come to a work like Hindess and Hirst, op. cit., it becomes transparent. The supposedly "theoretical" arguments of that work are unconvincing because they are in fact empirical claims which are too often patently false. The constant reference to some supposedly theoretical "necessity" cannot conceal the fact that this "necessity" rests on unsystematic, inconsistent, often incoherent, and not infrequently false, empirical premises.

148. *Grundrisse,* p. 197.

149. L. Althusser, Preface to volume one of *Capital,* in *Lenin and Philosophy.* One significant feature of this concept is its use to consign the theory of fetishism to the realm of ideology. This is ironic because it was theory, the centrepiece of the Althusserian theory of *Darstellung,* which was at the core of the version of marxism presented in the first edition of *Reading Capital.* The loss of this theory derives from its supposed implication of a "free social individual" contemplating the appearance as form of presentation of the essence. "Essence" and "appearance", it is argued, are simply scientific and ideological concretes-in-thought, which correspond to a single concrete-real, the real appearance. Later Althusserians abandon the distinction between science and ideology as an arbitrary one, so that "essence" and "appearance" are simply different, equally valid, points of view emerging from different discourses. This is the basis on which Cutler, Hindess and Hirst and Hussain, op. cit., reject any priority that might be claimed by marxism. While this is the logical consequence of the Althusserian version of Marx, based on the opposition of structure and process and of theory and reality (and so a nominalist view of theory), it has nothing to do with Marx's theory of fetishism, since (i) both essence and appearance are equally real, the essence describing the processes of which the appearances are discrete moments; (ii) fetishism does not implicate the free social individual contemplating a structure, but the social individual engaged in the practical activities which are the structure.

150. Rancière, *La leçon,* pp. 22, 24, 26.

151. *Réponse à John Lewis,* Paris, 1973, pp. 48-9 (cf. ESC, pp. (63-4).

VICTOR JELENIEWSKI SEIDLER
Trusting Ourselves: Marxism, Human Needs and Sexual Politics

The notes upon which this paper is based were an immediate and direct response to attending a Radical Philosophy Conference in Bristol in April 1977. I was left feeling deeply frustrated and angry. I had been intensely involved in political activity during the class struggle of the early seventies, and had come to the conference wanting political clarity and understanding. The speed with which the crisis had taken hold had surprised and disorientated many people. We had too easily assumed that theoretical understanding would flow from our political involvements. We needed to understand how the political movements of the late sixties and early seventies grew out of the changed conditions of monopoly capitalism.

I was already a graduate student in 1968. I was deeply influenced by the student movement. I took to heart its critique of the nature of teaching and learning. Learning has to be related to experience. Our ideas have to be integrated into our lives, if they are to be meaningful. If ideas are to be reproduced mechanically, very little will be learnt. Some of these ideas found echoes in my philosophical education, particularly my reading of Wittgenstein.[1] I had been made uneasy and suspicious of a certain kind of abstract theoretical work. Somehow concepts had to be related to the living contexts within which we grasp them. The meanings of concepts have to be investigated in the everyday contexts in which they are used. I was frustrated by the ahistorical character of this analytical tradition, but I felt that it was deeply significant in the ways that it grounded our theoretical discussions within experience. Sometimes I felt that it was reaching for insights that Marx in a very different idiom was raising about the relationship of theory to practice.

I learned not to identify theoretical work with abstract discussion. I found it difficult to challenge the theoretical style that my writing drifted into, discovering a more direct and immediate mode of communication. Somehow I knew that this was related to the very narrow class experience I had. In the early seventies I was increasingly frustrated by the abstractness of my politics, and my grasp of the realities of class experience. I felt the need for a political practice which would give me more understanding and experience of what I was talking about. I got involved in community and industrial politics in East London.

In these years of intense political activity I found it very difficult to recognise the importance of theoretical work. I was learning so much from my everyday involvements that it didn't seem important. When you face the brutal reality of thousands of people forced to spend their days as virtual slaves to the routines of assembly line production at Ford's plant at Dagenham, it can become difficult to give meaning to your own individual wants and needs. The dictates of the "class struggle" have such an overwhelming importance, that it's too easy to give meaning to your life through subordinating yourself. Even though, as a group, we had a deep commitment to sexual politics and to libertarian ideas about the importance of "struggling in different areas of your life", the everyday realities of political work forced its own form of "workerism".

The sacrifice of political work created its own forms of self-righteousness. It was easy to feel that if others were "serious" about politics, then they should be prepared to make the same kind of commitments. For some of us, our middle-class backgrounds and schooling prepared us well for this kind of self-denial. We had been brought up to sacrifice for high marks and a good career. For men it holds a particular fascination, because the kind of "objective analysis" of class forces meant that we were making our interventions at the most crucial points. We could proudly feel that we were where it was most "important" to be, whatever our individual qualities and gifts happened to be. The political practice of many groups forces this kind of negation, even though it may be at odds with the understanding that people have of themselves.

I was so conscious of how easy it had been for me to forsake my needs that the question of human needs in relation to class struggle and marxist theory was crucial to me when I went to the Radical Philosophy Conference. I was angry at the disdain for the "politics of the sixties", and at the abstractness of what passed for theoretical work. I felt deeply that we had to be able to learn from our own class experience, since this is what would situate us historically and politically. I felt that we had hardly begun to learn from the struggles of the late sixties and early seventies. I felt that the prevailing notions of "theoretical practice" seemed to make this crucial task unnecessary, and avoided all the painful issues of how to relate theoretical work to political practice, in the historical period we lived in.

I don't develop a detailed critique of Althusserian texts in this paper. However important it has been for some individuals in questioning a narrow economism and opening up areas of culture, ideology and politics for serious investigation, I don't think this is where a renewal of marxist theory is going to come from, or that the treatment of these crucial areas is well conceived. I can't show this adequately here. All I can hope to do is to show that Althusser's attempts to foreclose certain critical areas of discussion, particularly around the question of "humanism", is deeply misconceived. More positively I want to show how certain conceptions of libertarian marxism and sexual politics provide a critique of certain unifying conceptions of Althusserian marxism. They also promise us the renewal of critical concepts of marxist theory.

I am very aware of the divisions that exist within the women's movement, and within sexual politics more generally. I know that the conception of theoretical work that is fostered by Althusserianism is also strong within the women's movement. Nevertheless I think that the redefinition of the very nature of the "political" that has been fostered most clearly within sexual politics promises to transform our understanding of the form and content of class struggle within monopoly capitalism. It also promises a different conception of the relationship between theory and practice. I don't think that I make good on some of these grand claims. I hope I show that the crucial questions are still to be asked, if Althusser doesn't force us to lose our courage and nerve.

Edward Thompson's *The Poverty of Theory*[2] has shifted the whole locus of discussion. Hopefully this paper will be appearing in a very different climate because of his labours. It would have been too difficult to recast what I've written to integrate what I have learnt from his writing. However, one remark is relevant, which might throw into focus what I'm doing. I don't think that Thompson has learnt enough from 1968 and the movements that have emerged since about the making of socialism. This is crucial, because it means that the argument about "socialist humanism" tends to get set in the terms of the particular historical moment of 1956. I think that the experience of the Black movement, student movement, workers' movement and women's movement have very much shifted the terms of this discussion. I say something about how an understanding of racial and sexual oppression and powerlessness deepens our understanding of dependency, power, autonomy and liberation. It deepens our understanding of what has to be involved in the making of socialism.

There is always a danger that marxist theory loses touch with the realities of people's struggles for a more human life. It loses touch with the ongoing struggles, against the forms of exploitation and oppression, within capitalist society. Somehow the danger has developed in the early seventies, of marxism becoming an abstract theory that exists over and above the struggles of people to change their lives. For a generation of students who have read Althusser in place of reading Marx, marxism has become a theoretical discipline that barely connects up with the realities of working-class struggle, or with the contradictions that people live out as socialists in their everyday experience. Althusser's influence showed itself in the late sixties, but it has only been since the widespread defeats following 1974 that we have been forced to challenge its growing influence.

But it is too easy to understand the influence of Althusserian marxism as growing out of a politics of defeat. Perhaps it was also because of the exceptionally large gap between the hopes and the power, which was a feature of the group of people radicalised in the late sixties. There was a definite feeling in the air that, if only we were ready to commit ourselves enough, then large-scale social changes were almost inevitable. These hopes were fired by Paris in May 1968, and by the movement against the American involvement in Vietnam. It was easy to feel betrayed by history. Many people seemed to feel that they had been fooled. Many people who had received their political education within the student movement were to disown their experience as "naïve", turning away sharply from their experience, towards the certainties of a structuralist marxism, rather than to critically evaluate their own histories and experience. The past was to be dismissed as "voluntarist", and people were to make sure that they weren't going to be fooled again. Security and certainty was to be found in the realm of theory.

Althusser's influence in England has had a complicated history. Individuals have learnt creatively from his writings. It has helped some people break with an economism that was stifling. It has helped restore the significance of intellectual work on the left. But Althusserianism broadly conceived, as a prevailing current of thought, has damaged our grasp of the relationship of theoretical work to political practice. To accuse Althusserianism of being "theoreticist" is not to be anti-intellectual. It is to raise the theoretical issue of the inadequacy of Althusser's attempt to resolve the critical issues which Marx identifies, by renaming theory as "theoretical practice". Theoretical work threatens to become self-contained, and we avoid the critical issues of how to develop theory with a closer and more intimate relationship to class struggle in its different forms.

Althusser works within a fundamentally rationalist epistemology. This profoundly affects his conception of "knowledge", and his grasp of the relationship of "ideology" to "knowledge". It makes it difficult for him to grasp the direction and flow of Marx's thinking, about the relationship of "theory" to "practice". This is partly because Marx learns so fundamentally from Hegel, while he remains so critical of him. It's Althusser's rationalist education that makes him insist on the completeness of Marx's "epistemological break". He can't grasp or think through Marx's dialectical relationship to Hegel. This is also why he can't recognise his own rationalist presuppositions, in the critique Marx makes in the second of his "Theses on Feuerbach":

> The question whether human thinking can pretend to objective (*gegenstandlich*) truth is not a theoretical but a *practical* question. Man must prove the truth, i.e. the reality and power, the "this-sidedness" of his thinking in practice. The dispute over the reality or non-reality of thinking that is isolated from practice is a purely scholastic question.

What does it mean for thinking to be "isolated from practice"? Althusser fundamentally fudges this issue in his talk of "theoretical practice". His understanding of the ways in which different disciplines have their own theoretical objects which are, in some sense, actively created in the discourses of the disciplines, doesn't develop the sense of "practice" that Marx is developing. The sense of "activity" is a purely intellectual one, and remains fundamentally locked within a contemplative relationship to the social world. Because of this, his appeals to "class struggle" and his sense that "dialectical materialism represents the proletarian class struggle *in theory*" seem too mechanical.

Althusser's conception of "the theoretical domain" as existing on a level of its own, shows his difficulty in thinking the relationship between theory and practice. This is clearly illuminated in his "Interview on Philosophy", in *Lenin and Philosophy,* where he is asked:

> "You have said two apparently contradictory or different things: 1, philosophy is basically political; 2, philosophy is linked to the sciences. How do you conceive this double relationship?"
> "Here again I shall give my answer in the form of schematic and provisional theses.
> 1. The class positions in confrontation in the class struggle are *'represented'* in the domain of practical ideologies (religious, ethical, legal, political aesthetic ideologies) by *world outlooks* of antagonistic tendencies: in the last instance idealistic (bourgeois) and materialist (proletarian). Everyone has a world outlook spontaneously.
> 2. World outlooks are *represented* in the domain of *theory* (science + 'theoretical' ideologies which surround science and scientists) by *philosophy*. Philosophy represents the class struggle in theory. That is why philosophy is a struggle (*Kampf,* said Kant), and basically a

> *political* struggle: a class struggle. Everyone is not a philosopher spontaneously, but everyone may become one.
>
> 3. Philosophy exists as soon as the theoretical *domain* exists: as soon as a *science* (in the strict sense) exists. Without sciences, no philosophy, only world outlooks . . . The main battlefield in this struggle is scientific knowledge: for it or against it. The number-one philosophical battle therefore takes place on the frontier between the scientific and the ideological. There the idealist philosophies which exploit the sciences struggle against the materialist philosophies which serve the sciences. . . .
>
> 4. The science founded by Marx has changed the whole situation in the theoretical domain. It is a *new* science: the science of history. Therefore, for the first time ever, it has enabled us to know the world outlooks which philosophy represents in theory; it enables us to know philosophy. It provides the means to transform the world outlooks (revolutionary class struggle conducted according to the principles of marxist theory). . . .
>
> Marxist-leninist philosophy, or dialectical materialism, represents the proletarian class struggle *in theory*. In the unity of marxist theory and the Workers' Movement (the *ultimate* reality of the union of theory and practice) philosophy ceases, as Marx said, to 'interpret the world'. It becomes a weapon with which 'to change it': *revolution.*"[3]

This is schematic, but it gives a sense of the direction of Althusser's thinking. It demonstrates the hierarchies of knowledges, each with their own "domain". It shows the centrality of his conception of scientific knowledge, and his conception of marxism as "the science of history". It shows the gradual process of refinement from one level representing to the next, till we reach a conception of "marxist theory" which can form a "union" with "the workers' movement". This shows the "union" to be fundamentally external and mechanical, even if Althusser declares it to be "the *ultimate* reality of the union of theory and practice".

Learning from Gramsci

What does theory mean within marxism? If theory isn't to be simply the accumulation of scientific knowledge which can be applied in practice, what is the alternative conception? Gramsci has struggled with this issue most profoundly, though his formulations remain incomplete. He helps us focus our sense of frustration with the rationalist formulations of Althusser's "theoretical practice". Gramsci needed to develop a more dialectical relationship to the tradition of idealism, learning deeply from Hegel, Croce and the tradition of Italian idealism.[4] His appreciation of this tradition, rather than any idea of a complete break with it, allowed him to reformulate significant questions about the relationship of theory to practice.

Following Gramsci's discussion in the *Prison Notebooks*[5] about the "relation between science, religion and common sense" we can detect that Althusser has read Gramsci. We can discover certain of Gramsci's ideas, recast within Althusser's more rationalist idiom. On closer reading we discover that what *matter* are the radically opposed understandings that inform their writings. Not only are we led into a different conception of marxist theory and its relationship to political practice, but we are left with a completely different sense of the importance of Hegel in a marxist education. Gramsci develops a very different conception of the relationship of "common sense", "philosophy", "theory" and "science". These don't exist as independent "domains".

Gramsci questions the special status that is given to philosophy and theory. This is important to learn, given the developments of theoretical work on the left over the last few years. It's important for theoretical work to be demystified, without underestimating the kind of energies it involves. It isn't simply a matter of making ideas "accessible", but discovering a very different kind of basis for theoretical work than those offered in the conceptions of marxist science. Gramsci offers us a very different beginning:

> It is essential to destroy the widespread prejudice that philosophy is a strange and difficult thing just because it is the specific intellectual activity of a particular category of specialists or of professional and systematic philosophers. It must first be shown that all men are "philosophers", by defining the limits and characteristics of the "spontaneous philosophy" which is proper to everybody.

From the beginning Gramsci encourages us to have a critical relationship to our own experience. But we have to start with an understanding and appreciation of our experience, to discover how we have been brought up to take for granted the ways that we think, feel and act:

> Having first shown that everyone is a philosopher, though in his own way and unconsciously, since even in the slightest manifestation of any intellectual activity whatever, in "language", there is contained a specific conception of the world, one then moves on to the second level, which is that of awareness and criticism. That is to say, one proceeds to the question — is it better to "think", without having a critical awareness, in a disjointed and episodic way? In other words, is it better to take part in a conception of the world mechanically imposed by the external environment, i.e. by one of the many social groups in which everyone is automatically involved from the moment of his entry into the conscious world. . . . Or, on the other hand, is it better to work out consciously and critically one's own conception of the world and thus, in connection with the labours of one's own brain, choose one's sphere of activity, take an active part in the creation of the

history of the world, be one's own guide, refusing to accept passively and supinely from outside the moulding of one's personality?

So one develops a critical consciousness *through* a critical relationship with one's own experience. This is part of a process of making conscious what was all too readily unconsciously assumed. So, for instance, growing up in the middle class I might take it for granted that individual achievement brings happiness, almost as an inevitable consequence. This is something that might have been confirmed, within my own individual experience within the family, when I would get rewarded for bringing home a shining report. This might not be something that I have reasoned out for myself, but something that is simply taken for granted in the organisation of family and schooling.

It might only be in a consciousness-raising situation that I become aware of how this assumption is very much shared by others, particularly men, who have grown up within the middle class. I might recognise the ways that it continually spurred me to greater activity, thinking that the crossing of the next academic hurdle would bring happiness. In the sharing of experience, which is an integral aspect of "consciousness-raising", I become aware of the different ways I have been formed through my experience. This suggests a process that individuals have to go through themselves, discovering the particular and personal, but also the social and political formation of their experience. This suggests a challenge to the conception of knowledge as an accumulation of rational arguments which can be clearly taught. It suggests a more socratic conception, in which this understanding has to be gained through a sharing and locating of experience. This is an understanding that some people have reached through the practice of sexual politics. Gramsci must have already been aware of how this promised a different kind of educational practice, challenging the leninist ideas of *What is to be Done?*[6] that political consciousness is to be brought externally to the working class:

> The starting-point of critical elaboration is the consciousness of what one really is, and is "knowing thyself" as a product of the historical process to date which has deposited in you an infinity of traces, without leaving an inventory.

Gramsci recognises the disjunction that can often exist between what we say and what we do, between our theory and our practice:

> And is it not frequently the case that there is a contradiction between one's intellectual choice and one's mode of conduct? Which therefore would be the real conception of the world: that logically affirmed as an intellectual choice? Or that which emerges from the real activity of each man, which is implicit in his mode of action?

Gramsci recognises that you can explain this as self-deception when it is a matter of a few individuals, but that "it is not adequate when the contrast occurs in the life of great masses". This encourages Gramsci to ask fundamental questions about the relationship of knowledge to power. He demonstrates a keen awareness of the implications of subordination, dependency and relative powerlessness, upon the ways in which people think and feel about themselves:

> In these cases the contrast between thought and action cannot but be the expression of profounder contrasts of a social historical order. It signifies that the social group in question may indeed have its own conception of the world, even if only embryonic; a conception which manifests itself in action, but occasionally and in flashes — when, that is, the group is acting as an organic totality. But this same group has, for reasons of submission and intellectual subordination, adopted a conception which is not its own but is borrowed from another group; and it confirms this conception verbally and believes itself to be following it, because this is the conception which it follows in "normal times" — that is when its conduct is not independent and autonomous, but submissive and subordinate. Hence the reason why philosophy cannot be divorced from politics. And one can show furthermore that the choice and the criticism of a conception of the world is also a political matter.

This raises critical questions about the social conditions of autonomy and independence. They have been raised about the subordination of women in society, in questioning the definitions that women have accepted about themselves, their potentialities and their needs. Gramsci is hinting at a more general and intimate connection between forms of consciousness and knowledge, and relationships of power and control. He is also giving us a very different framework within which to raise issues about class consciousness.

This helps explain the importance of the relationship between theory and practice. Theory isn't something that can develop in a realm of its own, to be brought as a "science" to the aid of working people. Rather "science" must develop from closer contact and relationship with the problems and concerns of working people. It is this kind of contact which can renew marxist theory, developing it in a way that accounts for changes in capitalist society. This keeps us continually in touch with the historical nature of Marx's concepts. Gramsci puts this very clearly:

> It must be a criticism of "common sense", basing itself initially, however, on common sense in order to demonstrate that "everyone" is a philosopher and that it is not a question of introducing from scratch

a scientific form of thought into everyone's individual life, but of renovating and making "critical" an already existing activity.

This promises a fundamentally different understanding of the relationship of "common sense" to "science", but it also raises questions about the kind of relationship that intellectuals can have to class struggle. Gramsci develops an idea of organic intellectuals to express this relationship. It is the contact with working-class experience which for Gramsci has to be "the source of the problems is sets out to study and resolve".

It is through situating ourselves within the structures of power and domination that we gain a deeper grasp of their workings. In this way theory doesn't simply demystify external structures, but helps us recognise the sources of power, which will help transform the situation. Gramsci is very aware of this as a process of development. I shall set this out in his terms, and then I will endeavour to give an example which should help bring out what is involved.

> Critical understanding of self takes place therefore through a struggle of political "hegemonies" and of opposing directions, first in the ethical field and then in that of politics proper, in order to arrive at the working out at a higher level of one's own conception of reality. Consciousness of being part of a particular hegemonic force (that is to say, political consciousness) is the first stage towards a further progressive self-consciousness in which theory and practice will finally be one. Thus the unity of theory and practice is not just a matter of mechanical fact, but a part of the historical process, whose elementary and primitive phase is to be found in the sense of being "different" and "apart", in an instinctive feeling of independence, and which progresses to the level of real possession of a single and coherent conception of the world.

If we think for example about the dominating conceptions of "equality of opportunity" within education, then it's only "fair" that John has got himself in the top stream of the comprehensive school. He has proved himself to be brighter than his mates. John might be beginning to feel uneasy in his new class, without really being able to explain this feeling. He talks slightly differently from most of the others, and lives in a different part of town. He discovers that he feels ashamed about asking any of the others round to his house. It is only much later that John was able to make sense of this experience, and these feelings, in terms of learning to think about his experiences in terms of class. His consciousness of himself as being working-class, within a fundamentally middle-class school, has clarified some of his experiences. It hasn't changed his experience, but it has changed the way that he understands his experience. It has given him more of a grasp and understanding of his experience at school. It has also helped him understand why he was made to feel the way he did. This isn't simply a matter of learning that he is working-class, since part of him was fully conscious of this all the time. His theoretical grasp of the conception of class has also helped him understand the power that the middle class have in the larger society, to define the very meaning and character of education. He has more understanding of the ways in which class differences are reproduced within education, and that what seemed to him to be perfectly "fair" hides the class character of education. Very little in his education helped him grasp the class character of capitalist society. This is echoed in the very different context of Southern Italy, where schoolchildren report the following confrontation:

> *When a Test Gets a 4.* When the instructors saw the graph of achievement in school correlated with the father's occupation, they called it an insult to their fairness as impartial judges.
>
> The fiercest of them all protested that she had never sought out or received any information about the students' families. "When a test is worth a 4, I will mark it with a 4." She could not understand, poor soul, that this is exactly the charge against her. Nothing is more unjust than to share equally among unequals.[7]

Lived contradictions
The notion of "equality of opportunity" is institutionalised in the very organisation of schooling. Along with the conception of individual ability, it helps organise people's experience of schooling. Althusser is right to criticise the notion of ideology as a "veil" which covers over what's "really happening". He has helped some people recognise that ideology is lived, and is a "reality" that has to be grasped. But he's very unclear about the sense in which it is a reality. This is partly because his critique of the very category of experience makes it impossible for him to grasp *the ways* in which experience can be mystified. So John could blame his father because they didn't live in as large a house as the other families. It showed that his father hadn't worked hard enough, or else lacked ability. This is a reality in their relationship. John might even feel bitter and unforgiving. Only later might John realise how unfair he had been to his father, though this was almost inevitable, given the ways he was encouraged to think and feel about himself in school.

John had been schooled to accept that a person's position in society somehow reflected a person's individual abilities. This is a reality within John's experience, which has had consequences for his relationship to his family. It has left him sometimes feeling ashamed of his family. He doesn't like to remember this now, though he knows it's true. But he also knows that it's part of the "commonsense" of the school that has mystified him about his own class background and about the sources of inequality in society. Gramsci has offered him a more meaningful grasp of the structures of power within capitalist society, and the ways in which he has been mystified about them, than does Althusser's objectivist science. This is partly because Althusser doesn't claim to illuminate the nature of our *experience* within capitalist society. Somehow his science takes up a position which is superior to "experience", thereby situating us outside the struggles in society, observing the process. This means the theory no longer helps us to a sense of our own power through demystifying the character of capitalist social relations.

Althusser seems to want to dissolve the very category of "experience" as essentially individual, and thereby bourgeois. He wants to assert that our individual experience is a shared social and political experience. He barely allows it the reality he grants to ideology. This is a very different move from Gramsci, who can help me grasp the ways in which my experience is both individual, but *also* deeply social and historical. This transforms my sense of my individuality. Althusser doesn't grasp these dialectical possibilities within his rationalist tradition. He is forced to make unreal choices, which have very real effects on our understanding.

The danger for Althusser is that in presenting an overview of the "capitalist mode of production", the theory simply *asserts* that the ways in which we think about ourselves, (say) as "individuals", is simply generated automatically within the "capitalist mode of production". It doesn't help us grasp the social and historical processes through which this happens, or the contradictions that we find ourselves living out in our everyday lives. It gives us no sense of how we can change, or how this can be an integral part of a political practice. Rather we are left with an external and mechanical conception of the "capitalist mode of production". It is only within a different "mode of production" that people could have any hopes of living differently. So it's regarded as "naïve" for people to challenge the nature of sexual relationships, or if this is granted, then these are seen as "ideological questions", which exist in a specific realm of their own. We are left with a very technical conception of the "economy", within which questions of sexuality and ideology have no place.

Marx always understood how contradictions within capitalist society are *lived out,* in our experience. There is a danger in Althusserianism of simply identifying contradictions within the capitalist mode of production — i.e. as "structural contradictions", that have an existence *independently* of the struggles of people, to challenge and transform situations they are in. Marx's realisation that these contradictions work themselves out without the "conscious awareness" of people is taken — mistaken — to mean they exist "over and above" human social relations. They exist as features of a "system" or "structure", that exist over and above, or beneath human social relations. This follows Althusser's critique of the "common sense" of everyday life, wanting to unearth structures which somehow "determine" everyday life.

One of the ways Althusserian theorists assert their superiority over bourgeois social theory is in attacking conceptions of "human nature". They focus their attack on a classical conception of "human nature", as a definite set of qualities that has existed for all, at all times. This is taken as a feature of "classical philosophy" which can then easily be dismissed as inherently "anthropological". The early writings of Marx are taken as showing the same "naïvety", when they talk about "human essence" or "species being". This is one of the reasons that bright students and theorists, not wishing to be thought of by their fellows as "naïve", hurry to disown Marx's early writings without ever really giving them a careful reading. Somehow the very weight of Althusserian judgements intimidates our reading and understanding.

For all the discussion in Althusser's *For Marx*[8] about the development of Marx's thought, this development is very much presented in terms of a periodisation of his thinking. Althusser breaks Marx's development into various discrete stages. His rationalist framework encourages him to focus upon what he takes to be fundamental breaks in Marx's thinking. What remains very surprising is that for all Althusser's discussion of "this total theoretical revolution", it remains asserted, rather than shown through the critical discussions that Marx makes (say) in the "Theses on Feuerbach", where he is at great pains to clarify "the chief defect of all previous materialisms (including that of Feuerbach) . . . " Althusser doesn't help us enter into the process of Marx's thinking and development. Rather he passes judgements from a distance. You can't help feeling that Althusser wants to bury Marx's early writings, however formative they've been and however challenging they are to the categorisations that Althusser wants to impose. So in Althusser's essay "Marxism and Humanism" we discover the enormously self-confident statement:

> In 1845, Marx broke radically with every theory that based history and politics on an essence of man. This unique rupture contained three indissociable elements.
> 1. The formation of a theory of history and politics based on

radically new concepts: the concepts of social formation, productive forces, relations of production, superstructure, ideologies, determination in the last instance by the economy, specific determination of the other levels, etc.

2. A radical critique of the *theoretical* pretensions of every philosophical humanism.

3. The definition of humanism as an *ideology*.

These aren't the concepts of Marx's discussion. But why is Marx so rarely allowed to speak for himself in Althusser's *For Marx*? It becomes clear that Althusser wants to understand Marx as *replacing* one set of concepts by another, so that literally there is no "space" for these old concepts. There is no sense of a dialectical development in Marx's conceptions, rather there is a definite *replacement* of one set of concepts by another. Somehow this is involved with Althusser's understanding of what is involved in developing a "new problematic". But this is a pre-given understanding that he brings to his reading of Marx. He doesn't discover it in the development of Marx's own thinking. He is much more aware of Marx's own thinking in his *Reading Capital*, where he can feel that the decisive theoretical and political battle against "humanism" has already been won. By this time his audience has been secured, and few will think that it is worth time and effort to read Marx's early writings for themselves. But in *For Marx* the lines have to be sharply drawn:

> By rejecting the essence of man as his theoretical basis, Marx rejected the whole of this organic system of postulates. He drove the philosophical categories of the *subject*, of *empiricism*, of the *ideal essence*, etc., from all the domains in which they had been supreme.... This total theoretical revolution was only empowered to reject the old concepts because it replaced them by new concepts. In fact Marx establishes a new problematic, a new systematic way of asking questions of the world, new principles and a new method. ... When Marx replaced the old couple individual/human essence in the theory of history by new concepts (forces of production, relations of production, etc.), he was, in fact, simultaneously proposing a new conception of "philosophy".

Althusser leaves us thinking that we are "naïve" and "untheoretical" if we feel the need to continue talking about "human nature". Marx has replaced this kind of talk for Althusser, and with this has replaced the moral and political issues which were articulated through this notion. We simply have to accept that human nature is a "social and historical construct", existing in different forms in different societies, particularly within different modes of production. For many on the left this echoes the current but misleading idea that "human nature" in a socialist society is going to take on such radically different forms that we can't even begin to theorise, locked as we are within the prevailing realities of capitalist societies.

This dismissal can leave us uneasy. Part of me wants more to be said. I'm left feeling that fundamental questions about the very meaning of socialism and of the relationship of socialism to morality are being avoided, if they aren't being suppressed. We are forced into silence about some of the most painful and difficult evaluations about the experience of the Russian and Chinese revolutions. Our thinking and feeling is narrowed in a way that we are barely aware of, as a whole language of moral and human experience is declared redundant. Even if we accept in some form the critique of "human nature" as a shared set of inner qualities, wanting to recognise the historical formation of "human nature", we also want to give expression to a sense of shared human equality. This isn't easy to articulate, let alone to live out within the dominating realities of a class society. I reject the kind of choices that Althusser forces me to make. I think they are unreal. I think that we can question the notion of "human nature" as an ahistorical human essence forever unchanging, without thinking this makes the concept and questioning of "human nature" redundant. The terms of discussion will be transformed.

The discussion of human nature is vitally connected to the question of shared human needs. Our understanding of these issues has been fundamentally changed through the investigations of historians, anthropologists and sociologists. We have much more understanding of the very different kind of lives that people live in different periods and in different societies. We are all more conscious of how notions of "progress" and "civilisation" have been used to legitimate imperialism and cultural domination. It has been too easy within the "common sense" of a culture like Britain, which has had such a powerful colonising history, for there to be a switch to forms of cultural and moral relativism. It has become the common sense of those growing up in the 1950s and 1960s that different cultures and social classes have their own discrete moralities. This form of liberal relativism needs careful exploration. It is the equivalent, at the social level, of people saying that morality is a question of individual opinion.

Althusser's idea that human nature is simply a "product" of a particular mode of production goes very much with the grain of cultural relativism. The questioning of the very concept of "human nature" is tied to the attack on "humanism". This needs careful consideration. We can recognise the historical character of human qualities and needs and so recognise the competitive, individualistic, ego-centred "natures" that we grow up to accept as "normal", without concluding that "human nature" is simply a "product" of a particular mode of production. This would be to see people as passive objects, who are produced within a particular mode of production. It would be to share a misconception with much social theory which tends to deny, in different ways, the sources of resistance to the prevailing mode of determination and control, by assuming that people are "fitted" to a particular mode of production. This is to take up a fundamentally instrumental attitude towards people: people can only be "changed" with a transformation of the mode of production.

Althusser's rationalist critique of human nature leaves us with a flat alternative. Either human nature exists as a definite set of qualities, or else it is historically determined. We aren't left any room to consider the *nature* of the historical formation of "human nature". We are left feeling uneasy with the mechanical interpretations that Althusser offers, but we are trapped in a false logic. This is the very circle which Marx breaks in "The Theses on Feuerbach". But Althusser never explores the nature of Marx's critique, preferring to formulate Marx's "break" in his own terms. Marx can be read as giving a critique of Althusser, as much as of Feuerbach, in his powerful first thesis:

> The chief defect of all previous materialism (including that of Feuerbach) is that things (Gegenstand), reality, the sensible world, are conceived only in the form of *objects* (Objekt) *of observation,* but not as *human sense activity,* not as *practical activity,* not subjectively. Hence, in opposition to materialism, the *active* side was developed abstractly by idealism, which of course does not know real sense activity as such. Feuerbach wants sensible objects really distinguished from the objects of thought, but he does not understand human activity itself as *objective* (gegenstandlich) activity. Consequently, in *The Essence of Christianity,* he regards the theoretical attitude as the only genuine human attitude, while practical activity is apprehended only in its dirty Jewish manifestation. He therefore does not grasp the significance of "revolutionary", "practical-critical" activity.

This shows Marx's deeper appreciation of idealism, even if it "does not know real sense activity as such". This was something that Marx was to learn *how* to investigate in his later writings. He was to learn how to investigate the class relations of capitalist society. But this is the point at which he begins to define his position in relation to "all previous materialism", though Althusser avoids investigating this transition. He would have learnt that it is insufficient to want "sensible objects really distinguished from the objects of thought". This is something that Feuerbach manages. But neither Feuerbach nor Althusser have been able to "understand human activity itself as *objective* activity". This is something we have to grapple with, if we are to begin to grasp the nature of Marx's materialism.

The emphasis on human sense-activity as practical activity develops into an understanding of the centrality of class struggle in the transformations of capitalist society. This is a development and materialisation of the clarification that Marx is reaching for in his "Theses on Feuerbach". It is because human nature remains "human" that people will struggle against forms of injustice and exploitation. As long as a mode of production exists as a mode of domination, there is bound to be resistance. Because of the particular form of exploitation within capitalist society, people struggle in class ways. People are struggling against the workings of a particular capitalist mode of production, but they are also struggling as an assertion of their humanity. Marx recognised that people struggle against the concrete conditions of exploitation and wage labour. They don't struggle in the name of an abstract idea of "humanity". But it's the very ways in which people are *reduced* to wage-labour, so that their humanity is negated, that creates the conditions for class struggle This is the fundamental contradiction that is built into the iron fist of capitalist society.

Marx recognises that people are never simply "labour", nor can human labour be treated as a commodity, without reproducing the conditions of resistance. People can never simply be reduced to the "factor of production", which the capitalist economy requires. This is the profound moral understanding that moves everything that Marx wrote. People are constantly struggling against the dehumanising conditions of their lives, through struggling against the concrete conditions they are forced to live in. It is the task of theoretical work to clarify these conditions of resistance, always informed by a developing sense of what the social relations of a human society could be. This involves the careful clarification of historical experience.

The struggle against the concrete conditions of exploitation is the source of tension and opposition, which Marx comes to theorise as an integral part of the internal dynamic of capitalist society. Marx is continually learning how to "materialise" his understanding of alienation, to make it more historically specific. This doesn't make the notion redundant, even if it was to be continually clarified. So it is quite misleading for Althusser to characterise Marx's early writings as an attempt to outline an "anthropology". He doesn't assume a fixed nature for people, but explores the "nature" of people, through the need people have to express themselves through labour. He recognises this as "historical". The "means of expression" will differ in concrete historical conditions. In his later writings, he discovers ways of analysing these processes with greater historical specificity.

Marx recognised a fundamental need for people to express themselves through their activities. This is part of recognising "human sense activity" as "practical activity". In the *Paris Manuscripts* Marx recognises the needs people have to "realise themselves", even if it took longer to investigate the distorting processes through which this happens in a capitalist economy. There is a continuing discussion about identifying this "human sense activity" with "labour" and the ways in which "labour" and "work" are thought about in Marx's later writings.[9] It has been too easy in the difficult historical experience of socialism to identify "self-realisation" with ever increasing production, and so to reproduce within a different terminology the protestant ethic and all the sacrifices and denials that it involves. Althusser's implicit conception of socialism as a more efficient mode of production tends to silence these crucial discussions and suppress all-important moral discussion within a marxist tradition.

Marx recognised that people could only "realise themselves" *through* the conditions of everyday life. This was part of his critique of bourgeois morality, which wanted to think that the "realisation of self" could take place in a realm of its own, say through religion or art. In this way Marx was developing a specific critique of moral conceptions that were dominant, rather than a general critique of moral discussion. Marx felt that an escape into art or religion, however significant they might otherwise be in people's lives, could serve to legitimate injustice and oppression. Marx was struggling to find ways of describing and analysing the lived realities of people's lives within capitalist society. In a very real sense this remains the basis of his materialism, as the following sentences from *The German Ideology* show:

> The presuppositions with which we begin are not arbitrary presuppositions, they are not dogmas; they are real presuppositions from which one can abstract only in fancy. They are the actual individuals, their actions and the material conditions of their lives, those already existing as well as those produced by action.

Marx never saw people as the "products" of a particular mode of production. This is the deepest misconception, which makes it impossible to understand the contradictions and transformations *within* a particular mode of production. This is why structuralist marxists are much more confident when comparing different "modes of production", characterised by particular structures, than they are in understanding the struggles for control and domination that explain the developments, contradictions and transformations within the history of capitalism. As long as people are fundamentally conceived as the "products" of a mode of production, we fail to grasp what was fundamental for Marx. People aren't passive objects, but are human subjects, continually transforming themselves in the struggles against the conditions of exploitation.

Althusser doesn't help us clarify the issues around individual experience and class relations. It's as if discussion of "human sense activity" is to be *replaced* by talk of social classes, as if this is unproblematic. But Althusser often goes further in his discussion of the marxist theory of history, as in *For Marx* (pages 231-2):

> The "subjects" of history are given human societies. They present themselves as totalities whose unity is constituted by a certain specific type of *complexity,* which introduces instances that, following Engels, we can, very schematically, reduce to three: the economy, politics and ideology.

In this way Althusser creates his own sense of "complexity" but avoids the critical questions about human experience, human needs and class relations, through postulating a conception of "totalities" that exist in an analytical realm of their own. This leaves people as passive objects. It gives us no way of grasping the source of the struggles people engage in, and their power to transform the actual structure of social relations. Althusser limits our understanding through postulating a series of different "levels", so that "contradictions" always exist on a level of their own. It's because Marx grasped the mode of production as a mode of domination and control, that for instance he understood the centrality of the struggle going on *within* production, as capitalists have to legitimate their rights of control.[10] So that the "economy" isn't to be regarded as a discrete level of its own, determined by the technical needs of production. We have to understand the ways in which technology isn't a neutral gift of "science",[11] but has to be seen in the context of the capitalist's struggle to maintain a control which is being constantly threatened and challenged.

Dialectic of needs
In *Capital* Marx is analysing the forms which the struggle against wage-labour can take within a capitalist mode of production. But he also shows how the very forms of working-class struggle determine the developments within the capitalist mode of production. This isn't a struggle for an abstract conception of humanity, but it is a struggle against the forms of dehumanisation and exploitation, embodied in concrete conditions of wage-labour. Marx helps us recognise that in a modern factory, partly through the struggle for longer lunch breaks, lay-off pay and

nurseries and against speed-ups and mobility, people come to experience some of the power which they are dispossessed of, through the workings of the mode of production.[12] The very nature of collective struggle opens up new possibilities for relations, as it breaks and challenges the individualistic ways of thinking and feeling which people are brought up to accept as "natural". As the everyday routines are broken, as an assembly-line has been broken down, people might have more time to talk and appreciate their workmates.[13] Workers might have a glimpse of how things could be different. Possibly the very conception some white workers have of immigrants might change, as they see West Indian workers refusing to be pushed about by the foreman, as they are ordered back to work.

In a similar way young people at school, left alone because their teachers are striking for more pay, might be led to think about the ways that their school is organised. They might wonder about how much they can learn themselves, and about the whole organisation of teaching and learning. For the first time they might formulate such questions as "what do I want to learn?" or "what is worth learning?" or "what have I really understood in the lessons?" about would be exploring their needs for understanding, not simply assuming the routines of schooling. These different examples show that "needs" don't exist in some kind of historical isolation. Our sense of what we need and want in our lives changes, often with changes in the situations we find ourselves in. But this isn't to say that they are simply "created" by the situations we find ourselves in. We might well discover that we have different needs from those which we were brought up to take for granted. This can also be because we learn to know ourselves better, and come to have a more intimate understanding of what we want our lives to be.

In the late sixties and early seventies it was the women's movement, the gay movement and a smaller men's movement that raised issues about human needs and personal identity, in both theoretical and practical ways. These movements have challenged the kind of universalism often implicit in generalised talk of "human needs". They have offered in practice a critical relationship to empiricism, but a firm grounding in an understanding of experience, while showing how relationships of power and dominance have deeply influenced people's sense of self, individual worth and individual identity. This hasn't cut across an understanding of class, but has deepened our grasp of how our experience, feelings, expectations, longings, hopes, wants and needs have been deeply influenced through our class, sexual and racial formations. This has made it important to recognise "women" and "men" as locked into relationships of power which have often silenced the experience of women, through subsuming it under a dominant conception, identifying "rationality" in a way that is opposed fundamentally to emotions and feelings. This is one way in which the power that men have as a sex is legitimated. The ways that many of us, especially middle-class men, were brought up to assume the superiority of mental over manual labour can help us grasp the less self-conscious ways in which we assumed the superiority of men as a sex, because we were "rational" while women are merely "emotional".

Even on the left it has been a minority within a minority which has been prepared to see men as created beings, rather than as speaking for humanity in general. The intense rationalism of the Althusserian discourse makes it easy for a whole generation of theorists to put their experience at some distance from their theoretical work, rediscovering a new legitimation for a split between the "personal" and the "political". I shall talk about men as a sex, not to exclude women, but to avoid talking *for* people in general. This will be unfamiliar, but I hope that it will ground certain notions of "experience" that have been dismissed within Althusserian discourse. Very generally the ways in which the relationships between "knowledge", "power", "dependency", "class", "sexuality" and "identity" have been grasped within the practice of what's loosely called "sexual politics" shows a complexity, depth and reality which could promise a renewal of historical materialism.

It has been in the women's movement that women have challenged the prevailing definitions of "femininity" and the assumption of the naturalness of domesticity. It hasn't been enough to develop a theoretical critique of how the subordination of women is in the interests of the power of capital, but it has been necessary for women to challenge the ways in which their relationships with men have been organised, so that they could begin to live as independent and autonomous people. Women have recognised the necessity of challenging the ideology of women's subordination through challenging the relationships of power. It isn't simply a question of changing the ways that men "think" about women as sexual objects, but of changing the practice of sexuality. These practices have to change if women are to challenge their subordination, and if they are to realise themselves as independent people in their own right. This has reawakened a sense of socialism having to do with the "realisation" and "fulfilment" of people's needs. These fundamental questions are raised because women *can't* fulfil themselves if they remain subordinate and secondary to men, and if they are brought up to discover the meaning in their own lives through subordinating their own needs and wants to the men and children they are looking after.

The workings of subordination are subtle and deep. The processes of gaining a sense of confidence and individuality is risky and slow, if it's also exciting. This is a process that is threatening and scary as it challenges our own conceptions of masculinity as men. As this questioning has gone on for women and men, it gives content to the idea of a process of transformation that involves changing the structure and organisation of social relations, as people gain a sense of their individual power and strength, learning how to sustain each other in an identity which challenges the prevailing conceptions. Althusser has no sense of this process, as people attempt to separate themselves from the prevailing definitions of capitalist social reality. Althusser sees us as totally embedded in a capitalist society and its "modes of discourse". He leaves no room for the contradictions within people's experience, which help challenge people's conceptions of their needs and wants. His false conception of materialism gives him no grasp of the changes in social relations and human practices that are necessary if (say) women are to live a different kind of relationship with men.

I think it's partly because Althusser recognises the reality of ideology, thereby confirming women's experience of just how hard it is to change, and just how enduring and powerful are the institutions women are up against, and because he talks of ideology as a lived relation, that his writings have had significant influence within the women's movement. At another level this is surprising, because his writings confirm the necessity of women's subordination for the capitalist mode of production, and limit our theoretical understanding of the ways in which a growing women's movement could profoundly challenge the power of critical institutions in the society. If ideology is necessary, it exists in a realm of its own. We have little sense of how it is enmeshed within relationships of power, which have to be challenged if the ideology is to be questioned. In *For Marx,* Althusser closes these understandings:

> Marx never believed that an ideology might be dissipated by a knowledge of it: for the knowledge of this ideology, as the knowledge of its conditions of possibility, of its structure, of its specific logic and of its practical role, within a given society, is simultaneously knowledge of its necessity (page 230).

Althusser has raised interesting questions about the relationship of ideology to consciousness, which could easily be seen as relating to the woman's movement. He develops a significant critique of ideas that were all too readily reproduced within marxism. I think that Althusser's questioning has been important, even if it has served to substantiate false polarities:

> In truth, ideology has very little to do with "consciousness", even supposing this term to have an unambiguous meaning. It is profoundly *unconscious,* even when it presents itself in a reflected form. . . . Ideology is indeed a system of representations. . . . They are usually images and occasionally concepts, but it is above all as *structures* that they impose on the vast majority of men, not via their "consciousness" (page 233).

There are difficult questions of how we are to think about consciousness. Althusser acknowledges that there are questions, but he doesn't help us clarify them. As so often in his writing he offers us an alternative conception, almost in the hope that this will make the nagging questions just disappear. It doesn't help to talk about "structures" as somehow externally imposed, if we don't want to accept the implied contrast between "conscious" and "unconscious", but to think the ways in which ideology is both something unconsciously adopted (through the expectations of the family, say) and also something I'm vaguely conscious of. So, for instance, suppose I was brought up as a boy to feel that I've got to be continually doing things to prove myself. I've always got to show that I'm brighter than the next person. This is something that I might have lived out in my relationships with people, without ever really being conscious of it. But it is also something that I can *become* conscious of. This doesn't mean that even if I become aware of this, it's going to be something easy to change. It might create all kinds of anxieties for me.

I might discover that constantly proving myself against others makes it very difficult for me to get close to people. I might feel that I want to be closer to other men, while recognising that this need isn't going to be easily satisfied at work, because of the competitive organisation of higher education. So once I've questioned the liberal assumption that it's simply a question of "choosing" the kind of relationships that I want to have with people, I face the difficulty of creating closer relationships at work with the few people who may have discovered a similar need, while recognising that this challenges the organisation. It's also true that whatever relationships we might be able to sustain will be continually undermined and challenged through the social organisation of higher education. This means becoming acutely aware of our changing needs as we challenge the institutionalised definitions, but also being aware of how these definitions are strongly enforced in the social relations of power. We have to recognise *both* the structures of power *and* our growing awareness of what we need for ourselves.

Capitalist society reproduces class domination, and so distorts the kind of equal relationships we might want to have with people. These workings of the structure of power aren't transparent. It is partly through attempting to identify and change conditions of oppression, at work, school and home that we become more aware of the power which is opposing and limiting us, forcing us or seducing us into living the ways that capitalist society defines for us. So a woman can be told that she "should be happy" because she's got the husband, house and family that every woman wants. This can make it difficult for her to name her frustration and become conscious of its sources. She can so easily be left feeling "ungrateful", as if there must almost be something "wrong with her" for feeling miserable and bored, for not appreciating everything that her husband is doing for her. She will gradually recognise how she was brought up to accept this situation as "natural", but also how she has changed her sense of her individual needs as she has come to want more from life for herself. But as she changes, she's aware of the need for support and understanding.

Althusser sees capitalist society as a structured totality. Our "needs" are defined for us within the reality of capitalist society, and we can barely imagine, let alone live, the reality of a socialist society. This poses a fundamental division between different "modes of production" which blocks useful theorisation of what life within a socialist society could look like. At one level this recognises the truth, that it is impossible to talk about the character of sexuality, work, play, emotionality in a socialist society, while trapped in the relationships and experience of capitalist society. But too much can be made of this. Althusser poses too sharp a disjunction. The very conception of the society as a structured totality makes it difficult, both theoretically and practically, to grasp the very possibilities for social transformation that lie within the contradictions of capitalist society.

A false objectivism informs Althusserian work. The conception of society as a structured totality remains strangely out of touch with the realities of people's individual and class experience. Again Althusser poses a false choice between individual experience, which is taken to be "bourgeois", and the struggle between classes. It's this very polarisation, presented in abstract terms, which in the end makes his conception of "class struggle" so mechanical. I'll try to show this more fully through the Althusserian treatment of individual experience, since this poses more general questions of the ways in which all aspects of "individualism" are treated as inherently "bourgeois" on the left. We've been too hasty to contrast "individualism" with "communalism" without thinking carefully enough about the *nature* of this contrast. This has too easily forsaken discussions of "freedom", "individuality", "individual potentialities" and "choice" to the right. We've paid dearly for this kind of theoretical mystification.

Althusser encourages us into thinking that we are "rigorous" and "revolutionary" if we replace conceptions of the "individual" with concepts of "class". So it's important for theorists to "deconstruct" the conception of the individual, showing for example how a car worker might blame himself for not working harder at school, thinking that if he'd worked harder, he wouldn't be on the assembly-line. It's almost as if we are to *replace* this ideological understanding, making someone aware that it isn't their individual fault that they are forced to work on the assembly line, so they shouldn't blame themselves. Rather, it's because of the ownership of the means of production and the class character of capitalist society that he finds himself on the line. These aren't to be grasped as "alternative" accounts, as if it's simply a question of *replacing* one account for another. It *is* important to recognise the ways in which we've been brought up to legitimate social inequalities, through seeing them as flowing from individual differences of skill and ability. This is related to the ways in which education and ideas of equality of opportunity have come to have more centrally legitimating roles within monopoly capitalism. In a very real sense John might *live* this ideology, blaming himself for ending up in a dead-end job, seeing few possibilities for change.

The ideology of equality of opportunity can have a very real existence in the lives of people. It's an important force within contemporary society. If we say that this ideology "mystifies" John about the nature of his experience, we aren't saying that it is less "real", in the way that Althusser is anxious to establish. Rather we might want to talk about it mystifying John *to be able* to explore its contradictory reality. So that rather than thinking along with Althusser that the "individual" is a category of bourgeois understanding, so that we have to dissolve the very existence of the "individual" as a category of understanding, we want to *show* its power, through the hold that it has over John's experience. While Althusserian marxism isn't to have any connection with the experience of individuals, since this would be to remain trapped within "bourgeois" modes of thought, it becomes clear that we don't banish individual experience through a simple refusal to talk about it. It is too easy and too smug to think that the source of John's problems comes from the ways he thinks and feels about himself as an individual, so that somehow the problems disappear as soon as we learn to conceptualise our experience in different terms. In this way the sources of our problems — or at least our personal and emotional problems — are supposed to be "intellectualised" away, if we realise that we aren't "individuals" but our experience and feelings come from our class situation.

This will certainly challenge the ways we think and feel about ourselves. So John might realise that he didn't get on at school, not because he was "thick", but because he didn't really have a "fair chance", given the class character of our educational institutions. Thinking about the poor buildings, classes and teachers, will involve questioning the idea of "equality" in the notion of "equality of opportunity". So John might see through the idea that "if he had only worked harder at school, he would have ended up in a really good job". At the same time, it might be important for John to acknowledge that he didn't work enough at school and that he would have got more out of the experience if he had understood what he understands now.

This kind of questioning can radically affect our understanding of ourselves. We will no longer accept the "commonsense" we were brought up to assume, that an individual is totally responsible for the kind of life he or she has. But this clarity can tempt us into making too sharp a distinction between "individual" and "society", as if everything that we used to take to be the fault and responsibility of the "individual" becomes the responsibility of a class society. This is to contrast two kinds of understanding in an undialectical kind of way. It is to fail to grasp the process through which our understanding of our "individuality" is transformed, as we deepen our grasp of the class and sexual formation of our experience. So that for instance I increasingly grasp the ways in which my individual experience is shared with other men from roughly the same class background. This isn't to compare discrete individual experiences, but to recognise the ways in which our individuality has been formed through similar experiences and histories.

Althusserianism develops its own forms of passivity through its conceptual totalism. It isn't simply a question of learning to blame a "class society", where we used to blame ourselves. This too easily produces the answer that our energy has to go into "changing society", without giving us much grasp of what this means. The ways in which Althusserians want to obliterate the very category of the "individual" doesn't help people grasp their individual experience, as a deeply class and sexual experience. Somehow the critique moves people to a position of detachment, outside of captalist society, and estranged from our individual experience. It offers us an overview from which particular conflicts can be observed or placed, or particular discourses identified. So it allows us to situate any conflict within a total framework. This gives a sense of enormous power and importance to the theorist, who can remain strangely detached and all-knowing. This can encourage us into thinking that the only struggle which is worthwhile is the struggle against the "mode of production", to which everything else has to be subordinated. This reproduces a kind of political instrumentalism, since we never fully value and appreciate the significance of the struggles going on within (for example) education. These are partly generated through the conflict of liberal ideology, as new teachers are doing their best to give individual attention to classes of forty pupils or more, within the everyday realities of schooling. These are the kinds of experience which are politicising, as teachers develop a practice in which they can hope to be true to themselves in a situation that is fundamentally contradictory. If teachers want to put their liberal educational theories into practice, then class sizes have to be radically reduced. Rather than develop a politics of education out of these contradictions which helps support and strengthen socialist teachers, we are left with a fragmented conception of "politics" which exists in a realm of its own.[14] It has to do with traditional political organisations, as if the struggle against capitalism has little to do with the struggles within education, health, the media and the family. In a similar way, we are left feeling that nothing can be done about the "problems" we experience in relating to others, in forming closer and more equal relationships, until we live in a socialist society when our problems will either "disappear" or else be posed in such entirely different terms that we will barely be able to recognise them.

Althusserian marxists build too much out of their realisation that socialism will bring into existence a fundamentally different social formation. This insight connects with the critique of "human nature", to allow a conclusion that "human nature" will be radically different in a socialist society. This builds in an assumption of radical discontinuity that makes it nearly impossible to investigate important questions about "human needs" and their satisfaction and fulfilment within a socialist society,[15] even if it is recognised that these issues somehow remain to be addressed. What is more, this involves a systematic misunderstanding of the key notions of "dialectic", "contradiction" and "class struggle ". These notions get reinterpreted within a structuralist framework, so that dialectic means "dialectic" within a certain structure of the social formation, and contradiction is reinterpreted to mean a relationship between different "parts" or "segments" within the overall structure. These concepts allow a critique of the "surface" self-conceptions of capitalist society, embodied in different "modes of discourse", (say) of "individual blame" and "responsibility", *replacing them* by structural contradictions which are taken to be "embedded" within the structure of society. And so the deeper structures are supposed to "determine" the nature of our individual experience. It remains the task of the theorist to uncover these "structures". In this way our "experience" is supposed to be "explained", so that we can dispense with the very category of human experience. We are left feeling "naïve" if we remain sceptical about the validity of these kind of accounts. This shows that we are not serious about the development of a "marxist science".

Returning to the experience of school teachers in inner-city schools, we can begin to follow some of the implications of these theorisations. Althusser has helped people on the left, who would want to see teachers as "trade unionists" and "workers" in exactly the same situation as other workers struggling for wages. However significant it has been for teachers to see themselves as "trade unionists", it's also important to grasp the particular situation of teachers, and education, in capitalist society. Althusser has helped challenge a narrow economism which would simply assert that the more teachers struggle for higher wages, the more the profit margins of capital are squeezed. Althusser recognises the important role of teachers in reproducing bourgeois ideology. But the ways in which ideology is situated in a specific realm of its own makes it impossible to relate it to the social practice of teaching and the social relations of schooling. So the only alternative conceived for the teacher is to replace the teaching of "bourgeois ideology" with the teaching of "marxist science". We sacrifice the understanding of the educational critiques of the sixties which recognised how forms of knowledge related to the social relations of power in teaching. So it isn't simply an issue of what was taught, but of how we teach, and what kind of social relations of teaching and learning we are struggling to develop. This forces us to be self-conscious about our practice as teachers.

It's a deep consequence of Althusser's conception of ideology existing at a level of its own, that it can be thought that ideology is communicated in what is taught, but not in the very structure and organisation of schooling. The critiques of positivism that flourished in the early seventies showed that knowledge wasn't simply a commodity to be handed from teachers to pupils, but is socially produced. In this way, the marxist and phenomenological critiques of knowledge involved a critique of the social relations of teaching and learning, and so undermined the authority of the traditional relationship. These understandings haven't been engaged with. The institutionalisation of Althusserian marxism has led many to want to forget these insights as "naïve".

It's important to develop a critical relationship to certain of the ideas and practices about education that were current in the early seventies. I think they have tended to be too easily dismissed under the label of "progressivism". A marxist theory of education has to investigate the historical experience of these movements within education. Once we recognise how these were conditioned by an earlier, more affluent time, we also need to recover what we learnt about the theory and practice of education. So we also need to criticise those libertarian conceptions that thought it was "morally wrong" to involve yourself in the state sector, since this would necessarily involve you in authoritarian relationships in your teaching. We need to become aware of the sources for this kind of moralism, while remaining true to the understandings of the libertarian tradition. In a strange way this remains the other side of the coin, so that it can't be a total surprise that many people have switched from the libertarianism of the students' movement to the certainties of Althusserian marxism. Rather than develop a difficult critique of the politics of the sixties, people have been ready to switch positions. This means that little is learned for the making of socialism. On the one hand, we have a moralistic refusal of any involvement with authoritarian structures, which would only encourage a teacher to leave his or her job. On the other side, we have a legitimation for teachers adopting the same methods they were critical of when they were students, but teaching a content of marxist science. So politics doesn't have to do with the way you teach, but with the trade-union meetings that happen after work. Neither position takes to heart the experience of teachers or helps them grasp the contradictions that they find themselves in. It doesn't strengthen teachers to teach differently, recognising the realities of power they are involved in at school but appreciating that, as socialists, they need to develop different, more equal relationships of teaching and learning.

This isn't to suggest that when a teacher is brought to awareness about the contradictions in the situation, he or she will be "happy". But I am suggesting that the contradictions are *lived out*, though he or she might only remain aware of them as acute frustration. So it is possible for teachers to become conscious of the contradictions they face, which can be different from being provided with an analysis of capitalist education. Of course, it is important for teachers to gain some power in their situation, through both a grasp of the contradictions they face in their teaching situation, and from an understanding of the ways in which education is increasingly being used in a class society as a centrally legitimating institution for social inequality.

This isn't simply a matter of rediscovering the "social character" of learning, or of investigating phenomenologically the ways that teachers "make sense" of their situation.[16] Strangely enough this leaves us with too static a conception. It is often when teachers begin to put some liberal theories of teaching into practice, by reorganising the classroom, that they can come face to face with the structure of power which operates in the school. Sometimes they are forced to confront the contradiction between the image they have of themselves as being "free to teach whatever they want to teach" with the realities of power in the school, which are ready to impose their definitions of what should be taught. The subtle realities of power are more complex than the objectivism of the Althusserian analysis would help us understand. It doesn't help teachers develop an oppositional culture and politics within school, helping them recognise the kind of support they need from others if they are to challenge the competitiveness, individualism and ego-centred character of education. In posing the issue of power *within* the schools, they will bring into focus competing conceptions of the very nature and meaning of teaching and learning. Althusserian marxism too readily sees schooling as an "ideological practice", which has to be grasped on an ideological level. This fragments the experience of teachers, and doesn't illuminate the lived contradictions they find themselves in.

We can be left with a deeper appreciation of such books as Paulo Freire's *Pedagogy of the Oppressed*,[17] for the very reason that they help us *think* the relationship between what is taught and the social relations of teaching and learning. It can help us develop a fuller conception of relations of power within education, so that power isn't conceived as something "external" that one person has over another but is *intrinsic* within relationships. This means that relations of power are intrinsic to the very organisation of social life, rather than something which exists over and above it. This is an insight that has been most deeply assimilated and developed within sexual politics.

I want to question the Althusserian conception of power, social relations of power and social transformation. I argue that a recovery of the notions of personal relations as relations of power, as well as notions of "personal worth", "identity" and "human experience", which have been central to the historical experience of sexual politics, involve a deep critique in practice, as well as theory, of some of the central conceptions of Althusserian marxism. Against this is the fact that many people have looked to the influence of Althusser, Lacan and structuralism more generally, for a theorisation of the experience of the women's movement and sexual politics more generally. I think this is the wrong path. I hope to show that this involves a sacrifice of some of the basic understandings that have been learnt through sexual politics.

The women's movement has challenged a lot more than the ways we think and feel about women, as men. Changing the ways we think and feel, our "modes of discourse", has been an integral aspect of changing the relationships of power and dependency that have traditionally existed between men and women. As men, our power has been challenged, and we have been made aware of the power that we have been brought up to take for granted. Women have begun to transform a sense of their individual, personal and sexual needs, as they have challenged the assumption that they should subordinate their own energy, pleasure and desire, to serve our needs as men. It's become all too clear how the very structures of work and family reproduce the subordination of women. Capitalism has been developed upon a deep tradition of patriarchy. As women have challenged their subordination in individual relationships, we have been forced as men to reconsider and to change, if our relationships were to last.[18] This has been threatening. It has created bitterness and anger, as we are forced to learn to cook and clean. I know how deeply embedded is my feeling that "my work" is important. Part of me still expects to be served on, so that I can give my time and energy to working. Often this means that my energy has gone into reading and writing, so that I inevitably look to my relationships for recovery and nourishment. It's difficult to break these patterns, to realise that I don't give someone the kind of caring and love they want. As a man, I wasn't brought up to care for people, to be sensitive and aware of their different needs and wants.

Women have become aware of the ways they are treated as sexual objects. Too often we have uncritically reproduced property relations within our conceptions of socialism. Socialist equality is often seen in terms of the equal distribution of resources and material goods. We often think of the "satisfaction of human needs" in terms of the utilitarian formulations of the distribution of "satisfactions". We tend to see people's needs in terms of the passive consumption of "satisfactions", which in itself tends to deny activities and relationships in people's lives. Feminism makes us aware of how easy it has been for human relations to become objectified. It has made us aware of the fundamentally problematic character of "social relations" we have too easily assimilated into our understanding from Marx.

Feminism has raised fundamental questions about the nature of socialist equality.[19] We can't simply think about the distribution of goods, but have to also develop an understanding of the quality of human relations. We have been forced to think through the concept of "social relations", in the light of the realities of subordination, dependency and oppression, in what we otherwise conceived as more or less equal relations between the sexes. The deep liberal assumptions of the division between "public life" and "private life" have to be questioned, as we recognise that personal relationships have also been formed within relationships of power, not simply "shared interests" and "love". Questions of confidence, assertiveness, articulateness and self-assurance that we have easily assumed to be features of "personality" or "character" have to be reworked in the context of our understanding of the nature of power and dependency, within personal and social relations. So, as men, we can discover some of the sources of our arrogance, and the ease with which we can be condescending, even though we don't want to be. I learn how deep seated is the conception that men are basically rational, while women are fundamentally emotional, and therefore irrational. Even if I have begun to question this intellectually, I can discover myself "overlooking" what a woman is saying in discussion, waiting for the first moment to put my point.

The experience of the Black movement in the 1960s and the women's movement in the 1970s has forced us to rethink the nature of oppression. These movements have articulated their experience in terms of "oppression" and "liberation". The struggle for equal rights is an integral aspect of these movements, but it doesn't define their reality. This has promised a very different kind of basis for the discussions of "socialist humanism" than what went on in the late fifties. In some ways it promises us an even deeper and more sustained critique of stalinism. I think that we have been slow to learn the theoretical and practical lessons. I can't help feeing that questions of politics, and particularly questions of political organisation, are held so deeply as aspects of the male universe that the prevailing traditions on the left have done their best to control and domesticate the new movements, by understanding them in traditional terms.[20] It has been easy to identify the women's movement as part of a new "strategic sector of struggle", through which new "forces" can be brought into the struggle against capital. Very little is learnt. But unless marxism is prepared to learn from the ongoing struggles of each generation, it threatens to become a paralysing and abstract theory. Marx was always ready to recognise the historical nature of his theory. We are too anxious to disown our own histories before we have learned from them. This seems particularly true of the political generation of the late sixties.

It has been historically disastrous for the left to narrowly define our conception of socialism in terms of theories of surplus value. Marx always understood that the making of socialism involved more than the redistribution of wealth.[21] The women's movement gives us a much deeper sense of the ways that people are reduced, subordinated and denied, even within what we took to be "equal relationships". We learn about the painful realities of subordination and domination. We learn how women who in terms of capitalist society "have everything" experience themselves to be "worthless". We learn how dependency and power between the sexes can make people feel that they no longer "exist" in their own right, but only in relation to someone else. So we learn that power isn't something that men just hold over women. It's written into the very structure of relationships, and into the very formation of "character" and "personality". This deepens our sense of the kind of social transformations that are needed for more equal relationships to exist.

Althusser blocks our sensitivity and understanding of these experiences. Unwittingly he reproduces within marxist theory some of the damaging tendencies developing within monopoly capitalism. Althusser fundamentally misinterprets Marx's conception that people are to be understood as a set of social relations. He doesn't situate Marx's critique of the ahistorical and asocial conception of "human nature". Rather he uses Marx to develop a critique of the very notion of "individuality", which is taken to mean that you can "dissolve" individuals into their class and sexual relations. This is the deeper sense in which Althusser reproduces the *obliteration of individuality* that we also find in functionalist theory, making the individual an aspect of the larger structure. This prepares the subordination of the individual to the goals of the larger society. The social theory of capitalist society has to legitimate the subordination of people to the goals of production. Somehow people had to find their own fulfilment in the very sacrifices they were called on to make for increased production. This was the importance of Weber's analysis of the protestant ethic[22] and his recognition that hard work and self-sacrifice became "second nature", because life was accepted as a trial in which one proved oneself, for a realisation and fulfilment that could only come in the next world. In a very real sense Marx was attempting to challenge the hold of this conception, which has become the "common sense" of capitalist society, making people aware of the waste of human life this involved.

Althusserian theory furthers the very process of the obliteration of individuality that capitalist social relationships tend to produce, especially in periods of monopoly capitalism. This was something that Max Weber appreciated, though he tended to think that it was part of an inevitable process. It is this very experience of objectification, related to the experience that you no longer exist as a person in your own right, that was one of the driving contradictions of the women's movement. So the very assertion of individuality, of wanting to live as an autonomous and independent person, can challenge the prevailing relationships of power and dependency which want to reduce and obliterate this very "individuality". The social relations of capitalist society become more mystifying, as the social processes deny the reality that liberal ideology celebrates.

Marx's assertion about the ways in which, as individuals, we exist as a set of social relations, should be understood as a critique of bourgeois notions of "character" and "personality" as *fixed* qualities. For example, if a person is "shy", "insecure", "unsure", "dependent", then we shouldn't automatically assume that these are qualities that individuals have inherited. Sometimes we should think about ways a person is *made* shy, and maintained and sustained in their shyness, within a complex of social relations. A remark in *Letter to a Teacher* (page 17) illuminates this transformation of understanding:

> *Timidity:* Two years ago, when I was in first magistrale, you used to make me feel shy.
>
> As a matter of fact, shyness has been with me all my life. As a little boy I used to keep my eyes on the ground. I would creep along the walls in order not to be seen.
>
> At first I thought it was some kind of sickness of mine, or maybe of my family. My mother is the kind of person that gets timid in front of a telegram form. My father listens and notices, but is not a talker. Later on I thought shyness was a disease of mountain people. The farmers on the flat lands seemed surer of themselves. To say nothing of the workers in town.

The women's movement has deepened our understanding of class relations, as well as forced us to think critically about personal and sexual relations. The challenge to be "treated like a person" raises fundamental questions about "autonomy" and "individuality" that have been too easily assumed within liberal moral and political theory. Autonomy isn't something that is guaranteed in our capacity to live moral lives, even if the potentiality to live independent and autonomous lives is guaranteed. Social life bites more deeply into the lived reality of our relationships, and questions the very language in terms of which we understand our experience. From the beginning the women's movement of the 1960s challenged legalistic notions of equal rights, wanting to explore the lived reality and experience of subordination. The very division between the "public" and the "private", the "personal" and the "political" had served to legitimate the abstractions of liberal theory, making it difficult to grasp and theorise the lived reality of relationships. Women were to learn deeply from the experience of Blacks in America:

> Racism had never been legalised out of existence; in fact, its original virulence had remained virtually untouched, and, more important, the blacks in this country had never been able to shake off the slave mentality. He was born scared, he ran scared, he died scared; for a hundred years after legal emancipation, he lived as though it had never happened. Blacks and whites did not regard either themselves or each other differently, and so they in no way lived differently.... Black life is still marked by the "nigger mentality", the terrible inertia of spirit that accompanies the perhaps irrational but deeply felt conviction that no matter what one does, one is going to wind up as a 35-year-old busboy ... also characterises women's lives ... they have been trapped as second-class citizens, their minds have been deliberately stunted and their emotions warped.[23]

All this makes us suspicious of "formal" conceptions of "equality" in terms of "equal right". This isn't to diminish the historical significance of these struggles. It's important to investigate the tensions within, say, the nineteenth-century movements for equal rights. The Althusserians too easily "freeze" the struggles of the past, as completely determined within the "social formation". This makes it difficult to see how these struggles challenged the prevailing organisation of power, along with the conviction that women are born to subordinate themselves to men. If we analyse history, as a "mode of discourse" about women from the standpoint of the present, we are bound to misconceive the nature of the historical struggles. Althusserians tend to seek a point of "science", from which they can judge these "modes of discourse" within capitalist society. It's as if we can take a standpoint almost beyond her history from which we can see the nineteenth-century struggles as inevitably trapped within the limits of "bourgeois society".

By isolating "modes of discourse" about women we find ourselves locating our critiques in science, and we find ourselves somehow outside the ongoing struggles within capitalist society. And so it becomes too easy to ridicule liberalist struggles as "reformist", and as another way of retaining male power. The critiques inevitably become abstract, as we abstract from any genuine historical sense, comparing one "mode of discourse" with another. The danger of this form of ideological critique, from the vantage point of "science", is that we easily lose a sense of the reality of ongoing struggles. We lose a sense of the ways in which our language changes, as we change the ways we think and feel, in the context of changing relationships of power. We tend to misconstrue the complexity of challenges to power and prevailing conceptions of social reality, seeing them inevitably as changes in the "modes of discourse". It is not because of an abstract position of "science", but because of the struggles of the women's movement, that it has been possible to analyse how dependency and subordination are perpetuated through domesticity and sexuality.

The women's movement has challenged our language, as it has challenged the relations of power within relationships. Language doesn't exist in a realm of its own, somehow mirroring the realities of the social world. We are brought to integrate into our thinking and feeling the meaning of Marx's conception of "social relations", rather than to simply assert it abstractly. This helps challenge some liberal moral psychology that we tend to take for granted within our "common sense". So it isn't simply that some people are "dependent" and others "independent", and these people happen to be "women" and "men", but often a person is made dependent within the *workings* of a relationship. So it isn't just because of individual weakness that a woman might realise that she doesn't "exist in her own right", but is a part of a *shared situation of invalidation* that is often shared by women in relationships. This isn't simply a matter of the "inner qualities" of individual women, but of the social relations they are involved in with others. And it isn't simply a matter of replacing one set of qualities for another, say, "independence" for "dependence", but of learning about the social relations of autonomy and independence. It isn't a question of somehow rooting out our feelings of dependency, as if these are "bad feelings" that we shouldn't have. (This is to reproduce a Kantian conception of morality,[24] in which we are encouraged to believe that we can change through an act of will, and that we have to live up to certain ideal conceptions of ourselves.) It isn't a question of redefining the qualities which are "good" and living up to them, through not giving into temptations to think and feel differently. There are situations in which we need the help of friends, and it is vaulable to be able to draw on this help, admitting our need for it. This can be particularly difficult for men, who have been brought up to identify needing things from others as a form of weakness. This, in itself, can make it difficult to get closer to people. It can create its own fears of intimacy. We can fail to grasp that it's very much a question of the *ways* in which we are "independent" and "dependent". There are ways of being "independent" *and* "dependent" that can be crippling in our relationships. It isn't a question of making a choice.

The women's movement has taught us about the *social relations of autonomy*. The very struggle against dependency, can be a struggle "to be oneself". It's only when a person exists in his or her own right that we can think about being "dependent" or "independent" in a way that is appropriate to the situation. Autonomy isn't something that can be assumed. It is something that has to be struggled for. Nor is it assured in the respect or the regard which others are prepared to give, as if respecting someone as an equal will somehow *make* someone an equal. But nor is this a matter of realising the liberal ideas of "autonomy" and "independence", since the very meaning of these notions will be transformed. Understanding and accepting one's sexuality, for example, becomes an integral aspect of one's "individuality", since we learn to appreciate just how significant it has been in our formation. The women's movement shared with the Black movement a sense of the connection between "autonomy" and "responsibility".

> Where is black manhood?... How can it be retrieved? The answer lies in one word, responsibility; therefore they have been deprived of serious work; therefore they have been deprived of self-respect; therefore they have been deprived of manhood. Women have been deprived of exactly the same thing and in every real sense have thus been deprived of womanhood. We have never been prepared to assume responsibility; we have never been prepared to make demands upon ourselves; we have never been taught to expect the development of what is best in ourselves because no one has ever expected *anything* of us — or for us. Because no one has ever had any serious intention of turning over any serious work to us. Both we and the Blacks lost the ballgame before we ever got up to play. In order to live you've got to have nerve; and we were stripped of our nerve before we began. Black is ugly and female is inferior. These are the primary lessons of our experience.

In its own way this is a critique of the forms of work which exist within a labour process of assembly-line production and routinised office work, which systematically deny this very "responsibility" to people. This makes it clear that it isn't simply a matter of the ownership and control of the means of production, but of the quality of work and experience within a reorganised mode of production.

A structuralist marxism tends to see "contradictions" as "static" characteristics of a particular social formation. It does not see them grounded in the lived experience of people, and as a moving force for the transformation of society. The women's movement generated a different conception of "politics" which *rooted us* in our experience, as sexual and class experience. In exploring our experience with others, we weren't simply sharing what is usually personal, we were also incovering the larger structure of power and dependency, and the ways in which they work in the formation of individuality. In discovering *our* need for a transformation of social relations so that we can live more human lives, we grounded our politics, and could recognise more realistically the problems of our relationship to working-class struggle. The very claim to have more control over one's life questions the liberal rhetoric which wants us to think and feel that we've already got the control we ask for. We recognise, for instance, that it's very difficult for men to participate equally in childcare, unless the organisation of work is radically transformed.

Althusserian marxism limits our understanding of contradictions, making us think that we gain a clearer conception of the "contradictions" of capitalist society, if we are ready to remain detached and aloof. We prove our "seriousness" through being ready to abstract ourselves from our lived experience, conforming to notions of "rigour" and "objectivity", which gives us a sense that we've got "knowledge" while others simply have experience. A generation has emerged since the early seventies whose commitment to marxism is a theoretical commitment to a superior "analysis" of capitalist society than can be offered by bourgeois theory. The connections between a moral rejection of social inequality and injustice, and the development of revolutionary politics, are derided. So people are offered the self-confidence of "objectivity", while protected from any recognition of how narrow their class experience has been. Our experience has been safely separated off as "personal experience", with little bearing upon our grasp of the prevailing contradictions of capitalist society. If Althusser has made us more aware of some deeper assumptions that so easily get reproduced within our political practice unless we become critically aware of them, he has also separated us from learning seriously about the politics and experience of the new left. We are led to disown our histories in search of an "objective analysis", which locks us back into situations we struggled hard to escape from in the late sixties.

The women's movement, the gay movement and sexual politics more generally helped us understand that we weren't simply dealing with the contradictions of a capitalist economy, we were confronting the injustice, oppression and contradictions in people's experience. Capitalism wasn't simply an external set of economic institutions which had to be fought. Sexual politics recovered a central insight, often painfully and insecurely, that the revolution wasn't simply a matter of reorganised economy, but was about a transformation of social life. We had a deeper basis to understand capitalism as a totality of social relations. Politics wasn't simply an external and alienated practice, to do with abstract notions of "political work", but connected up with the ways people were living, attempting to create forms of collective living and support. So politics was grounded in the realities of people's experience, even if it developed in critical relationships to this experience. This wasn't simply a question of sharing personal experience, but of *grounding* our understanding in the realities of people's experience. Gramsci recognised the importance of grasping the needs, aspirations and emotions of people. It's largely because of the ways the society dispossesses us of this understanding of ourselves that it's hard for us to grasp the realities of a class experience which is very different from our own. In a letter to his sister-in-law Tatania, Gramsci wrote:

> I do a great deal of reading. But I enjoy it much less than I used to. Books and magazines contain generalised notions and only sketch the course of events in the world as best they can; they never let you have an immediate, direct, animated sense of the lives of Tom, Dick and Harry. If you're not able to understand real individuals, you can't understand what is universal and general.[26]

Sexual politics has the possibility of renewing our understanding of certain central ideas of Marx, as well as giving us the basis for asking new kinds of questions of Marx's writings. The politics of the late sixties suffered deeply from its own form of political moralism. Even though there was a lot of talk about the politics of experience, there was a very strong sense of political principles. People often believed that you could change through an act of will, once you had recognised that it was "wrong" to be possessive, or even jealous. Politics was too often a matter of abstract political and moral principles. People felt that they could avoid the contradictions of living differently within a capitalist society. It took time for people to recognise material realities, and to learn that we can't change through simply changing the external realities of our lives. However important it was to gain the experience of living collectively, it took time for people to realise that the structures of our emotions and feelings don't change so easily. We had to learn for ourselves that it was much harder to change than we thought. This involved challenging the kind of naïve psychological understanding that prevails on the left. We had to learn the influence of our own histories, and we had to deepen our understanding of Marx's conception of people as a complex of social relations. Marx was already expressing his realisation that people can't change through "acts of will", trying to bring us to recognise the importance of changing the ways we relate to people, the character and form of our everyday relationships. But it was already a deep misunderstanding of historical materialism, to think that once we change the situations then people will change. This kind of mechanical understanding that sees people as "products" of "social forces" is still implicit in Althusser's understanding.

The libertarian politics of the early seventies hadn't fully integrated Marx's critique of moralism. It carried a sense of itself as presenting a break with previous political traditions, coming to terms in its way with the new realities created through monopoly capitalism. With living through the excitement of living differently, people learned that it was far harder to change. We could either withdraw into communities we created, or else we had to find ways of developing an oppositional politics, through coming to terms with the contradictions of developing different practices, while living and working within a capitalist society. This wasn't simply a matter of compromising our "principles", but of learning how easily a politics of principles becomes a form of moralism. This was more easily learned in the practice of consciousness-raising within sexual politics, where people could more readily admit the problems and difficulties of living up to the ideals that they set themselves. It became possible to criticise the conception of socialism which saw it very much in terms of replacing bourgeois ideals by another set of socialist ideals. This too easily involved inheriting notions of self-sacrifice and self-denial, in the name of living up to these "ideals". Within sexual politics it became possible to realise the difficulties of living more equal relationships, while the structures of work remained fundamentally the same. Through consciousness-raising groups it was more possible to share the reality of our experience, e.g. as men attempting to relate more to children. We could more readily admit the difficulty of changing the depths of our feelings that child-care isn't really important, and that children are a drain on our energies.

Implicit within the practice of consciousness-raising is a transformed psychological understanding. Rather than changing through an act of will, our changes are more likely to be genuine if we share the difficulties and joys of our shared experience. As a man, I very rarely shared what I was thinking and experiencing with other men. Drink would sometimes make it possible, but not often, since a very different kind of relationship can be established in a situation of a consciousness-raising group, in which men learn to trust their vulnerability with each other, not feeling that they will be made to look silly, or that others will take advantage of them. I know that this gives me more understanding and grasp of my experience, as it has helped me gain love and support for living more equal relationships, in the contradictory contexts of capitalism.

The practice of sexual politics has given people an experience which, if they dwell on it, can make it easier to understand the importance of an understanding which is both "dialectical" and "materialist". It can help us preserve our grasp of the meaning of historical materialism, because it helps us grasp the ways in which our "individual experience" is a social and historical experience, while we remain "individual". This challenges the kind of reductionism of individuality that we discover in Althusserian work. However correct Althusser's critique of the implicit teleology within Hegel's writings, it's important to realise that an essential aspect of the dialectic isn't the inevitability of the process, but the nature of the struggle to *negate* the situation and state of affairs that an individual or class is involved in, so that they can become more of themselves.

Learning from Herbert Marcuse's discussion of Hegel, we can say very crudely that if John is a slave, then John is always *more than* a slave.[27] It is because John is a human being that he will be constantly in tension and contradiction with the condition of slavery. This is the moral understanding that informs both Hegel's and Marx's grasp of the dialectic, and which gives them a continuing sense of the ways in which people are reduced and negated within different modes of production. This is directly opposed to the Althusserian understanding of dialectical materialism, which substitutes a structuralist conception for Marx's understanding. This is why Althusser is left with such a mechanical understanding of "class struggle", which is always at the heart of Marx's understanding. But this is something that we can only understand in Marx if we also appreciate his grasp of the dialectic.

John can't become a subject or exist as a person in his own right without negating the social and historical conditions of slavery. He can't realise himself individually, but only through social and historical changes. Hegel tended to see this as an inevitable process of the realisation of the "notion". It was Marx who challenged the idealistic form of this inevitability and showed the necessity of the material struggles. It is the contradiction between the demands of John's humanity and the social and historical subordination that creates the constant instability and tension, since John can never be reconciled to the condition of slavery without sacrificing his humanity. So we have to grasp the "psychological" process of "liberation" as an integral aspect of the social and historical movement. Althusser is quite wrong to contrast these moments. Marx grasped that John couldn't liberate himself individually *without negating* the social and historical conditions of slavery.

The women's movement has recovered some of these connections in practice. It doesn't separate the "psychological" transformation of women from the social and historical movement. Rather than abandon the notion of the "psychological" we have to reformulate it, though I'm not sure that this involves developing a "marxist psychology". I think we have to ask different questions from those that Marx would have recognised. When Marx talks about "social relations", he is also talking about *relations of power*, material relations. The women's movement has helped us transform our grasp of the workings of these relations in respect of such issues as subordination, dependency and identity. It also makes us aware of how ideology penetrates every area of our experience, so that our very dreams, passions, anxieties and fears are deeply influenced by the prevailing ideology. Capitalist relations have a much deeper hold upon the very sense we have of ourselves than we ever imagined within the narrow conception of "material self-interest". Marxism was too easily assimilated into prevailing utilitarian conceptions of the self. This is something we need to understand historically. Althusser has recognised some of this, in his awareness of the importance of our unconscious lives. But again, understanding of the formation of the unconscious too easily sees it as a "mirroring" of the structures of the capitalist economy. This yields powerful and suggestive insights, but is incapable of understanding the difficult and painful processes of change and transformation, which are "personal" but involve a reorganisation of social relations at the same time. For this it is important to recover the significance of the discussion between Freud and Reich.[28]

We learn that capital isn't simply an "external enemy" but exists in the very structure of social relations, as much as in the ways that we've been brought up to think and feel about ourselves. As soon as even small changes are suggested in our relations, we can realise how the patterns of power have been institutionalised within the relationship. These patterns have deep roots. For instance we can think of the conflict created sometimes because a woman hasn't cooked her husband's dinner. With so many women working and earning money, the traditional relations of power have been challenged in many working-class families. Women are making more demands that childcare and housework be shared. Jim might feel threatened if his dinner isn't waiting for him. He knows that he's been working all day, so that he deserves to have his dinner waiting for him. He feels all choked up to find that she hasn't cooked the dinner again. You can't separate the way that Jim sees his wife from the material organisation of their relationship. They aren't different "levels" which have to be related to each other. Jim's consciousness begins to change *as* his social relation changes, as he's forced to come to terms with Kate's refusal to do all the cooking and cleaning. The Althusserians are in danger of separating "social being" from "social consciousness", and are thereby weakening our understanding of the processes of change. Jim feels that his authority is being thwarted. He thinks that it's a question of "who's wearing the trousers" in the family. Jim might try to turn it into a joke, thinking that she's only kidding. At other moments he might be furious, thinking there must be something wrong with Kate, since other men at work don't seem to have this kind of "problem" with their wives. Part of him might feel "what have I done to deserve this kind of treatment", as his anger comes near to the surface. This is a difficult moment in many relationships. It's a situation that shows similarities in our experience in growing up as men, however significant the class differences are.

It might only be when Kate has left Jim for a while that he begins to realise just how much "work" is involved in looking after the kids and doing the housework. This separation might help Jim to see Kate as an independent person with her own needs, interests and life, not simply as a "wife" and "mother". It might be different to see her as an independent person, but he might realise that only if he can change might their relationship have any chance of continuing. So the conception that he has of Kate will alter *as* the power in the social relation is challenged. He will be forced to see Kate as a person in her own right, not simply as *his* wife. This won't be easy. Jim might go through a period of feeling really hateful, feeling that she's been ungrateful for all the sacrifices that he's made for her and the children. This might help him rethink his masculinity, once he realises how much his life seems to be a "sacrifice" for others. As they change their relationship this will involve *both* ideological and material changes. As she demands to be treated differently, he will have to learn to do housework and spend time with the children.

None of these changes are easy. They involve considerable difficulty and confusion. Many people are involved with these changes, usually precipitated by the refusal of women to continue subordinating themselves in domesticity. Sexual politics has gives us a chance of helping people recognise and articulate this experience. It needs to become much more central in the politics of the left. The right is grasping the significance of these broad social changes, through a reassertion of traditional male power.

Ideology and power

Ideological struggle can't be separated, even analytically, as a particular *kind* of struggle that takes place in a realm of its own at another "level" from "material struggles". This forces us to misconstrue the social relations of power, in their involvement with questions of consciousness and ideology. Nor is it simply that "knowledge" or "ideology" *is* power, because it has its own characteristic reality, or because it shows the ways in which we conceptualise the social world. Rather "social consciousness" can't be separated in this way from "social being", and ideology can't be separated from its inextricable involvement with ongoing social practices. So we have to be ready to relate changes in our understanding to changes in the situation of power within particular social practices. This is the point which Marx makes when he warns us about separating questions of "ideology" or "consciousness" from social relationships. Marx is much less clear about social relations *as* power relations, and about the ways in which they affect the very formation of "self". So that it has been possible to separate the "ideological" from the "material", which has misled us about the relationship of ideological critique to ongoing political practice. Althusser has had to painfully learn some of these connections for himself,[29] but it shouldn't have been so necessary.

Even if Althusser's critique of notions of ideology as a "veil" for underlying material struggles has helped people to a sense of the significance of ideological and cultural questions, the general effect of his discussion has been to isolate these discussions to a "level" of their own. In doing this Althusser has actually preserved the traditional separation of economistic struggles. It is still as if "ideology" has to be criticised, to open the space and prepare the way for the struggles at the point of production to take place. The task of theorists is still very much to lift the weight of ideology. Although Althusser wants to recognise the importance of "ideological struggles", he tends to see these as parallel struggles, carried through in a relatively autonomous realm of their own. The "material struggle" is still very much identified with a technical notion of economic struggles.

This is bound to involve a theoretical and practical underestimation of the sources of power for the transformation of capitalist society. So for instance the "materiality" of women's struggles isn't sufficiently acknowledged if it is seen as a part of the ideological struggle against patriarchy. It is the very fragmentation inherent in the Althusserian account, which would see capitalism as a set of economic institutions somehow related to patriarchy, as an independent ideology. This has given important support for challenging a narrow economism which would want to reduce women's struggles to forms of wage struggles, because this is the way they become "material". But it is also mystifying to see patriarchy as an "ideological structure", because this inevitably limits our understanding of sexual divisions and sexuality within production, as well as in other aspects of capitalist social reality.

Too often the notion of "relative autonomy" that Althusser invokes reproduces a structuralist understanding of the relationship of different institutional structures. This involves a redescription of Marx's conception of the dialectic. At the different "levels", structures tend to remain in static relationship to each other. So ideology is conceived of as a more or less coherent structure. We easily get trapped into thinking about "structural analogies" and in seeing the different levels as more or less "coherent" within a particular "social formation". This search for structural analogies inhibits our understanding of how "ideology" is *lived out* inextricably within everyday social practices. Searching for direct homologies between different structures is to maintain the autonomy of each "level" in a misleading way. For example, it can be important to think how changes in sexuality have taken place, in relation to other changes in capitalist society. But it can be misleading to think of sexuality as having a definite "structure" whose changes can be set against changes in the structure of capital. This is to assume the autonomy and independence of different "structures" whose relationship we want to investigate. So we implicitly reinterpret the meaning of "dialectic", to refer to the existence of homologies between independent structures.

It is because of the weakness of Althusser's conception of the "dialectic" that the notion of "relative autonomy" so easily leads to a fragmentation in our understanding. If we want to avoid economic determinism, we also want to avoid the fragmentation of Marx's understanding. It is in this deeper sense that Althusserianism reproduces some of the conceptions of the orthodox marxism of the Second International, whatever the strengths of Althusser's individual criticisms. Perhaps it is because Korsch already detects this possibility in *Marxism and Philosophy* that he has to be summarily banished. One of the terrible effects of Althusser's critiques seems to be that they seem to banish the thinker, rather than the way of thinking. There is still so much that can be learnt from Korsch:

On the other hand, it has to be said that the supporters and followers of Marx, despite all their theoretical and methodological avowals of historical materialism, in fact divided the theory of social revolution into fragments. The correct materialist conception of history, understood theoretically in a dialectical way and practically in a revolutionary way, is incompatible with separate branches of knowledge that are isolated and autonomous, and with purely theoretical investigations that are scientifically objective in dissociation from revolutionary practice. Yet later marxists came to regard scientific socialism more and more as a set of purely scientific observations, without any *immediate* connection to the political or other practices of class struggle.[30]

There is also a danger in understanding "language" as some kind of conceptual totality, even if we relate it to a mode of production. We lose a textured understanding of the ways in which language — discourse — is a feature of ongoing relations of power, so that it becomes very difficult to talk about the features of language generally. This is what we can learn from Wittgenstein's development, from the *Tractatus* to the *Philosophical Investigations*.[31] This shows that language has to be grounded in our lived experience and relationships, so that we have to recognise how differently it enters different areas of our lives. It also shows how deeply mystifying it is to search for a single relationship between "language" and the "social world", between "thoughts" and "experience". So we can recognise in sexual politics the ways in which the challenges of women have begun to affect and transform how we "see", "talk to", "recognise" and "objectify" women.[32] This highlights the danger of separating language as a "mode of discourse" from the concrete social practices within which it lives. Once you isolate "discourse" as a "separate realm", you separate yourself from the structures of social practices. The temptation, present in Althusser, to see social practices as somehow "constituted" by language, makes it difficult to understand how we have been forced to change the ways in which we "see" and relate to women, because of the ways in which we have been questioned and challenged as men. It hasn't simply been a matter of changing the ways we "see" women, but of changing our relationship as men to housecare, childcare and sexuality.

As women, through the women's movement, gain more sense of their independence and power, they gain more sense of their own individual needs. As you begin to claim your autonomy as a person, you clarify your individual needs and wants. This involves a questioning of what you are brought up to need and want for yourself. It also involves thinking about how you have been brought up to accept certain needs and wants as "natural".

> What I learnt, ultimately, was that it was the prime vocation of my life to prepare myself for the love of a good man and the responsibilities of homemaking and motherhood. . . . No woman could possibly be happy without a man to love and children to raise. . . . How did I learn this? . . . The lessons were implicit and they took place in a hundred different ways, in a continuous day-to-day exposure to an *attitude* shared by all, about women, about what kind of creatures they were and what kinds of lives they were meant to live.[33]

Women were questioning these traditional notions of female subordination, recognising how these conceptions involve a denial of power and individuality. The Black movement had already learned the depths to which they had been brought up to despise themselves, so that they could live up to an image of themselves created by those who had power over them.[34] In a similar way women were refusing to define their femininity in a way that suited the interests, needs and demands of men. So women were beginning to separate themselves from men, so that they could claim the space to define their needs and wants.

The concept of "autonomy" has been of critical significance in the struggles against monopoly capital. The political theory of the left is only just beginning to appreciate its importance. It was Gramsci in his article "Americanism and Fordism" who first asked whether the changes taking place in the world of production were so profound as to constitute the beginnings of a new historical period. Gramsci was talking about the importance of the assembly-line production introduced by Fords, and the implications of scientific management:

> In America rationalisation has determined the need to elaborate a new type of man suited to the new type of work and productive process. This elaboration is still only in its initial phase and therefore (apparently) still idyllic. It is still at the stage of psycho-physical adaption to the new industrial structure, aimed for through high wages. Up to the present (until the 1929 crash) there has not been, except perhaps sporadically, any flowering of the "superstructure". In other words, the fundamental question of hegemony has not yet been posed.[35]

You can't say this after 1968. Gramsci recognised that these processes of "rationalisation" would involve a powerful transformation of work-processes within the state, hospitals, education, media and office. The routinisation of work and the subordination of people to machines undermined traditional conceptions of work and traditional forms of hierarchy. In some situations the hierarchies have to be artificially created by management because they no longer have a basis in the technical organisation of production.[36] The struggles against corporate capitalism were to take on a different form, as the very experience of work was to be transformed. The process of "de-skilling", particularly within assembly-line production, drained work of whatever skill and meaning it could have had in earlier periods. These developments are obviously uneven, and it's important not to generalise too hastily.

However it becomes crucial to challenge the Althusserian notion of the "economy", and to explore the relations of power within production. So the introduction of assembly-line production isn't simply a "technical" advance, but has to be seen against the background of the increasing success of skilled workers in challenging capital's right to "manage" and "control" in the period around the first world war.[37] So we become aware that "class struggle" isn't simply an issue around the distribution of surplus value but affects the everyday organisation and running of the plants, schools and hospitals in which these new labour processes have been introduced. This means we have to question the idea that the wage-struggle is the critical moment, since it's the point at which the surplus is to be distributed. We musn't simply focus upon the wage contract, nor must we assume that the willingness to strike is the only sign of workers' militancy. Possibly we should expect this kind of ahistorical understanding from a politics that develops outside the experience of work, and which makes the assumption that consciousness within work can only reach a limited trade-union consciousness.

We have to question the meaningfulness of the traditional left distinction between the "economic" and the "political", which gets reproduced ahistorically within Althusserian work. This involves a deeper understanding of changes in the labour process and experience of work. Often workers prefer to hit production without hitting their own pockets. It is absurd to assume that this is "reactionary". We should be ready to question the identification of "militancy" with notions of self-sacrifice. Or rather we should recognise the ways in which the protestant work ethic has been increasingly questioned. This has been one of the aspects in the developing crisis of trade unionism, which tends to assume traditional conceptions of work. It becomes increasingly blind to the changes in the experience of work.

Workers' struggles have increasingly separated themselves from the needs of capital. This has been a feature of these fundamental changes in the labour process, and it is partly what necessitates a different kind of discussion about the meaningfulness of socialism, when people so deeply experience work as a waste of time and energy. Traditional conceptions of socialism have been deeply connected to a meaningful work experience, promising the ownership and control of this work. The notion of workers' autonomy is articulated to express the separation between the needs of workers and the needs and requirements of capital.[38] This was a point of contact between the Turin workers at Fiat and the students in Turin in 1969. The students were redefining their education, wanting it to meet their needs rather than the needs of industrial capital. The workers were ready to talk about their needs for better housing and equal wages, separating themselves from the needs of capital. Both were ready to challenge hierarchies, and both talked in terms of a political language of needs. This wasn't a discussion about the abstract needs of humanity, but a discussion about the material and personal needs that people experienced in a definite historical situation. It's easy to romanticise this situation. We live in a very different period of economic crisis. But I can't help thinking that something important can be learnt about the more fundamental changes that have taken place in monopoly capitalism.

This was graphically shown in the struggle over lay-off pay at Fords plant in Dagenham in 1976. Workers had been laid off after coming into work late at night, because there were problems in supplies of components coming from the Midlands. The workers were fed up. They occupied the plant for the night, locking the manager in his office and insisting to be paid for their time. This developed into a strike over lay-off pay. As far as the workers were concerned these were the company's problems of supply and they shouldn't be made to pay for them. This created a problem for the trade unions, who felt the strength of the ideology of "a fair day's work for a fair day's pay" and so felt that they had to call the workers to work to *prove* to the management that there was still unfinished work to be done which should be paid for. There was a near riot on the day that men were called in to work. Many of the people felt that they should get "40 hours' pay, work or no work". They had separated themselves from the needs of the management, and felt that they should be paid regardless. This feeling was very strong. So there was a challenge to the prevailing ideologies of work, as an integral aspect of the assertion of workers' power.[39] The struggles over "ideology", "legitimacy" and "control" have to be seen as an integral aspect of the ongoing struggles, not something happening in a "realm" of their own.

In a similar way Althusser misleads us into looking for "structural contradictions" which move us out of touch with the transformations that take place in labour processes. It becomes increasingly difficult within the Althusserian language to understand people's changing relationship to work, and the contradictions that emerge between, say, "work" and "home", "workmates" and "family". We find that our thinking becomes blunted and insentitive to historical changes as we are searching for "contradictions" of the "social formation", with little way of connecting to the historical experience of people. Many people experience their work as direct alienation. In a strange way Marx's early discussions help articulate an experience of work in which people want to be paid as much as possible for working as little as possible. This has to be grasped not simply as a change of "attitude" or " orientation", but as a specific historical response to changes in the organisation of work.[40] Our socialist theory has to come to terms with these changes and has to be able to redefine the meaning of socialism in this new historical context. These questions have become pressing, especially to a younger generation, because work can no longer provide this meaning and identity for people. What is more, people are more ready to define themselves independently of the needs of work and production, wanting to have more sense of their own needs and lives. This has been an aspect of enormous significance in the counter-culture generally.

It has largely been within sexual politics that this kind of qualitative discussion about the meaningfulness of relationships has taken place. The women's movement, gay movement and men's movement have all in their different ways challenged prevailing definitions of "femininity" and "masculinity", of "sexuality" and "love", of "power" and "worthlessness", of "dependency" and "independence", of "friendship" and "community". It has also developed practices that help people face the difficulties of their experience, as they begin to define a sense of their own needs. Different movements have felt the need for "autonomy", to help discover and define their reality, in a situation in which they are protected from the power of others. In direct opposition to Althusserianism, there is deep respect and understanding of individual experience, not as something to be reduced but as something to be appreciated and learned about in the process of change. It is this very sense of experience and recognition of human needs which, in contrast to Althusser, connects with a deep tradition of historical materialism which can still learn from Morris and Carpenter, Gramsci and Lenin, Lukács and Korsch, Reich and Marcuse, Kollontai and Serge, Berkman and Goldman.[41] This becomes a question of rediscovering our own theoretical tradition of historical materialism, which can uncover and illuminate the struggles for a new life in the everyday contradictions of life in a capitalist society. We must begin by trusting ourselves and our experience of others. We must keep our nerve in face of being made to feel that we aren't clever enough, or theoretical enough, to offer our own understanding and experience. But we must also be ready to ask fundamental questions about the meaning of socialism in the times that are ours.

Notes

1. The most crucial work has been Ludwig Wittgenstein's *Philosophical Investigations* (Oxford, Basil Blackwell, 1963). Some idea of the context of this work is given in Norman Malcolm's *Ludwig Wittgenstein: A Memoir* with a bibliographical sketch by G. H. von Wright (London, Oxford University Press, 1958).
2. E. P. Thompson's *The Poverty of Theory and Other Essays* (London, The Merlin Press, 1978).
3. See the interview with Louis Althusser conducted by Maria Antonietta Macciocchi, "Philosophy as a Revolutionary Weapon" in *Lenin and Philosophy and Other Essays* (London, New Left Books, 1971), pp. 15-25.
4. See Alastair Davidson, *Antonio Gramsci: Towards an Intellectual Biography* (London, The Merlin Press, 1977), and Giuseppe Fiori, *Antonio Gramsci: Life of a Revolutionary* (London, New Left Books 1970). For a more general background to the political situation in Italy, see John M. Cammett, *Antonio Gramsci and the Origins of Italian Communism* (Stanford, Stanford University Press, 1967) and Gwyn A. Williams, *Proletarian Order* (London, Pluto Press, 1975).
5. Antonio Gramsci, *Selections from the Prison Notebooks* (London, Lawrence and Wishart,1971), particularly "The Study of Philosophy",pp. 321-78 and "Problems of Marxism", pp. 378-472. Both these sections have enormous relevance for our understanding of the nature of theory within a marxist tradition.
6. V. I. Lenin, *What is to be Done?* (1902), (London, Panther, 1970). This continues to have a deep hold upon the revolutionary left's conception of consciousness and political organisation. Somehow it has become an ahistorical manual of political principles.
7. See *Letter to a Teacher* by the School of Barbiana (London, Penguin Books, 1970, p. 50).
8. Louis Althusser, *For Marx* (London, New Left Books, 1977).
9. The writings of Horkheimer, Adorno and Benjamin within the context of "The Frankfurt School" have tried to face some of these questions. I think it can be said that in order to avoid a narrow economism, they never develop a full enough grasp of the significance of changes within the capitalist labour process. Marcuse comes closest to doing this. I think this has prevented a full enough appreciation of the significance of their insights. In *Dämmerung* Horkheimer wrote: "To make labour into a transcendent category of human activity is an ascetic ideology. . . . Because socialists hold to this general concept, they make themselves into carriers of capitalist

propaganda." For a general discussion, written with considerable understanding in the tradition of the history of ideas, see Martin Jay, *The Dialectical Imagination* (London, Heinemann Educational Books, 1973). Wilhelm Reich was also acutely aware of some of these issues. His work has far too easily been set aside as "biologistic", largely through the growing influence of Lacanian interpretations of Freud. See Wilhelm Reich, *The Sexual Revolution* (New York, Farrar, Straus and Giroux, 1974).

10. See Harry Braverman, *Labour and Monopoly Capital* (New York, Monthly Review Press, 1974). Also Bob Young, "Labour and Monopoly Capital" in *Radical Science Journal,* no. 4 (1976),pp. 81-93, and Russell Jacoby, "Essay Review of Braverman", *Telos* (Fall 1976), pp. 199-206. Georg Lukács's critique of Bukharin's *Historical Materialism,* for its reduction of the social relations of production to features of technology, is helpful in sorting out the weaknesses of Althusser's notion of "economy". See Lukács, "Technology and Social Relations" in *Marxism and Human Liberation,* ed. E. San Juan, Jr. (New York, Dell Publishing Company, 1973), pp. 49-71. Also Simon Clarke's piece in this collection.

11. See the discussion provoked by Herbert Marcuse's "Industrialisation and Capitalism in the Work of Max Weber", in *Negations* (London, Allen Lane, The Penguin Press, 1968), pp. 201-26, and Jürgen Habermas, "Technology and Science as 'Ideology'", in his *Towards a Rational Society* (London, Heinemann Educational, 1971), pp. 81-122. See also Bob Young, "Science *is* Social Relations", in *Radical Science Journal* no. 5 (1977), pp. 65-118. Includes a useful bibliography.

12. See Brighton Labour Process Group, "The Capitalist Labour Process" in *Capital and Class* no. 1 (Spring 1977), pp. 3-26, and the collection of articles brought together as *The Labour Process and Class Struggle,* CSE Pamphlets no. 1 (London, Stage 1, 1976).

13. See, for instance, *Workers' Struggles and the Development of Ford in Britain,* Red Notes Pamphlet no. 1 (London, Red Notes: Box 15, 2a St Paul's Road, London N1), and Andrew Friedman's *Industry and Labour* (London, Macmillan Press, 1977).

14. These issues are thought about in Michael Young and Geoff Witty (eds.), *Society, State and Schooling* (London, Falmer Press, 1977).

15. Important questions about the notion of needs in Marx are raised more directly in Agnes Heller's *The Theory of Need in Marx* (London, Allison and Busby, 1976). There is also an important discussion relating directly to the situation of monopoly capitalism in Herbert Marcuse's *One Dimensional Man* (Boston, Beacon Press, 1964), ch. 1.

16. See for instance Michael Young (ed.), *Knowledge and Control* (London, Collier-Macmillan, 1971).

17. Paulo Friere, *The Pedagogy of the Oppressed* (Harmondsworth, Penguin, 1970) and his *Education: The Practice of Freedom* (London, Writers' and Readers' Publishing Co-operative, 1974). Also Martin Hoyles (ed.), *The Politics of Literacy* (London, Writers' and Readers' Publishing Co-operative, 1977), and Chris Searle's *Classrooms of*

Resistance (London, Writers' and Readers' Publishing Co-op., 1973).
18. See Paul Atkinson's article "The Problem with Patriarchy" and my article "Men and Feminism", both to be found in *Achilles Heel* no. 2 (7 St Marks Rise, London E8, 1979).
19. See for instance Sheila Rowbotham, *Women's Consciousness, Man's World* (Harmondsworth, Penguin Books, 1972), and Zillah Eisenstein (ed.), *Capitalist Patriarchy and the Case for Socialist Feminism* (New York, Monthly Review Press, 1978).
20. See Sheila Rowbotham, Lynne Segal and Hilary Wainwright, *Beyond the Fragments: Feminism and the Making of Socialism* (London, Islington Community Press 1979, also Merlin Press, 1979).
21. See particularly Karl Marx's *Critique of the Gotha Programme* in Karl Marx, F. Engels, *Selected Works* (Moscow, 1935, vol. 2, pp. 29ff, London, Lawrence and Wishart).
22. Max Weber, *The Protestant Ethic and the Spirit of Capitalism* (London, George Allen and Unwin Ltd., 1930).
23. Vivian Gornick, "Women's Liberation: The Next Great Moment in History is Theirs" (New York, *The Village Voice*, 27 November 1964).
24. Kant's Groundwork of the Metaphysic of Morals" in H. J. Paton (ed.), *The Moral Law* (London, Hutchinson and Co., 1948).
25. Vivian Gornick, op. cit.
26. Lynne Lawner (ed.), *Letters from Prison by Antonio Gramsci* (New York, Harper and Row, 1973), p. 136.
27. Herbert Marcuse's *Reason and Revolution* (London, Routledge and Kegan Paul Ltd., 1955). I learned of the death of Herbert Marcuse while rewriting this piece. I was deeply saddened. I felt an awful sense of loss. I dedicate this writing to his enduring sense of the importance of philosophical work and to the smile he gave to so many in his wonderful TV interview.
28. See Wilhelm Reich's important historical discussion in the early sections of *The Function of the Orgasm* (New York, Farrar, Straus and Giroux, 1970), and the long interview which appears in *Reich Speaks of Freud* (London, Souvenir Press Ltd., 1972).
29. Althusser, *Essays in Self-Criticism* (London, New Left Books, 1976).
30. Karl Korsch, *Marxism and Philosophy* (London, New Left Books, 1970), page 54.
31. Ludwig Wittgenstein, *Philosophical Investigations* (Oxford, Basil Blackwell 1963). For a helpful interpretation there is Rush Rhees, *Discussions of Wittgenstein* (London, Routledge and Kegan Paul, 1970), and Stanley Cavell's essay "The Availability of Wittgenstein's Later Philosophy" in *Must We Mean What We Say?* (Cambridge University Press, 1977).
32. Sheila Rowbotham's early essay "Women's Liberation and the New Politics", reprinted in *The Body Politic: Women's Liberation in Britain 1969-1972* (London, Stage 1, 1972).
33. Vivian Gornick, op. cit.
34. See, for instance Malcolm X and A. Haley, *The Autobiography of Malcolm X* (Harmondsworth, Penguin, 1968), and George Jackson, *Soledad Brother* (Harmondsworth, Penguin, 1971).
35. Antonio Gramsci's essay "Americanism and Fordism" in *Prison Notebooks* (London, Lawrence and Wishart, 1971), p. 275.

36. See André Gorz (ed.), *The Division of Labour: The Labour Process and Class Struggle in Modern Capitalism* (Hassocks, Harvester Press, 1976), and the articles collected in the special issue of *Insurgent Sociologist* devoted to Harry Braverman's work, nos. 2 and 3 (Fall 1978) and the special issue *Monthly Review*, 28, *3*, 1976.
37. Sergio Bologna, "Class Composition and the Theory of the Party in the Origin of the Workers' Councils Movement", reprinted in CSE, *The Labour Process and Class Struggles* (London, Stage 1, 1976).
38. See, for instance, *Working Class Struggles in Italy*, a wide-ranging pamphlet published by *Radical America*, 7, 2, 1973.
39. See, for instance, *The Little Red Blue Book: A Short History of the Ford Workers' Fight against Layoffs,* a Red Notes Pamphlet (Box 15, 2a St Paul's Rd, London N1), and *The CIS report on Fords* (Counter-Information Services, 9 Poland St, London W1, Anti-Report no. 20, 1978).
40. A study such as Lockwood's and Goldthorpe's *The Affluent Worker* (Cambridge, Cambridge University Press, 1971) can help us recognise some important changes, but they will tend to make sense of them in terms of a changed "orientation" of workers towards finding "satisfaction" in the home. We are left with little real understanding of the sources and meaning of these changes. Huw Beynon and Theo Nicols, *Living with Capitalism: Class Relations and the Modern Factory* (London, Routledge and Kegan Paul, 1977), offers us more understanding.
41. Althusser has attempted to construct his own tradition of marxism which is consonant with his reading of Marx. Both need to be carefully challenged. This doesn't simply involve a reassertion of "Hegelian marxism", though it does involve an appreciation of the importance of Hegel. It is damaging to our understanding of the rich history of Marx's work to allow Althusser to define the terms of discussion. There is more to be learned from Lukács, Korsch, Reich and the Frankfurt School, as there is from an English tradition that E. P. Thompson has helped us appreciate recently. With a deeper sense of the problems we face in defining and making socialism in the very different conditions of post-war monopoly capitalism, we will be able to learn from the past.

Many friends have given me support, understanding and criticism in writing this essay. It hasn't been easy and I've drawn heavily on their encouragement. I want to thank Paul Atkinson, Larry Blum, Steve Gould, Paul Morrison, Jonathan Ree, Sheila Rowbotham and Bob Young for their comments on an earlier draft. In their very different ways, they helped me trust my understanding. I want to thank Abel and Anna for living with me through the difficult days of rewriting.

KEVIN McDONNELL AND KEVIN ROBINS

Marxist Cultural Theory: the Althusserian Smokescreen

Introductory Note[1]
Our interest in Althusserian theory began around 1973-74 when we both started work on theses in the area of the marxist theory of culture. Althusserianism and semiotics were the most developed and rigorous and, apparently, most useful approaches available. Over the next few years, we had growing doubts about these approaches, which were crystallised when we attended the 1975 Edinburgh Film Festival event. In our work on our theses we found Althusserian concepts extremely abstract and impossible to apply in practice. We came to realise that Althusser's work was not progressing. His self-criticisms did not stop him remaining rooted in the same space. We also began to question more the political implications of Althusserianism: the inability to break away from the isolation of the intellectual, and the emphasis only on theoretical work. The growing discussions on the British left about the nature of the crisis demonstrated that Althusserian theory had little to say about anything but ideology. From 1975 onwards our movement towards a different approach was aided by our involvement in various working groups of the Conference of Socialist Economists and the new debates we encountered there.

Our final break with Althusserianism came around 1976. Why have we written this essay? It is a way of settling our debt with our past. After having devoted three years to Althusserian theory, we had gained a considerable knowledge of it and felt this should be used in some way. We were dismayed by the growing domination of cultural theory by Althusserianism and saw the need for it to be challenged. It was for these reasons that we decided to offer a paper at the 1978 BSA Conference. Now, in 1979, as we complete the rewrite of the paper for this book our feelings towards it are ambiguous. We must apologise for the length to which it seems to have grown. There is an immense sense of relief now that writing it is over. We found it extremely hard to continue reading *Screen* when we were no longer convinced of its usefulness. What is more, we now have doubts about the whole enterprise. Is such a long, detailed critique of Althusserianism just another version of "the class struggle in theory"? Despite these worries we do believe that a critique of Althusserian marxism and *Screen* in particular, does raise fundamental questions which any alternative approach to a marxist theory of culture must address.

Marxism and Althusserianism

The last decade in Britain has been marked by the proliferation of writings on culture. We write from a marxist position and our assessment of this work will be in terms of its adequacy as a basis for a marxist approach to culture. It would be impossible to consider all the developments which have occurred so we focus on what has become the dominant tendency in radical cultural studies: Althusserian marxism, frequently supplemented by semiotics and Lacanian psychoanalysis.

This paper concentrates on one particular journal, *Screen*. We have chosen *Screen* as the best known and most influential journal working within this current. We believe that many of the criticisms we make of *Screen* can be extended to the other individuals and journals that take related approaches. Our concentration on *Screen* is justified not only by the key role it has played in cultural studies in Britain, exerting a major influence over all the newcomers in the field, but also because it synthesises all three of the currents which, as we shall see, define the dominant set of positions. A *Screen* editorial speaks of "the three discourses which *Screen* has most consistently used in its enquiry into the epistemology of representation — historical materialism, semiotics and psychoanalysis" (18,*1*, p.6).[2]

Before we examine the impact of Althusserianism on cultural theory, and *Screen* in particular, it will be useful to make some comments on the work of Althusser himself. Given the recent publication of E. P. Thompson's *The Poverty of Theory* and the presence of the other essays in this collection these comments can be brief. We will restrict them to two aspects of Althusser's work which are most relevant for a theory of culture: the conception of the social whole and of ideology.

Althusser has described the marxist whole, in contrast to the Hegelian one, as "constituted by a certain type of complexity, the unity of a structured whole containing what can be called levels or instances which are distinct and 'relatively autonomous', and co-exist within this complex structural unity, articulated with one another according to specific determinations, fixed in the last instance by the level or instance of the economy".[3] It is through the combination of two concepts — on the one hand, the "relative autonomy" of the superstructures and, on the other, "determination in the last instance" by the "economic" — that Althusser attempts to overcome the problems of reductionism.

Althusser's concept of the whole is premised on the existence of three levels of the social formation — the economic, the political and the ideological, each having a "relative autonomy" from the others. This represents a re-theorisation of the base/superstructure metaphor[4] as theorised by Marx in the 1859 Preface to *A Contribution to the Critique of Political Economy*. Althusser's whole is a syncretic one, composed of parts that are defined as external to each other. The parts are theorised *before* the totality, and they take precedence over the totality. For this reason Althusser's conception retains all the problems of the base/superstructure metaphor.

The main danger for those who, like Althusser, are trapped in the base/superstructure metaphor, is that it only grasps surface appearances:

> These categories only grasp the surface, that is the manner in which "economy" and "politics" appear as separate entities and not as specifically related. The totality of the reproduction of capital appears on the surface as the totality of the ongoing social process. The relation between the inner structure of "our capitalist society" and its superficial appearance cannot be unproblematically equated with the superficially appearing relation of "base" and "superstructure" or "politics" and "economy". This misunderstanding leads to the idea that marxist analysis is purely economic, as a particular form of "political economy" which can be compared to other "social sciences".[5]

It is precisely this appearance that Althusser reproduces with his separation of economic, political and ideological. The marxist principle, in contrast, is that one must first grasp the totality and then the way it appears as fragmented: "It is not social links, in Marx's view, that need to be explained, but the division or separation that occurs with the appearance in history of capitalism and 'civil society'."[6]

Althusser's division of society into separate levels marks a clear departure from Marx's emphasis on totality. On this point we side with Lukács when he claims: "It is not the primacy of economic motives in historical explanation that constitutes the decisive difference between marxism and bourgeois thought, but the point of view of totality".[7]

Althusserianism is only the most recent of a series of reformulations in marxist thought that have failed to grasp the centrality of the concept of totality and to understand the concept of "social relations of production". The marxism of the Second International conceived the "economy" as "one isolated factor, separated from the other 'moments' and thereby emptied of any effective 'socio-historical' content, representing... an antecedent sphere, prior to any human mediation".[8] The level of the "economy", of the forces of production, and thus of capital accumulation is externally related to social relations, the superstructure, which may inhibit or support the production process.

The basis for this error is a return to Ricardianism which sees production in purely technical, natural terms and relegates social relations to the sphere of distribution (i.e. of the appropriation of the product), which is externally superimposed on the eternal structure of production. It thus separates the "economic" from the social, failing to realise that, for Marx, production is simultaneously the production of things and of social relations.

Elsewhere in this book Simon Clarke describes how Althusser operates entirely within this Ricardian framework: "the process of production as a technological process determines certain functions. The 'relations of production' assign agents to these functions by distributing these agents in relation to the means of production. The relations of production do not therefore determine the *production* of surplus value under capitalism, but only its *appropriation"*. For Althusser relations of production are *"relations of distribution mapped on to production* by law or custom which assign rights to shares in the product by virtue of the *ownership* of factors. Hence 'relations of production' can only be legal or ideological relations". Production as the realm of necessity is separated "from the 'political' and 'ideological' or distribution and exchange, as the social realm". Because Althusser treats the "economic" as a technical and asocial process, he evacuates social relations from this level. Social relations then gravitate upwards to the political and ideological levels, thereby privileging them as the *only* spheres where social relations are to be found.

The emphasis on different levels allows the reintroduction of the bourgeois division of intellectual labour between the study of "economics", "politics" and culture, marking a regression from Lukács's insistence that "marxism does not acknowledge the existence of independent sciences of law, economics or history, etc: there is nothing but a single, unified-dialectical and historical-science of the evolution of society as a totality".[9]

Given this external relation of the (Ricardian) theory of the economy to the (Althusserian) theory of the superstructure or culture, then the way of keeping them together is to use the concept of "determination in the last instance" by the "economic". It is this concept which aims to prevent its twin concept i.e. "relative autonomy" from becoming total autonomy. The problem is solved terminologically. The new terms take the problem into theory rather than confronting it. Knowledge about social formations is achieved by juggling theoretically with "relative autonomy" and "determination in the last instance" rather than through empirical and historical research. Such research would lead to a questioning of the original terms. The easy consignment of aspects of social reality to particular levels becomes more problematical when faced with the complexity of reality. For instance, E. P. Thompson in his work on eighteenth-century law found that the law "did not keep politely to a level but was at *every* bloody level".[10] The difficulty of making reality fit neatly into the model of levels constantly forces the focus back on to theory, where the problem can be "solved" in the permutation of abstract concepts.

The positivism of Althusserians has prevented them from understanding the importance of the concepts of *critique* in Marx's work. For Marx, the (scientific) analysis of bourgeois society and its modes of thought is inseparable from a political and ethical critique. At the heart of this critique are the theory of alienation and, subsequently, the theory of value. Value is taken up, however, not only as a quantitative problem, in the manner of the political economists. Marx's real advance on Smith and Ricardo resides in his *qualitative* elaboration of value relations, as they express themselves through commodity fetishism. Coletti has demonstrated the importance of these concepts for Marx's critique of the irrational reality of bourgeois society:

> For Marx . . . the essential problem, prior to that of exchange rates of commodities is to explain why the product of labour takes the form of the *commodity,* why "human labour" appears as a "value" of "things". Hence the decisive importance for him of his analysis of "fetishism", "alienation" or "reification" *(Verdinglichung)*: the process whereby, while *subjective* human or social labour is represented in the form of a quality intrinsic in *things,* these things themselves, endowed with their own *subjective* qualities, appear "personified" or "animated", as if they were independent subjects.[11]

Marx's critique of capitalist society depends crucially on the notion of "determination of form",[12] the process, revealed by Hegel, whereby content gives birth to forms already latent within it. Thus, *Capital* describes the process of an increasingly complex determination of forms, the ever "more concrete *forms*" of the commodity (money, capital, profit, interest, rent etc.), corresponding to the increasing complexity of the social relations of production. It is the theory of commodity fetishism which is the key to these "forms of human life", the forms in which capitalist social relations present themselves. It allows us to comprehend the way in which relations between people assume "the *form* of a social relation between the products of labour", "the *fantastic form* of a relation between things".[13]

The objective of a marxist social analysis is "to develop from the actual, given relations of life the *forms* in which these have been apotheosised".[14] Hence, when we come to those social relations which are the state, law and, in our case, culture, we must understand them, too, as specific forms assumed by the relations of production. The state, law and, in a more complex way, culture are aspects, *constitutive* parts, of the relations of production. And because, in capitalist society, they are increasingly mediated by the category of value, the concept of fetishism is a critical tool for analysing them. This mode of investigation has been undertaken by Pashukanis for law, and by the German "state derivation" theorists (e.g. Altvater, Müller and Neusüss) for the state (although, as we argue below, we are critical of the abstract and ahistorical tendency of some of this work).

In his discussion of fetishism, Marx brings out the way in which it obscures or *mystifies* the real relations of production and the real source of value. In the process of exchange the relation between owners of commodities, including labour power, is one of equality. The real (and unequal) relations are "concealed by the process of circulation", for "in the process of circulation [the capitalist] forgets the process of production". He/she is unaware that "in the depths entirely different processes go on, in which this apparent equality and liberty disappear". Marx draws an analogy between the (fetished) form assumed by social relations and the "misty realm of religion", arguing that both come to "appear as autonomous figures endowed with a life of their own".[15] Moreover, these relations actually *do* assume this form in capitalist society. The mystification comes from giving the fetished forms a natural rather than a social explanation.

The state, law, and culture must also be seen in this manner, that is, as aspects — albeit more mediated — of the social relations of production, exchange and consumption. These particular social relations also present themselves as "autonomous figures": but they have further *autonomised* themselves, become apparently divorced from the social relations of production — drifting up to that "heavenly" realm called the superstructure. Bourgeois society presents itself, then, as a *fragmented* structure, and it is this mystification which is reproduced in the base/superstructure model and in the Ricardian view of society. The notion that "economics", "politics" and culture (or ideology) are external to each other is a constitutive illusion of capitalist society.

The "relatively autonomous" ideological or cultural "level" is thus the *result* of a long *struggle* by capital: the struggle to detach working-class culture from working-class control, by removing it from the context of work and community experience. And it is now "politically decisive for bourgeois society that the appearance of the separation of areas of life, the break in the cohesiveness of life, which has been objectively produced through the circulation of capital, should be maintained subjectively".[16] It is, then, necessary for a cultural politics to refuse the sectoralisation, the ghettoisation of culture — and this is one basis for our criticisms of *Screen*. It is necessary to reassert the point of view of the totality, the interrelatedness of areas of social life; to recreate at the subjective level the unity of life experiences.

Thus culture like every other area of social life is the site of a struggle. Realising this means promoting class struggle to a central place in our analysis. Althusser, on the other hand, despite various rhetorical declarations about its importance has been unable to change the fact that class struggle is external to the main body of his work.[17] In bourgeois society there is a particular, and dominant, *modality* through which the class struggle is articulated as an expression of the capital relation. This is the modality of fetishism, predicated on the formal equality of capitalist and labourer established by the conditions in which they exchange their respective commodities, money for labour power. The class power of capital is assured through a constant struggle to assert and reassert the validity of this fetish appearance of equality — a validity which, because it is repeatedly seen through in the daily course of struggles, is always threatening to break down. Heide Gerstenberger has shown how this process operates in the case of the state and law (the "state-fetish") with their fetishised appearance of autonomy and social neutrality:

> The class character of the state is inherent in its very form, in its separation from society which is constituted through its basic form of action, the law. The fundamental difference between a pre-bourgeois state apparatus and the bourgeois state is given with the formal equality of all citizens before the law. And it is exactly this formal equality which constitutes the class character of the bourgeois state, because in denying the fundamental differences between those who own the means of production and those who are forced to sell their labour power, it is constantly reproducing the basic differences which have historically been brought about in the process of original accumulation.[18]

The same argument applies to cultural and leisure activities — that is, in so far as they are brought under the capital relation. Culture presents itself as a distinct sphere of activity, "outside" "economics" and "politics" — the sphere of human values and truths (high culture) or of leisure time, entertainment and distraction (mass culture) — in which all are equal as consumers, since all can buy a theatre ticket or television licence. The domination of capital is achieved through asserting the validity of fetishised appearances, and not, as Althusserians would have it, through institutions, i.e. the "ideological state apparatuses". Franz Droge has described how the appearances generated in exchange and consumption define, and simultaneously obscure, the class character of mass media. In the "formal generality" of the media "is preserved the claim to equality, based on the capitalist principle of exchange, which has long since been liquidated in reality: all get the same commodity for the same price, and all pay the same price for the same commodity".[19]

There is, of course, the danger that the approach we have indicated will become functionalist, as in some versions of the "state derivation" theory. It is, therefore, necessary, at this point, to make two qualifications to our argument. The first is to reaffirm that we understand the capital relation, as a relation of class struggle, to be a historical, and not just a logical, category. That is to say, our discussion of fetishism as an aspect of class struggle remains abstract, describing a *tendential* process within the capitalist mode of production. Joachim Hirsch made this point in relation to the state: "Beyond the general definition of the bourgeois state, derived from the concept of commodity producing society, it is necessary to derive *concrete definitions of its functions* from the historically variable conditions of the capitalist accumulation process..."[20] It is essential to further develop capital theory in order to account for the changing class composition, and for the historical specificity of struggles, as they are expressed in those movements of accumulation, reproduction and crisis which constitute particular phases of capital accumulation.

The second point is to stress that capital theory accounts only for the organisational attempts by capital to contain the working class within the confines of the capital relation. It *cannot* deal with that movement by which the working class asserts its autonomy, denying its status as variable capital by externalising (estranging) itself from the capital relation. Moishe Postone has quite correctly criticised those theories which view capitalism "only in terms of deformation and reification. In Marxian language, they grasp only the value dimension — a moment of a more complex totality — as that totality itself". He continues:

> The capitalist social formation not only entails reified forms of consciousness and needs, but also socially formed, historically changing other needs which are neither "natural" nor pre-capitalist and which form the bases for oppositional, critical and revolutionary forms of consciousness.[21]

The only way to examine the more concrete forms of the capital relation and how the working class attempts to break from the confines of the capital relation is through empirical and historical research. This is another area in which Althusser's writings have been shown to be totally inadequate.[22]

Althusser's theory of ideology has undoubtedly been the principal inspiration behind the recent upsurge of cultural theory in Britain. However, there is by no means a single theory of ideology within Althusser's work: his followers have all extracted particular elements for their own theoretical purposes. If it is generally accepted that his work is incomplete, it is none the less generally welcomed as an important advance. Criticisms of specific aspects of Althusser's theory have done nothing to diminish the acceptance of his general conceptual framework, which starts from the assumption that ideology is an autonomous "region". In our view, it is important to make the obvious, but commonly disregarded, point that Althusser's formulations bear little relation to those of Marx.

The principles (what he calls "a few schematic theses") of Althusser's theory — "a theory of ideology in general" — are presented in the essay on "Ideology and Ideological State Apparatuses".[23] Althusser attempts to situate his theory of ideology in relation to the reproduction of the conditions of production and in particular the reproduction of the relations of production. His "central thesis" is that "all ideology hails or interpellates concrete individuals as concrete subjects". Ideology "has the function (which defines it) of 'constituting' concrete individuals as subjects"; in doing this it simultaneously subjects them to a Unique, Absolute, Other Subject, e.g. God, the State.

This thesis, which is an expression of Althusser's "theoretical anti-humanism", is complemented by an anti-empiricist thesis: "Ideology represents the imaginary relationship of individuals to their real conditions of existence". Enigmatically, Althusser maintains that ideology is not a representation of people's real conditions of existence, but of "their relation to those conditions of existence". Two further theses are relevant for the discussion of *Screen*. The first asserts that "ideology is eternal" and "has no history". By this Althusser means it is "omnipresent, trans-historical and therefore immutable in form through the extent of history". The second is that "ideology has a material existence" which means that ideology "always exists in an apparatus, and its practice, or practices". Althusser labels a series of institutions, including the church, schools, the family, political parties, trade unions and the mass media, as Ideological State Apparatuses (ISAs).

The question of ideology is a prism in which are focused all the problems that characterise Althusserian theory. What is immediately striking is the *a priori* and deductive nature of Althusser's formulations. Admittedly they have their own elegant, internal consistency, but they are insensitive to the historical real world — and to their own status as mediated (historical) products. Althusser's fear of empiricism leads him to subordinate historical and social reality to his own abstract and inflexible theoretical principles. The mystified result, to borrow a phrase from Marx's criticism of Hegel, is that "the real world is only the external appearance of the idea".

A second point to be made is that this theory is fetishised in that it sees ideology as a distinct social "level" or practice. For Althusser, "ideology is not the reflection of real social relations, but the reflection of the social imaginary of its subjects. The image of an image, it is deprived of all real denotation".[24] Ideology is defined as a parallel sphere (or struggle), in a realm of its own, rather than as an organic part of *all* social practices and struggles. This problem is particularly acute in Althusser's theory of the ISAs. We believe it is totally contrary to the spirit of marxist method to separate, as he does, the sphere of reproduction, the domain of the ISAs, from the sphere of production.

And finally, it is important to be aware of the significance of the Althusserian tendency to equate ideology with the whole symbolic or cultural order — important precisely because of the manner in which this approach is taken up by *Screen*. In striking similarity with the sociology of Comte or Durkheim, ideology is characterised as maintaining social cohesion.[25] This functionalist conception regards ideology, like culture, as *something* to which we are passively subjected: there is little suggestion that it is possible to transform ideological consciousness. This functionalism is particularly apparent in the notion of interpellation. The subject is seen as unproblematically responding in an identical way when hailed by a whole series of larger Subjects, including the family, law, religion and education. On the contrary, the relationship of an individual to these various institutions must be the site of a complex array of contradictions and struggles.

The Althusserian position, firmly located within the scientific tradition of marxism, sees ideology only in positivist fashion (as a reified entity). Opposed to this, the critical marxist tradition regards ideology in a pejorative sense, as a reality to be negated through (practical) critique. This latter tradition sees the phenomenon of fetishism as the basis on which ideology is articulated in capitalist society. This in no way implies, as Althusserians would claim, that ideology is treated as pure illusion. It is more than this, both because it has social effects and because it does provide knowledge about reality, albeit only a *partial* knowledge (i.e. it does not perceive the totality, provides natural rather than social explanations, and so on).

Ideology is thought which is dominated by the fetishised surface appearances produced by social relations in capitalist society: the fragmentation of social existence, the apparent equality of individuals in the sphere of circulation, the apparent domination of things over people, etc. Fetishised social relations have, according to Colletti, an existence and a reality, albeit an "unsubstantial reality", like that of value. When Marx discusses the process of abstraction in society "he has in mind... a process of real abstraction, something which actually goes on in reality itself". Alfred Sohn-Rethel has convincingly argued that Marx's originality lay in grasping an abstraction that occurs *other than in thought:* that is, the concrete or "real abstraction" effected through commodity exchange, which becomes the basis for deriving forms of thought.[26] Marx himself makes this point in a discussion of Thomas Hodgskin:

> The capitalist, as capitalist, is simply the personification of capital, that creation of labour endowed with its own will and personality which stands in opposition to labour. Hodgskin regards this as a pure subjective illusion which conceals the deceit and the interests of the exploiting classes. He does not see that *the way of looking at things arises out of the actual relationship itself: the latter is not an expression of the former, but vice versa.*[27]

The consequence of this is that it is the overwhelming presence — the imposed reality — of concrete fetish forms, that effectively structures, and thereby controls, people's daily lives. Jean-Marie Vincent has argued that the force of political and juridical forms — and we may add cultural forms — "rests less on mechanisms of ideological inculcation (via what Althusser calls Ideological State Apparatuses, or ISAs) than on the complementary play of the different modalities of fetishism".[28] In this context, ideology becomes a less total phenomenon than it is for Althusserians, who identify it with the cultural or symbolic as a whole. We take ideology to be an *abstract* concept, referring only to the (fetishised) forms assumed by thought which uncritically confronts the necessary constraints of capitalist social reality: it stands in need of elaboration and supplementation through historical observation and analysis of the content of this thought.

We also understand ideology to be a conscious process, and not a factor of the unconscious as Althusser maintains. This latter position would, indeed, make class consciousness impossible. And if ideology is a conscious phenomenon, it is not one which permeates people's minds: the working class does not find it impossible to unmask the ideological mystifications of capitalist society. For ideology is far from watertight; it requires an incessant struggle by the capitalist class to maintain its precarious validity. A validity that is constantly called into question, *not in a separate sphere of ideological struggle, but throughout the daily struggles in the workplace, the community etc.* — for ideology is an organic and integral part of all social practices. The problem remains, of course, that although it is possible to demystify ideology, one does not thereby change social reality: one is still confronted with the imposing and dominating reality of the "real abstractions". The ultimate objective must be to *practically* subvert these concrete fetish forms of bourgeois society.

Whilst initially Althusserian marxism seemed to mark an exciting break with vulgar marxism, it now stands as a barrier to knowledge. We believe Althusserianism to be distant from marxism. We say this not to make Marx the source of all true knowledge which cannot be challenged, but in the belief that Althusser and his successors have discarded from his work almost all that is of value: the tradition of critique, the concepts of the totality, of social relations of production and of fetishism, the emphasis on class struggle and on historical specificity.

In using the term "Althusserianism" as we do in this paper we realise there is a danger of reductionism. Many of those Althusser has influenced have taken on board only parts of his work, and have, from the start, criticised other aspects. Many regard themselves as post-Althusserians, believing they have developed beyond Althusser. They no longer take any interest in the latest modifications Althusser continues to make to his own position. All those who have been influenced by Althusser invariably unite in rejecting the term "Althusserian" as being of no value, on the grounds that Althusser's project was only to reconstitute marxism from its empiricist, historicist and humanist distortions, and not to establish any new system or school.[29]

However, we believe it is still useful to retain the term even though it applies to a broad theoretical space, a spectrum of positions, rather than to a single phenomenon. There are numerous authors who share the same conceptual framework, in the sense that they all situate themselves and recognise their specificity within an internally referential network of positions. Apart from these positive principles, certain negative criteria operate, whereby Althusserian positions can be defined according to those particular theoretical directions are ruled out of court. The easiest definition to give Althusserianism is a negative one, in terms of positions rejected. An anti-empiricism rejects the connection between knowledge and reality; an anti-historicism fragments the totality; an anti-humanism denies people the role of active subjects. An interesting test case for the term "Althusserianism" is the work of Hindess and Hirst. They see themselves, and have been described by others, as only remote descendants of Althusser. We believe that the relationship is closer to that between Frankenstein and his monster.

In the discussion above we have seen how Althusser frequently attempts to juggle with crucial contradictions in his theory. Hindess and Hirst draw out the full implications of these contradictions. By doing so they turn his work against itself. Hindess and Hirst's successive books, from *Pre-capitalist Modes of Production* onwards, can be seen as a process of using Althusser to criticise more and more of Marx, and of Althusser. We believe it is important to include some discussion of Hindess and Hirst because it is increasingly their writings rather than those of Althusser himself which are cited in *Screen*. We will concentrate on the same two aspects of their work which we focused on with Althusser: the conception of the social whole and of ideology.

Hindess and Hirst have made a critique of Althusser's reformulation of the base/superstructure model on the grounds that this still does not avoid the problem of economic reductionism. They argue that the notion of structural causality turns the social whole into an "expressive totality" as distinct practices are reduced to an essence — the structure of the social whole. Any general, universal form of causality which specifies *a priori* the relationship between different practices in the social whole (such as "determination in the last instance") is rejected. In its place they put the concept of "conditions of existence". All that is implied by this concept is that understanding a particular object in the social whole will include the effects of other objects on it. Just what these other objects are and what these effects will be cannot be determined in advance.

Whilst Althusser struggles to retain a conception of the social whole, the impetus of Hindess and Hirst's critique is to completely fragment the social formation. They ask, "Why is the study of whole societies epistemologically superior to the study of half societies?" Graham Burchell spells out the consequences of following their approach: "The idea of totality seems increasingly fragile. It is often claimed that the 'superiority' of marxism resides in its grasp on the 'totality'. One wonders how far is this conception a consequence of a rationalism unthought in its implications? ... The idea of the object of theory as a totality arises from a rationalist epistemology which represents the conceptualisation of social relations in terms of a general theory, or 'science', of so-called society... If we reject the epistemologicalisation of discourse we also dispose of the necessity to conceive of its objects as totalities".[30] We regard the rejection of the concept of totality as an abandonment of one of the key tenets of marxism.

Another aspect of Althusser's work which is criticised is his theory of ideology. In an article entitled "Althusser and the Theory of Ideology", Paul Hirst argues that in still seeing ideology as a misrepresentation of the real, Althusser retains the idealist notion of ideology as false consciousness. He has been unable to escape the empiricist notion that ideology is a representation of the real. Furthermore, Althusser does not escape the humanist problematic, in that his notion of the interpellation of subjects already implies the prior existence of the subject. Finally, Hirst believes that emphasising the role of ideology in reproducing the relations of production and presenting the ISAs as simply representing class interests, is functionalist, and, thereby, historicist.

Many of these points are valid, but what is Hirst left with as an alternative? He writes: "We use the word 'ideological' to refer to a non-unitary complex of social practices and systems of representations which have political significances and consequences". As with the concept of "conditions of existence", no attempt is made to specify what these practices and systems or political consequences are. He goes on to argue: "There is no necessary relation between the conditions of existence of the means of representation and what is produced by the action of those means, no necessity that they 'represent' those conditions".[31] Whilst we acknowledge that there is struggle within "the means of representation", we are unashamedly "reductionist" to the extent we believe that who owns and controls the means of representation is of more than a little significance. This theory of ideology, like Hindess and Hirst's theory as a whole, refuses to specify in any way relationships which are essential for an understanding of society, and is therefore unable to move beyond the level of surface appearances.

In all these points we can see how, despite quite important differences, Hindess and Hirst remain firmly caught in the Althusserian problematic. Every move they make bears the imprint of their starting point. And the more they try to wriggle free, the more surely they hang themselves in the Althusserian noose.

The most significant characteristic of contemporary marxist cultural theory in Britain is the almost unquestioned dominance by Althusserian positions. Historically there were very good reasons why cultural theorists turned to Althusserian marxism. By granting a (relative) autonomy to culture, it allowed marxists to operate without the need to constantly refer back to the "economic". Marxists were able to deal with the specificity of culture, to take it seriously. Furthermore, Althusser opened up marxism to the influence of other disciplines, which given the then largely impoverished state of marxist "superstructural" theory helped to establish the importance of cultural analysis. Historically, the intervention of Althusser into cultural theory was, for a short period, a positive gain: it has now ceased to be such, and is a fetter on the further development of marxist cultural theory.

There are at least three distinct currents within Althusserian cultural theory (although by no means all Althusserians fit neatly into one of these currents). The first is the one we shall concentrate on in this essay and is best represented by the work of *Screen*. It combines the work of either Althusser or Hindess and Hirst with semiotics and Lacanian psychoanalysis. The second trend, most prominent in *Red Letters,* draws more on Althusser's own, frequently neglected, writings on art and, particularly, on the work of Pierre Macherey. The third current takes up Althusser's essays on "Contradiction and Overdetermination" and on Ideological State Apparatuses, and combines them with ideas drawn from a particular reading of Poulantzas and Gramsci. This trend includes the work of Stuart Hall and most of the contributors to later issues of *Working Papers in Cultural Studies* (although this journal has followed a highly varied course and has also included articles deriving from the first current and from approaches unrelated to Althusserianism).

In its more recent issues there is some indication that *Screen* is attempting to broaden its coverage to include articles which are closer to the third current. In many ways we find this current more attractive than the other two, as it does at least place a considerable emphasis on empirical research. However, we believe it to be problematical in that it still focuses its analysis on texts and fails to locate culture within the relations of production. When its empirical research does provide interesting results, this work has often had no necessary relation to — and sometimes even seems to be in spite of — its conceptual apparatus.

In this paper we focus on the first current, and, in particular, the journal *Screen*[32]. We will begin with the question of its relation to marxism and Althusserianism. *Screen* normally cloaks its adherence to marxism behind the term "historical materialism", but it does clearly see itself as a marxist journal: "as 'professed marxists', we take marxism in our situation to be a political commitment to a materialist analysis of the contradictions and overdeterminations of capitalist societies and to the transformation of those societies" (17, 2, p.112). *Screen* has, however, contained very few references to Marx's work. Occasionally a quotation from him is slipped in to support a theoretical point, but his writings are never a fundamental point of reference or subjected to detailed examination. When he is cited he is clearly being read via Althusser, who has been a more constant influence, although again this is not usually by explicit references to his writings but more frequently through continual use of terms such as "problematic", "practice", "conjuncture", "instance", "historicism", "empiricism", etc.

The first aspect of Althusserianism which we believe has had an important impact on *Screen* is the emphasis on theory and the role of intellectuals. *Screen* first began to resemble its present form when in 1971 it underwent a fundamental transformation. This change of direction, begun under the editorship of Sam Rohdie, was defined in terms of a new emphasis on theory rather than any shift in political position: "*Screen* is committed to the development of theoretical ideas and more systematic methods of study" (12, *1*, p.5). *Screen* has always rejected other approaches to film criticism, such as that of *Movie*, because of their lack of theoretical rigour. In the earlier issues, *Screen* saw its task as relating to film education: "The practical work of *Screen* is education. It is not primarily a journal for professional intellectuals, film critics, cinephiles, but for practising teachers" (12, *1*, p.12). It was stated that "the decision to emphasise theoretical and critical issues in *Screen* was taken after a long debate about the prime needs in film education" (12, *3*, p.10).

Screen has, however, increasingly moved away from this concern with education. On the basis of SEFT's decision to bring out a companion journal, *Screen Education*, orientated towards the practical teaching of film and television, *Screen* has turned towards *purely* theoretical criticism, towards an audience composed of academics and cinephiles. It is only able to relate to education at the very highest levels. Despite the fact that the editorial board has dismissed the charge that the journal took no serious interest in educational matters as "largely invective and, as always, this can be categorically refused" (17, 2, p.116), it doesn't seem to be far from the truth. *Screen*'s strong theoretical emphasis, combined with its exclusive preoccupation with foreign sources, has meant that it has become increasingly a forum for none but theoretical specialists, hermetically sealed into their own internal debates on film theory — a theory with its own built-in obsolescence, such that each article is a critique or autocritique of a previous one. Without knowing about the latest theoretical trend surfacing in France, it is difficult to participate in discussions.

The emphasis on developing theory, even if this means that the journal is accessible only to a small group of fellow theoreticians, demonstrates the key role *Screen* attributes to the work of intellectuals. It is a position that is quite consistent with *Screen*'s theoretical premises. Its critique of empiricism is premised on the argument that the true nature of reality is revealed — if at all — only to those armed with the appropriate set of theoretical concepts. It is, of course, only intellectuals who have access to science, or theoretical practice, to illuminate social reality, in order to map out strategies for political intervention. To tread a path through the webs of ideology in capitalist society requires, it would seem, a detailed knowledge of Althusser and Lacan. Thus, to intellectuals falls the crucial role of developing theory, which is then passed down to others, to be put into practice.

Because Althusserianism places great emphasis on theory and theoretical work, it bestows a special status on intellectuals. Althusser talks glowingly of the "working-class intellectual" — a term which "denotes a very specific type of militant intellectual, a type unprecedented in many respects". Invoking Lenin, Althusser assigns to these intellectuals a special task in refining theory, for "occasionally, the whole world class struggle may be summed up in the struggle of one word against another word".[33] It is the Althusserian notion of "theoretical practice" which has bolstered the role of intellectuals. This concept gives those who engage in "the class struggle in theory" a central place in the class struggle as a whole. Rancière has described how Althusser's conception of the "class struggle in theory" was eagerly seized on by the Maoists of th UJCML for whom "an immense class struggle was opened up: combating revisionism in theory, defending scientists against their exploiters, even preserving the materiality of writing".[34]

As we have seen *Screen* resembles other forms of Althusserianism in stressing theory and science. Colin MacCabe has given as the reason for *Screen*'s neglect of the contemporary situation in British film and television: "a severe shortage of people with the competence to produce the kind of article *Screen* was trying to promote". However, he now believes that thanks "in no small measure" to the work of *Screen,* the situation has changed and there is now an abundance of potential writers with the necessary "competence" (17, *1*, p.101). In addition *Screen* shares the common Althusserian position that working-class experience is of no value as a guide to political strategy. This is most apparent in the judgements it makes of works of art it wants to criticise (which, incidentally, invariably amount to parodies of the positions under attack). Thus MacCabe condemns the television play *Days of Hope,* for being concerned "to demonstrate the falseness of institutions (the TUC, the Labour Party) beside the truth of working-class experience".[35] Similarly, as we shall in the next section, *Screen*'s critique of realist films is in part based on the accusation (by MacCabe again) that working-class people are seen as "simple possessors of truth", or (by Johnston and Willemen) that working-class consciousness is believed to be "the sole basis for struggle".

We have dwelt at length on this emphasis on the role of intellectuals and devaluation of working-class consciousness because we believe that it has significant political implications for Althusserians. For many it leads to a stance derived from Lenin's *What is to be Done?* Althusser gives Lenin as his authority for the claim that "the 'spontaneous' ideology of the workers, if left to itself, could only produce utopian socialism, trade-unionism, anarchism and anarcho-syndicalism", and that because "marxist theory is produced by a specific theoretical practice *outside* the proletariat, marxist theory must be 'imported' into the proletariat".[36]

We do not feel able to adjudicate on the arguments about whether *What is to be Done?* is untypical of the rest of Lenin's writings, or whether many of the groups who identify themselves as "leninist" today distort his writings, but clearly the mode of operation within these groups is often very different from our interpretation of socialism.[37] This conception of the role of the intellectual serves only to reflect and reinforce the distinction between mental and manual labour in capitalist society. Socialism will only ever come about when a large part of the working class sees it as a realistic alternative and begins to sense "its right to govern". To achieve this the priority is not to build any existing group until it becomes "the party". Rather it is to build working-class confidence and independent self-organisation through forms of "popular power" as existed for a time in Portugal and Chile. On the role of socialists in this process, we agree with the Italian socialist organisation Lotta Continua that the aim should be to "be at the head of the masses", not to "put ourselves at the head of the masses".[38] The latter implies jumping into the middle of a struggle with the automatic right to lead, whilst the former means earning the right to be taken seriously by being inside the development of the struggle. Socialists should not bring preconceived demands from outside, but attempt to express working-class needs in a way which generalises and unifies them and advocates ways of fighting for them which increase working-class power.

We are not advocates of pure spontaneity. We recognise that any struggle involves organisation. Our main criticism of the views of the people we have been discussing is the way they discuss working-class experience. For us there has to be a constant dialectical relation between the development of forms of organisation and working-class experience. Organisation must flow from and meet the needs of struggles as they develop if it is not to be a bureaucratic imposition from above, but its forms must constantly be questioned and reassessed and not inherited and passed on as a pre-fabricated model from the past. In criticising the conception Althusserians have of the role of intellectuals we do not deny that there are problems for intellectuals in trying to relate themselves to the working class. However, the task for those seriously attempting to do this is rendered more difficult by Althusserian theory.

There are two areas in which specific concepts developed by Althusser have been most obviously taken up by *Screen*. These are *Screen*'s understanding of the nature of social formations (although there was rarely any attempt to elaborate it), and (more self-consciously) its understanding of ideology. When *Screen* first began to theorise ideology what it presented was extended summaries of Althusser (e.g. 15, *2*, p.23; 15, *2*, pp.113-15), but, as we shall see later, Althusser's writings came more and more to be a jumping-off point for a concentration on Lacan and a theory of the subject.

Over the last few years the star of Hindess and Hirst has risen higher than that of Althusser. The move towards Hindess and Hirst has not been without opposition on the *Screen* editorial board. For example, a former editor of the journal, Geoffrey Nowell-Smith, has called their challenge to the validity of historical enquiry a "destructive development".[39] Nevertheless, there have been a number of articles which endorse Hirst's critique of Althusser's theory of ideology (e.g. 18, *1*, pp.102-03; 18, *4*, p.71; 19, *3*, p.139). Similarly the work of Hindess and Hirst has been increasingly used as a reference for the theorisation of the nature of social formations. It is worth recounting in some detail a recent debate within the *Screen* editorial board as it illustrates how differences which from our external position seem quite narrow are seen as being of the greatest significance.

The contours of the "debate" are given in an article by Paul Willemen, in which he makes the very reasonable point that "the 'concrete experience' of the individual, determined by his or her place in the relations of production, his or her place in the real, will determine in its turn to a large extent which institutions, which discursive régimes, etc., he or she will encounter and in what order". The claim that the ideologies people encounter is related to their position in the relations of production might seem elementary for a marxist. But Willemen in fact qualifies this statement with another: "Having recognised the determining power of the real, it is equally necessary to recognise that the real is never in its place, to borrow a phrase from Lacan, in that it is always and only grasped as reality, that is to say, through discourse" (19, *1,* p.67).

Willemen's partial recognition of the real in fact proved highly controversial within *Screen.* It is the theoretical tendency represented in the second quotation, expressing an agnosticism towards the real, that predominates in the journal. In defence of this latter position Ben Brewster and Elizabeth Cowie criticised Willemen for "reproducing the now surely discredited notion of ideology as the misleading phenomenal form of the real movement of the relations of production" (19, *1,* p.69). According to Colin MacCabe, Willemen is "forced to resurrect the topography of the base/superstructure model"; "[this] use of a spatial metaphor is indicative of the cost of ignoring the reality of discourse" (19, *4,* p.35). He rejects the attempt to retain the concept of "determination in the last instance"; and deplores the "disturbing tendency for these difficult relations [of cinema, discourse, politics] to be resolved by postulating an ideological/political space 'outside' the cinema which determines the reading of any particular film" (p.33). MacCabe's own position, which draws extensively on that of Hindess and Hirst,[40] "does not understand cinema to have an ideological function determined by its representational relation to other ideological, political and economic struggles. Rather it is concerned with interrogating the conditions of existence of that representational relation, conditions which are ideological, political and economic but which are also specifically discursive" (p.32). The question of determination within the social whole becomes a question of epistemology, as social practices are subsumed into discourse. In fact, the problems of the social context and determination of film texts is "solved" by making it a non-problem.

The Althusserian emphasis on the autonomy of each practice within the social whole lends support to *Screen*'s tendency to restrict its analysis of film solely to the "reading" of texts. It has been unable to escape the confines of immanent analysis, inherited from the tradition of literary criticism, and which is, as we shall see, reinforced by the methodologies of semiotics and psychoanalysis. In its analysis of film texts *Screen* has always bracketed the social structure in which they exist. By default — because *Screen* has merely ignored or neglected the question of social context — these texts have assumed an autonomy, they have become detached and separated from the societies in which they are produced, distributed and consumed.

An early *Screen* editorial emphasised that "film criticism" is not enough: "Criticism is but one element in the study of cinema which also involves locating film in a specific system of production and consumption and of seeing it in relation to the other arts and to the culture it reflects and relects upon" (12, *1,* p.5). But from the perspective of textual analysis it is extremely hard to move "back" to examine the social relations of cultural production. There have been some studies of the film industry in *Screen,* but we have only to compare their number with studies which apply psychoanalytic concepts to textual analysis to see how *Screen*'s priorities have developed. It has paid no attention to the whole wider context in which film and film studies are situated. There is no recognition of film's relation to other mass media and to forms of working-class leisure and culture. Nor is there any acknowledgement of the relation between film theory and the broader contexts of mass communications research (as a whole) and the sociology of culture.

Screen's inability to escape from a narrow focus on texts is a clear consequence of its rejection of the crucial concept of the totality. We believe this rejection to be one of the main characteristics defining Althusserianism and also one which frequently has certain political consequences. Althusserianism has a fragmented conception of the social totality in which political, ideological and economic levels are externally related. Particular variants may place emphasis on any of these levels, or regions — although it is politics and ideology that are generally taken up by Althusserians. This conception of the "social formation" links up with Eurocommunism, which in turn is composed of two theoretical approaches which fragment the totality. The first is the theory of state monopoly capitalism which sees the increased role for the state and the increased concentration of capital in contemporary capitalism as the basis of a distinctly new stage of capitalist development.[41] State monopoly capitalism theory implies that the state is autonomous from the base and that gaining control of the state and introducing new (socialist) personnel enables the base to be transformed in the direction of socialism. We believe that the capitalist state is a form of the social relation between capital and labour, in that it not only performs certain material functions for capital but, more importantly, it reproduces certain social relations which enable capital's domination to continue.[42] Therefore, it is wrong to see the state as an entity detached from "the economy", which can then be used as a neutral instrument to change it.

The second political current is that of neo-Gramscianism, which poses the ideological or cultural level as outside the "economic", and confines its struggle to the "war of position" in this sphere. In the attempt to achieve hegemony in the cultural sphere a wide range of classes and political forces are to be brought together in the building of a "new historical bloc". Both state monopoly capitalism theory and neo-Gramscianism represent an inversion of the economism they set out to oppose. Both believe that power and the transformation of social relations are concerns of "the superstructure" and underestimate the effect of the "dull compulsion" of the sphere of immediate production.

We have previously indicated that one characteristic of Althusserianism is its rejection of historical and empirical research. *Screen* shows little interest in analysing specific films or specific historical situations, except as a way of substantiating its highly abstract theoretical and philosophical positions. Thus it falls between two stools, being characterised by a combination of philosophical and aesthetic analysis, of theoretical exposition and the study of films. In our view it fulfils neither of these functions adequately, in so far as the discussion of particular films is always subordinated to — provides illustrations for — philosophical positions, whilst the elaboration of such positions is never sufficiently developed, and recourse is always necessary to *Screen*'s philosophical mentors in order to comprehend its arguments.

In a list of the work which needed to be continued in its pages an early *Screen* editorial included the development of a history of the cinema (13, *1*, p.3). Only a very few articles have been published which attempt to contribute to this history, and they have usually come from writers outside the editorial board. Rather than developing historical distinctions *Screen* has tended to reduce everything to a single pattern. *Screen*'s inability to cope with historical specficity is particularly vividly illustrated in its discussion of realism which we will examine in the following section. Can this deficiency be remedied? According to a report on a SEFT weekend school in 1978, dealing with "Ideology/ Discourse/Institution", there was a marked emphasis among those present on the need to engage in conjunctural analysis (19, *3,* p.133). Such ambitions can only be taken seriously when there are signs of a significant change in the contents of the journal, which so far has not occurred.

There might appear to be another cause for optimism in that the topic for the special event for the 1977 Edinburgh Film Festival, with which *Screen* writers were closely involved, was "History/ Production/Memory". Before rushing to the assumption that this signals a renewed emphasis on the importance of history, it is necessary to realise that a very particular meaning was given to the term "history". In a talk at the event Keith Tribe argued for a rejection of the position that "history is something real and tangible, that can be effectively recapitulated, discovered, or of course distorted" in favour of one which believes "'history' is something perpetually constructed in a specific conjuncture" (18, 4, p.12). A report on the same event noted that there was a "polemical insistence" that history "is neither the past as such, nor yet a discourse in which the past is revealed, but rather a set of discourses in which the past is constructed not simply from 'the past' itself, but from the various discourses that the past has thrown up" (18, 4, p.77). This notion of history comes from the critique of "empiricist" theories of history by Hindess and Hirst, and from an interpretation of Lacan's claim that the history of the subject is always being rewritten as memory is continually reconstituted.[43] For *Screen,* history has ceased to be anything real and has become yet another discourse.

There is one more aspect of Althusserianism which we believe has had a significant effect on *Screen*. We are referring to the role that Althusserian theory has played in opening up the space for incorporating new disciplines into marxism, which is particularly important. Initially it was a positive step, but increasingly it has, in fact, led to the displacement of marxism by advanced bourgeois disciplines. Beginning with the *a priori* assumption that there exist three or more separate levels in the social whole, it is an easy next step to concentrate on developing the "regional science" of a particular level, suspending consideration of its relation to the other levels. Graham Burchell shows where an Althusserian position can lead, when he suggests that after "the rejection of the services of the 'totality'," the considerable contortions and questioning about whether or not psychoanalysis or Foucault are compatible with marxism, may no longer be necessary.[44] If, in addition, Marx's work is seen only as a continuation of political economy, a theory of the "economic", then it is obvious that it must be supplemented by theories of the political and ideological "regions". Thus, space is opened up for the importation of disciplines like semiotics and Lacanian psychoanalysis to fill the "gaps" left by "traditional marxism". The next two sections of this paper will examine the way these two disciplines have been incorporated into marxist cultural theory by *Screen*. We will aim to show how they converge with Althusserianism in the pages of the journal, generating and reinforcing the same basic problems.

Semiotics

Before we discuss the parts played in *Screen*'s development by semiotics and Lacanian psychoanalysis, a few preliminary comments are necessary. First, a general discussion of semiotics and psychoanalysis is obviously beyond the scope of this article. We can only hope to deal with these disciplines in so far as they have become operative within the theoretical work of *Screen*. Secondly, there coexist within *Screen* two distinct "generations" of semiotics: the early positivist and methodological semiotics, of which the best known examples are Roland Barthes's *Mythologies* and *Elements of Semiology;* and the philosophical, critical semiotics associated primarily with the French journal *Tel Quel*, notably the work of Julia Kristeva, and Barthes's later writings. When it is necessary to bring out the contrast between these two forms of semiotics, or to avoid confusion, we shall use Kristeva's term, semanalysis, to refer to the latter. It is difficult to assess the extent to which *Screen*'s contributors, despite their severe criticisms of early semiotics, still consider it to be theoretically acceptable or useful. Nor is it clear how the "fundamental importance" of Kristeva's theory of language can be separated from the "anarchic" implications, for which, as we shall see later, it is criticised. It should also be pointed out that the way *Screen* has introduced these theories means no attention is given to the historical context in which they arose. As Andrew Britton writes: "There has not been the slightest attempt to place Freud, Lacan, Barthes, Althusser, Kristeva, etc., ideologically. Each of them might be taken as an individual working in an ideological vacuum producing 'knowledge', whereas one is subjected to endless vulgar and trivial misreadings of, say Leavis, in relation to his class position."[45]

Our third point is that *Screen*'s pages are characterised by a complex, and confusing, mélange of qualifications and counter-qualifications to theoretical assumptions that have themselves never been justified, or even clearly presented. *Screen* has not considered it a political or pedagogic priority to articulate and debate theoretical choices and refusals, such that an active and participating readership can be fostered. To prove their intellectual seriousness — and stamina — readers are expected (presumably) to turn to *Screen*'s theoretical mentors and sources for further clarification.

In the early seventies, under the editorship of Sam Rohdie, the "new" *Screen* undertook to shift British film culture away from the *practical criticism* of individual films, to the *theoretical analysis* of film in general. In this project, *Screen* took aim at two major targets. The first was "the dominant aesthetic of British art", realism, which according to Rohdie "conceived the artistic text primarily as a means to convey a certain social, ethical or philosophical content. Attention to the art object was sacrificed for a concern with the significance of the world created by the art work and the meaning and relevance that world had to the external world" (13, *4,* p.135). The other target was the *politique des auteurs,* developed in *Cahiers du Cinéma,* to be assimilated into Anglo-Saxon criticism by Andrew Sarris, in the early sixties, as the *auteur* theory. This "theory", which saw film as an art form of which the director is the author, had two main schools: "those who insisted on revealing a core of meanings, of thematic motifs, and those who stressed style and *mise en scène".* In *Screen's* opinion both of these currents had reached an impasse.

This was not merely an internal dissension within film theory. It had a resonance beyond that small world because it was taking up the challenge presented by Perry Anderson in *Components of the National Culture,* and attacking the "empiricism" and "traditionalism", that were at the heart of the British ideology. It was aiming at that mode of criticism, represented by Robin Wood and V. F. Perkins, which was firmly in the Leavisite tradition. In the article referred to above, Rohdie describes this form of criticism:

> This view of the art work as an "organic" whole, expressing important "truths", the essence of which the critic is positioned to grasp and, thereby, to correctly position the spectator, connects back to Romantic aesthetics and to its heir, Realist aesthetics. The art work in *Movie* was a kind of decal, a transparency, with an ideal or original "content", which the critic could decode, clarify, and, to an extent, restore. (13, *4,* p.138)

It was into this context that semiology was introduced. "Both formalism ... and semiology have revealed the essential realist and hence ideological impulse involved in the species of romantic aesthetics and at the same time, in work on the sign systems of art, have theoretically demonstrated the untenability of that aesthetics" (13, *3,* p.3). Semiotics differs from this traditional aesthetics in its theoretical objective. "Rather than an authorial statement about human nature (totality) or a reflection of the particular society in which it was produced (exterior), the semiologist regards the text as the contradictory interplay of different codes." (15, *1,* p.4).

It was semiotics that provided the central impetus and inspiration for British cultural and film studies, promising a theoretical revolution that would break with its ideological prehistory. But it also provided a theoretical snare, within which *Screen* continues to struggle. For, despite the vigour with which *Screen* sought to break with the organicism and empiricism of the Leavisite Eng. Lit. tradition, it was unable — or did not see the necessity — to break with that tradition's primary, and exclusive, *focus on texts*. With this debilitating theoretical weakness at the heart of its inability to make a decisive break with the literary tradition, *Screen*'s project became the much narrower one of turning from speculative criticism to a more "rigorous" and "scientific" investigation of texts. Science would struggle against ideology on the terrain of culture. Peter Wollen in his influential book *Signs and Meanings in the Cinema* asked "whether it is possible to dissolve cinema criticism and cinema aesthetics into a special province of the general science of signs".[47] The trajectory of *Screen* shows that it certainly has been possible, with a vengeance — the operative word being "dissolve"!

This early film semiotics followed very closely in the shadow of linguistics, the reason for this being that the latter was "at present the most advanced branch (and likely to remain so) of semiology" (14, *1/2*, p.3). Its major theoretical source was the work of Ferdinand de Saussure, which supposedly set linguistics on a rigorous, scientific basis by taking as its analytical object *langue,* a system or a set of interpersonal rules, as opposed to *parole,* which consists of the actual manifestations of the system in speech and writing. *Langue* is constituted by a network of signs, comprised of "signified" and "signifier" (the concept, object or person referred to and the word or symbol used to represent it), which exist in an arbitrary or "unmotivated" relation to each other. Developments in semiotic theory have been based on the appropriation of these methodological principles for the examination of other social systems. Jonathan Culler has shown what underpins this shift in perspective, to view culture as language:

> The notion that linguistics might be useful in studying other cultural phenomena is based on two fundamental insights: first, that social and cultural phenomena are not simply material objects or events but objects or events with meaning, and hence signs; and second, that they do not have essences but are defined by a network of relations, both internal and external. Stress may fall on one or the other of these propositions — it would be in these terms, for example, that one might distinguish semiology and structuralism.

The attraction of this form of semiotics for marxist cultural theory lies in the way it is able to denaturalise social phenomena. "In the case of non-linguistic signs there is always a danger that their meanings will seem natural; one must view them with a certain detachment to see that their meanings are in fact the products of a culture, the result of shared assumptions and conventions."[48]

Although this owes more to the Durkheimian notion of "collective consciousness" — which also lurks at the heart of the Althusserian theory of ideology — than to Marx's view of social phenomena, it was taken up as a tool for "ideology critique", for the demystification of bourgeois social reality. Influential in this direction was Barthes's analysis, in *Mythologies,* of bourgeois "myth", or ideology. It was also Barthes, in *Writing Degree Zero* — "a mythology of literary language" — who showed how myth is present in literature. Laying the foundations of a "problematic" that will be so important throughout the development of *Screen,* he argues that "traditional literature" is characterised by the "spontaneous assent to myth". Given this, "the subversion of writing was the radical act by which a number of writers have attempted to reject Literature as a mythical system".[49]

This form of semiotics was most fully taken up for cinema theory in the work of Christian Metz. According to *Screen,* Metz established "a break in the history of ideas relating to the object film". Before his intervention "film had never been regarded as a text, i.e. ... the question of pertinence had never been asked with regard to the cinematic discourse, [and] individual critics assumed that no knowledge was required other than the 'general culture' of the 'well-educated' gentleman/woman". Drawing on linguistics, Metz sought to analyse the production of meaning in film texts, "to describe the system of relations constituting the cinematic discourse" (14, *1/2,* p.2,3).

In seeking to use linguistics as a paradigm for film semiotics, Metz had to confront the fact that film has no *langue,* or underlying system. His initial solution was to regard the articulation of cinematic images, i.e. the narrative, as the basic principle around which "film language" is organised. A later formulation argued that cinema was composed of a plurality of "codes" and "sub-codes". For both formulations, however, it can be said that through his reliance on linguistics Metz is "forced into a situation where a rigorous method confronts an object which constantly refuses to be stably systematised".[50] And it was largely for this reason that Metz abandoned this kind of "problematic", in favour of a psychoanalytic approach to cinema.

What then, are our criticisms of this form of semiotics? What is its effect within the theoretical discourse of *Screen?* And how does it relate to, or develop out of, the underlying Althusserian paradigm? We have already referred to the complicity between the Althusserian conception of ideology and the semiotic (and structuralist) conception, which is strongly influenced by

Durkheim's sociology. We shall now look at three further areas where Althusserian theory and semiotics overlap, on the basis of their common origin in structuralism. It should be pointed out that the period in which *Screen* assimilated Metz, was also a period when indebtedness to Althusser was at its most explicit.

The first distinctive trait that we can identify in this "generation" of semiotics is its positivistic, and even *scientistic*, nature — resulting from its origins in "scientific" linguistics, and reinforced through the invocation of Althusser's complementary scientism. For *Screen* makes explicit reference to Althusser's conception of science when trying to establish the scientific status of "cinesemiotics". It has argued that film study should become a systematic discipline in the manner of biology, physics etc. (13, *2,* p.12). So, Metz's theories are presented "as being solely descriptive, as being not in any way *normative* or *prescriptive*" (14, *3,* p.7). And, whilst *Screen* recognises the difficulties in such a formulation, this scientific tendency is never far from view: "*Screen* sees theory not as a system for providing values, but as a system for providing knowledge" (17, *3,* p.120). *Screen*'s reaction against "organicist" criticism, just like Althusser's reaction against socialist humanism, merely produces a fantastic inversion of the position under criticism. This dismal scientism is an absurdity, for anyone but the most crude positivist. To call it marxist theory is a travesty. Marx's whole work is imbued with the ethical dimension of critique, as is proven by those who, in seeking to weed out "humanist" residues, find themselves left clutching only tattered fragment of *Capital,* and two short works, Marx's marginal notes on Adolph Wagner and the *Critique of the Gotha Programme.* The whole binary opposition of science (theory) and ethics is as destructive for cultural theory as it is for marxism in general.

A second characteristic of this semiotics resides in its *formalism* — again deriving from its origin in Saussurean linguistics, and again a trait of Althusserian marxism, particularly its theory of ideology. *Screen* is concerned with the mechanics of the production of meaning in general, at the expense of dealing with the meaning of particular films. The activity of the semiologist is distinct from that of the spectator, in that he/she aims to produce an analytical "understanding of how the film is understood, of how it signifies, of its system(s) of intelligibility" (14, *3,* p.7). This exclusive concern with the formal mechanics of signification runs throughout the journal's career.

There is clearly a much closer relation between this approach and the explicitly formalist work of Noel Burch[51] than *Screen* would care to admit. Chuck Kleinhans's observations on Burch certainly have resonances for our discussion of *Screen:*

> Burch is symptomatic of... a new formalism which not only separates form from content and elevates form above content, but one that also takes pure film form as itself a sufficient political weapon to overthrow bourgeois ideology (and perhaps even the ruling class itself?).[52]

Screen clearly recognises the dangers of such a position, and is characterised by a more complex and qualified position. By making certain criticisms of Burch (Heath, 17, *3*), and of avant-garde cinema and theory (Wollen, 17, *1*), *Screen* presents its work as more at variance with formalism than it really is. And it suggests that the concern with content, or signification, marks a significant advance over the positions criticised — when, outside the confines of *Screen,* it is a theoretical commonplace, and could only seem to be an advance to those who have first to break out of the straight-jacket of formalism.

Our third criticism is directed at the way in which semiotics privileges *immanent criticism,* the notion that cultural analysis can be made purely through the study of texts. The French film theorist, Thierry Kuntzel, maintains that "the *before* and the *after* of film do not interest semiotics". Invoking Barthes's *Elements of Semiology* as his justification, he claims that the semiologist studies

> neither the various pressures of production and distribution nor the ideological impact of film (these external studies being left to sociologists, economists and psychologists) but the ideological interplay within the filmic fact itself (14, *3,* p.44).

This treatment of texts in isolation from their social conditions of production, distribution and consumption, finds further theoretical justification in Althusser's conception of a (relatively) autonomous ideological instance. *Screen* is not insensitive to the problems of isolating texts through immanent analysis — and this marks its superiority over the work of Noel Burch. However its initial premises turn the question of how film can be related to the social process into a complex and insoluble problem.

Second generation semiotics or semanalysis developed out of the moment of May 1968, which brought a radicalisation of intellectuals. The theory of Kristeva, and of *Tel Quel* more generally, sought to give intellectuals an active, revolutionary role through their association with the supposedly subversive practice of avant-garde texts:

> Through a specific practice which touches upon the very mechanism of language (in Mallarme, Joyce, Artaud) or the mythic or religious systems of reproduction (Lautreamont, Bataille), the "literary avant-garde" confronts society — even if only on its fringes — with a subject

in process, assailing all the stases of a unitary [*unaire*] subject. The avant-garde thus assails closed ideological systems (religions), but also social structures of domination (the state), and accomplishes a revolution which, however distinct from or up to now unknown to the socialist or Communist revolution, is not its "utopian" or "anarchist" moment, but designates its blindness to the very process which sustains it.[53]

We are not arguing that *Screen*'s position can simply be equated with that of Kristeva. Whilst initially, in *Screen* 14, *1/2*, for example, there is quite considerable enthusiasm for her work, and whilst some of *Screen's* contributors regard it as a necessary basis for a materialist theory of signification and ideology, others such as Paul Willemen have equated it with the "romantic-anarchist project of eternal and universal subversion/transgression" (19, *1*, p.68).[54] There are, indeed, various stances, within *Screen*, to Kristeva's semanalysis, many of which distance themselves critically from it. For us, the problem lies in *Screen's* failure to explicitly assess the status of her work, to articulate clearly what it (or rather its contributors) considers to be her virtues and deficiencies. To what extent are its "anarchist" implications *implicit* in its theoretical premises? Since *Screen* follows Althusser so assiduously in criticising the Hegelian residues in Marx's work, why does it find the strong influence of Hegel — and of Husserl and Heidegger — in Kristeva so unobjectionable? And it is not unfair to point out that second generation semiotics has been enthusiastically appropriated by non-marxists, in such journals as *Semiotext(e), Substance, Glyph, Oxford Literary Review, Enclitic, Diacritics*, etc.

Despite all qualifications, Kristeva's work *does* play an important and complex, role in the pages of *Screen*. It is present not through direct references, but as a *distant* authority to which *allusion* is made — hence the elusive and subterranean nature of its existence is the journal. It is a "reference-text", with which *Screen*'s readers must *already* be familiar to fully understand the journal's dense, theoretical articles. The influence of this current can be found in *Screen*'s predilection for, and its theory of, avant-garde and "deconstruction" (non-realist) texts (which we shall discuss below). Of course, we are aware that *Screen* recognises the danger of overestimating "the radicalness of works which strongly exhibit the 'deconstruction' of the reigning codes" (17, *3*, p.5). But, although it has moderated and qualified its position, *Screen* has not radically broken with this "problematic" that provided the initial rationale for its whole attack on realism and "organicism".

Kristeva presented her semiotics as a critical and reflexive theory that would avoid the faults of early, positivistic semiotics by its constant self-awareness and self-questioning. "The whole time it is being produced, semiotics is aware of its object, its tools, and their relation; and thereby it is aware of itself, becoming through this self-reflexivity the theory of the science that it is".[55] This theme is taken up in *Screen* 14, *1/2,* where semiotics is accepted as "a rigorous theoretical framework" that "constantly questions its own discourse in its very formation: being the science of signification its own discourse necessarily forms part of its object" (p.5).

Kristeva's work also takes up the Althusserian conception of science in its claim to be a "science of meaning (and consequently of knowledge) in its material conditions and development" (14, *1/2,* p.5). It regards scientific procedure as "the process of elaborating models, along with the theory that underlies those models".[56] Whatever critical edge semanalysis may initially have had, it is this emphasis on its scientific status that predominates in *Screen*'s assimilation of it. Semanalysis is taken up as a superior science: the all-embracing science of meaning and knowledge that is also the science of itself.

Second generation semiotics shifted the focus away from semiotics as a methodology to regarding it as a philosophical, or ontological, theory. It claims to be a social theory, able to provide an adequate basis for the articulation of signification/language/ representation with the social process out of which it is generated: and it claims to give theoretical access to *all* social practices. Kristeva maintains that semanalysis is at the centre of a major shift in philosophical perspective: "The semiotic project replaces the fundamental philosophical question, that of Being (as Hegel and Heidegger have constantly emphasised), with the question of signifying" (14, *1/2,* p.27). It is in the critique of the sign, of the linguistic basis of early semiotics, that one can see the basis for this shift. Barthes has written, in a reflection on his earlier *Mythologies,* that the purpose of semiotics has changed such that it is now "less the analysis of the sign than its dislocation":

> It is no longer the myths which need to be unmasked (the doxa now takes care of that), it is the sign itself which must be shaken; the problem is not to reveal the (latent) meaning of an utterance, of a trait, of a narrative but to fissure the very representation, is not to change or purify the symbols but to challenge the symbolic itself.[57]

This recognition has developed out of Jacques Derrida's claim that the relation between signifier and the signified is the basis upon which Western metaphysical discourse is based. Saussurean linguistics and early semiology are based on the notion that there is "a truth behind every sign: a moment of original plenitude when form and meaning were simultaneously present to consciousness and not to be distinguished". Such "logocentric" thought "assumes that we should try to pass through the signifier to the meaning that is the truth and origin of the sign and of which the signifier is but the visible mark, the outer shell".[58] At a more general level this "metaphysics of presence" sees language "as instrument of the natural expression of some absolute subject, of the individual, Reality, or whatever, a reference in which the processes of the production of meanings, of the articulation of the individual, Reality, or whatever, are occulted" (14, *1/2*, p.122). The subject is seen as the founding source of meanings, the signified, which are then expressed through the signifiers. Derrida's project, like that of Lévi-Strauss is the "dissolution of man", the disruption of this metaphysical humanism, which is expressed most completely in the cartesian *cogito*. It is a theoretical refusal of the idea that thought (the signified, meaning) can pre-exist language (the signifier).

It is this predominance of the sign that is considered to be the foundation upon which bourgeois culture and civilisation rests:

> The distinction between signifier and signified, form and content, regulates Western discourse (furnishes its rationale); civilisation of the sign: a whole régime — a metaphysics of presence, of meaning, and of the subject.[59]

In order to make an epochal break with this "logocentric" civilisation, it is necessary to fracture, to subvert, the metaphysical essentialism of the sign. Against this sign, which is *centred* on meaning (the signified, consciousness), post-structuralist semiotics juxtaposes a conception of language as the *decentred* play of signifiers. This interpretation is developed from Saussure's "radical" insight — which he, himself, did not carry through to its logical conclusion — that language is a "diacritical" system in which there are no positive terms, but only differences. Signification is not pre-given, but is an effect of the infinite play, and resonances, within the network of signifiers:

> If meaning is a function of differences between terms and every term is but a node of differential relations, then each term refers us to other terms from which it differs and to which it is in some kind of relation. The relations are infinite and all have the potential of producing meaning.[60]

In contradistinction to the idealism of the sign, this theory is put forward as the basis of a *materialist* theory of signification. It is this theory which underlies the developments of semiotic, and psychoanalytic, cultural theory in both *Screen* and *Tel Quel*.

For *Screen,* this "radical" theory of language has two important dimensions. Firstly, it provides the philosophical context for a "radical" and "disruptive" critique of bourgeois culture, to show the insidious nature of bourgeois ideology, the manner in which it secretes itself at the very heart of language itself, in the sign. Moreover this radical structuralism has a distinct resemblance to Althusser's structuralist form of marxism in the emphasis it puts upon "theoretical anti-humanism":

> The subject is no longer assumed as full immediate presence, point of origin and source, but is grasped in his (*sic*) construction in the series of signifying systems, in a multiplicity of structures (taking "structure" there as "that which puts in place an experience for a subject whom it includes"), dispersed, in Foucault's words, in "a plurality of possible positions and functions". (14, *1/2,* p.11).

This neat compatibility with Althusserian theory — and, by implication, with marxism — prevents *Screen* from ever assessing the problems of post-structuralist philosophy, particularly with respect to its compatibility with Marx's theoretical work. A clear difficulty resides in the level of abstraction at which this philosophy operates, its critique being aimed at no less than Western metaphysics and culture as a whole. Its empty formalism, which sees language as the decentred play of signifiers — no longer having any referential relation to the real world — has led to its easy absorption as a radical bourgeois theory.

The second, and most important, sense in which the "radical", diacritical theory of language was important for *Screen,* resides in the manner in which it becomes the foundation for an *aesthetic.* Of great importance was the way in which it gave a rigorous basis to *Screen*'s critique of realism and of the *auteur* theory. Because "radical" semiotics denies that there can be any pre-given meaning prior to signification, the notion that film texts can express reality, or that they express the intentions of an "author", becomes ideological in its complicity with metaphysical modes of thought (see 14, *3,* pp. 24-5). In the case of the *auteur* theory Heath argues:

> consciousness and language are confused as an immediate unity in the flow of expression (this immediacy of consciousness is that bourgeois conception of "man" as the punctual subject of history which Marx attacked, in, for example, the *German Ideology;* "man" and "author" go hand in hand, the latter a particular instance of the former)" (14, *3,* p.87).

In contrast to this *Screen* sees the author as a construct or effect of textual systems: a subject constructed "in a series of signifying systems", not a homogeneous, punctual source of meaning, but a "dispersed" subject, "in process in a movement of assumption and contradiction, over the instances imposed by the set of [signifying] systems" (14, *1/2,* pp.11-12). It should be pointed out, however, that despite this theoretical critique of authorship, *Screen*'s whole rationale for selecting and categorising films is based on this principle. Its more complex notion of the author as a "subject" produced by, and in, the text, amounts only to a more sophisticated *"politique des auteurs"*: it even has an (implicit) pantheon of directors (Straub/Huillet, Godard, Oshima etc.). Its strategy is — to borrow from Geoffrey Nowell-Smith's criticisms of *Screen Education* — to travel the auteurist route, but then to "turn round and bar access to that route to anyone who would follow them" (17, *1,* p.28).

It was in the context of its ongoing concern with realism that *Screen* absorbed the lessons of this new semiotics most thoroughly. It refuses any "ideological" notion that film is a simple expression of the real, that it can be adequate to the real, as in the aesthetics of André Bazin. Any such proposition exhibits its complicity with the metaphysical conception of the sign, in which meaning, in Bazin's case the essence of reality, is pre-given, and for which the film (signifier) is merely a vehicle, an expression: "The subject is then Reality: Reality speaks" (14, *3,* p.24). Moreover, in revealing reality "all aesthetic devices are simply there to unmake themselves so that we too [the audience] can experience, as the artist experienced before us, that moment at which reality presents itself as whole" (17, *3,* p.11).

Screen argues that "reality" is not given, but *produced,* the "realisation of a social praxis"; and cinematic realism is the "repetition of the forms of the ideological ('naturalised') representation of reality dominant in a particular society" (14, *1/2,* p.11). The notion that realism is in fact a product, an *effect* of a discourse, and not a reflection of the "real world", converges at this point with the Althusserian refusal of language/discourse as being in any referential relation to social reality. Thus, Althusserians are compelled to refuse the adequacy of literature or film to the real world, positing in place of this conception, the idea of the construction within given texts of a "reality *effect*". For Althusser's co-workers, Balibar and Macherey, literature is the production of "fiction effects" and "reality effects": "fiction, realism, are not so much *the concepts of* literary production, as notions *produced* by literature".[61]

In its own attempts to identify the mechanics behind the "reality effect" — attempts which coincide in many ways with the purely Althusserian formulations of Balibar and Macherey — *Screen* found Barthes's *S/Z* to be of particular value. In this text Barthes looks at the realist text as process rather than as product: he moves "from a semiology of products to a semiology — a semiotics — of production, from structure to structuration".[62] He does this by examining the realist text from the point of view of — as a variant of — the avant-garde text; the transparent, denotative language of the former, from the point of view of, and in the light of, the diacritical play of language in the latter. The realist text is regarded as a text with a limited, or circumscribed, plurality of meaning (production). Barthes shows how meaning is produced in the realist text, only to obscure its own productivity and to pose as natural.

It is from this perspective that Colin MacCabe in *Screen* 15, 2, attempts to outline the manner in which realist cinema produces the effect of a natural reproduction of external reality. The plurality of signification within this form of cinema is inhibited by one dominant discourse, narrative, which "simply allows reality to appear and denies its own status as articulation": "in the claim that the narrative prose has direct access to a final reality we can find the claim of the classic realist novel to present us with the truths of human nature." Such a discourse fixes the viewing subject in a position of "pure specularity", in "a point of view from which everything becomes obvious." It is this position of specularity that corresponds to Althusser's formulation by which an individual is fixed, or "interpellated" by the mechanism of ideology (the "ideology effect"). This notion of film fixing individuals in subject positions is central to *Screen*'s theory of realism and will be discussed more fully in the following section which takes up its use of psychoanalysis.

MacCabe argues that the realist text is politically reactionary because it is unable to deal with the real as contradictory: "The only problem that reality poses is to go back and look and see what *Things* there *are*". By "dealing with the real as contradiction", he means the articulation of the formal mechanics by which the real is represented in discourse. He indicates what he does *not* mean when he says that there is one kind of discourse with which the realist text can cope:

> This is the contradiction between the dominant discourse of the text and the dominant ideological discourse of the time. Thus a classic realist text in which a strike is represented as a just struggle in which oppressed workers attempt to gain some of their rightful wealth would be in contradiction with certain contemporary ideological discourses and as such might be classified as progressive.

Discussing those realist films made from a socialist perspective, MacCabe argues that as they are unable to offer any perspective for struggle: "It is thus not surprising that these films tend either to be linked to a social democratic conception of progress — if we reveal injustices then they will go away — or certain *ouvrieriste* tendencies which tend to see the working class, outside any dialectical movement, as the simple possessors of truth" (15, *2*, p.16). In another article, Claire Johnston and Paul Willemen, writing about agitprop documentary films, link "their dependence on *cinéma-vérité* forms which purport to capture the world as it 'really is'," and their belief in the "unproblematic, immediate transparency of the image", with a strategy "aimed at producing the impression that individuals and groups participate in some mythical unity of consciousness", and thus "an ultra-leftist idealism which poses the notion of working-class consciousness as the sole basis for struggle" (16, *4*, pp.103-04). Thus not only is the "progressive realist text" associated with a political position which is rejected but, in addition, it entails an inadequate theory of the working class and working-class experience which is the crucial link allowing "ultra-leftist" or "social democratic" politics to be reproduced in the aesthetics of realism.

While these films are classified in terms of their *content,* which may serve a certain progressive function, MacCabe's "revolutionary text", however, is such because it is able to achieve an articulation of the *formal* mechanics by which language appropriates reality. Thus a "revolutionary text" would operate "much in the way that James Joyce in *Ulysses* and *Finnegans Wake* investigated the contradictory ways of appropriating reality through an investigation of the different forms of language". At this point we have returned to Kristeva and texts of pure subversion, transgression or deconstruction.

Because *Screen* defines realism in purely formal terms — "classic realism should be considered as centrally defined by a certain formal organisation of discourse" (17, *1*, p.98) — then, all that can be put in opposition to it is a purely formalist alternative. That is, the dislodging of realism by its formal deconstruction, through "strategies of subversion". It is in this way, for example, that *Screen* appropriates the work of Brecht: it is interested in his anti-illusionist technique above his political content. The consequences of such a formalist conception is that films become arranged in an abstract typology. In MacCabe's case this is a typology consisting of realist texts, which are implicated in the dominant ideology; of a kind of film which refuses any dominant discourse and "as such, remain[s] essentially subversive of any ideological order"; and, possibly, of "a revolutionary film which would subvert the traditional position of the spectator in a more positive fashion than the simple deconstruction of the subversive film" (17, *3*, p.25). Such typologies have characterised *Screen*'s whole approach to the cinema, from the time it took up a similar categorisation from Comolli and Narboni of *Cahiers du Cinéma*, in *Screen* 12, *1* and 12, *2*. And despite *Screen*'s efforts to distance itself from the position of the formalist critic Noel Burch, the typologies it has formulated bear a remarkable resemblance to Burch's hierarchical taxonomy of films: those totally informed by dominant codes; films which intermittently escape the dominant codes; and aesthetically superior films, which deconstruct them. Such taxonomies are quite unreal, and say more about *Screen*'s — and Burch's — theoretical preoccupations than about actual films. With any text there are a range of possible readings, and, at the same time, particular readings towards which readers are encouraged by the text itself. Differences between texts are a matter of degree and not of fixed, separate categories.

Screen's discussion of realism highlights a number of problems relating to the appropriation of semiotics in general. Colin MacCabe is aware of one such problem when he observes, in *Screen* 17, *3*, that his earlier article on realism (15, *2*) was "contaminated by formalism; by a structuralism that it claimed to have left behind". In this article he "made the subject the effect of the structure (the subject is simply the sum of positions allocated to it)"; the text is seen as "immutable structure determining reality and author/reader in their positions". MacCabe now recognises that "it is a question of analysing a film within a determinate social moment so that it is possible to determine what identifications will be made and by whom". The realisation that films must be analysed in terms of their effect at a particular social moment led to a reassessment of the positive evaluation given to films aiming at pure subversion. *Screen* began to realise that there was the danger of "an overestimation of the radicalness of works which strongly exhibit the deconstruction of reigning codes" (17, *3*, p.5); and that emphasis on the "exposure of the device" could easily lead to "the celebration of the self-cultivation of the aesthetically aware individual spectator" (17, *2*, p.7).

Thus, quite characteristically for *Screen*, we have what should in fact be an obvious and fundamental theoretical premise being presented as a significant theoretical breakthrough. This partial escape from the straitjacket of formalism should provide the occasion for a reassessment of *Screen*'s earlier "problematic". But no! This insight is in fact seen, not as calling into question the previous work of the journal, but as a logical progression, which renders the earlier position more sophisticated and flexible.[63]

MacCabe's break with formalism remains incomplete, however.

While he can maintain, in his self-criticism, that "realism is no longer a question of an exterior reality nor of the relation of reader to text, but one of the ways in which these two interact" (17, *3*, p.25), *Screen* is unable to find a way of theorising the relation of cinema to empirical reality, which will remain consonant with its principle of theoretical anti-empiricism. Consequently, it always falls back into the narrow confines of textual and discursive analysis, in which socio-historical reality (e.g. the production or consumption of films) can only be considered in so far as it is "represented" in and through the textual codes.

It is this question of immanence that is the basis for the first of three final observations we want to make about *Screen*'s general appropriation of semiotics. An index of the underlying theoretical weakness of immanent criticism is to be found in the manner in which semanalysis is forced to use marxist concepts metaphorically: the mode of production of the text, the economics of language, the production of symbolic surplus value etc. Similarly, Marx is translated into semiotic language: "the economic system is thus a semiotic system: a chain of communication with a sender and a receiver and an object of exchange — money — which is the sign of a piece of work" (14, *1/2*, p.35). This confusing and mystifying transference of concepts from one theoretical discourse to another is particularly characteristic of *Tel Quel,* but it also plays an important role in *Screen*. Thus we have references to "that other industry", which is the "mental machinery" which spectators have internalised; there are references to the "machine" between industry and text; references to signifying *practice* (adopted from Althusser's concept of practice), which takes film as a work of production of meanings.

This reference to the film as a productivity of meanings is particularly prevalent. Geoffrey Nowell-Smith has argued that *Tel Quel* fails to differentiate the production of signs as *analogous* to commodity production, from the production of signs within the social relations of commodity production. Emphasis on the former leads to recourse to the idea of a dynamic produced within the text (the text "produces" itself) or in the spectator-text relationship (the spectator actively produces meaning out of the text).[64] The same may be said of *Screen*'s focus on "film as meaning-production", and it clearly shows how *Screen* is theorising from the point of view of consumption. Because it cannot theoretically incorporate the real (industrial) production of films, *Screen* is able to utilise the marxist concept of production only by subsuming it into the discursive. Such a notion of meaning production has the advantage of making film viewing (consumption) appear to be an *active* process.

This rhetoric of "production" is supplemented by a further device, the constant assertion that both *Screen*'s theory and the films of which it approves are *materialist*. Materialist because they see meaning as production. *Screen* needs to reassure us that its project is materialist, that semiotics can provide a materialist theory of language. Evidently, because it is difficult in reality to see why it is materialist. Bernard Sichère has commented, ironically, that "everyone today sees themselves as more or less a materialist. Writers because they deal with the material of language. Painters because they touch colour. Musicians because they manipulate notes. Psychoanalysts because they deal with drives... we are all materialists without realising it".[65] It is difficult to see how this "materialism" can be understood in any way as being marxist.

A second point that needs to be made about *Screen*'s use of semiotics is that it lends support for the suppression of history. *Screen* operates with an abstract notion of the "classic realist text" which is seen as a simple progression from the realist novel (MacCabe, 15, *2*) or the Quattrocento perspective in painting (Heath, 17, *3*). Thus, all distinctions within, and between, art forms are submerged in one mode which has been dominant since the nineteenth century — or even the Renaissance. Stephen Heath takes up this approach to characterise the distinctive communications media of the twentieth century: "cinema reproduces and produces the novelistic",[66] and "television is an apparatus used for the production/reproduction of the novelistic" (18, *2*, p.58). He is extremely fond of quoting Godard's remark: "When the bourgeoisie had to find something else besides painting and the novel to disguise the real to the masses, that is, to invent the ideology of the new mass communications, its name was the photograph".[67] *Screen* takes this epigram literally and constructs a "history" solely on this basis.

Works advanced as counter examples to realism are treated in the same undifferentiated way. At the "Brecht and the Cinema/Film and Politics" event at the 1975 Edinburgh Film Festival, organised by *Screen,* films by Godard, Oshima, Straub/Huillet and others were shown and discussed. Despite the denial that these *auteurs* were being compared on the basis of an "essential Brechtianism" (16, *4,* p.34), the films were in fact examined in terms of an abstract conception of what it means to subvert realism, rather than as specific interventions in particular societies in particular periods.

Contrary to *Screen* we would argue that whilst all the "realist texts" produced over the last one hundred and fifty years may well have much in common, what differentiates them is surely more significant. It is our belief that the category of the "classic realist text" is a barrier to knowledge, rather than an aid. Individual films are regarded only as examples of the general category of realism, as evidence for the validity of a theoretical category. To restore a historical dimension to analysis it is necessary to break out of the textual world of literary categories; to progress from this narrow focus to an examination of films in their social and historical context of production and consumption.

As our final point we want to raise the question of semiotics as politics, which is in fact the question of the relation between theory and practice. *Screen's* project has been that of elaborating a materialist *theory* of film. It has confined itself to the hermetically sealed world of "theoretical practice", making no significant attempt to involve itself in the practical sphere of film-making. From within this theoretical perspective it has formulated a set of complex and sophisticated propositions on the nature of political or revolutionary cinema. In *Screen*'s opinion such a cinema entails the subversion or disruption of the dominant semiotic codes of the (bourgeois) realist cinema: it is a "practice" which occurs entirely within texts. The films of a Straub/Huillet or an Oshima continue to be shown at film festivals, thence to become the "objects", or raw material, for theoretical discourse by film semioticians, who expound on the subversive nature of code breaking... A political film which remains confined to the subversion of film language remains, however, within the safe world of the avant-garde. It fails even to confront the broader political question of the nature of cinema in capitalist societies: of film within the social and class divisions of leisure consumption. Film remains a separate area within the "arts"; and art, or culture, is accepted as a distinct and autonomous sphere of leisure, separated from "economics" and "politics".

More important than the categories of realist and non-realist texts are the social relations in and through which those texts are experienced. More important than the subversion of textual practices is the subversion of the traditional subdivisions of the arts, and thereby of traditional patterns of production and consumption.[68]

In this essay it has by no means been our intention to criticise semiotics as such, since it can obviously be a valuable *methodological* tool for analysing *some* aspects of social phenomena. Nor are we dismissive of the integration of new disciplines into marxist cultural theory. Indeed, we believe that taking into account the alternative approaches to film which predominated at the time, *Screen*'s initial interest in semiotics did, for a short time, represent a "small step" forward — although not the "giant leap" it has been made out to be. The object of our

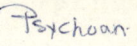

criticism is, rather, the manner in which *Screen* subsequently appropriated and expounded semiotic theory. It is our contention that semiotics — as it now exists in *Screen* — has become an end in itself (i.e. reified), too inflexible and intractable to provide a means for responding to empirical material. For this reason it has become necessary to critically undermine the false obviousness, the naturalness, with which semiotics has been taken by many to be the indispensable, central component of marxist cultural studies.

Lacanian psychoanalysis
If it was not possible to give more than a schematic discussion of semiotics, then this is even more the case with psychoanalysis. In the following we shall, therefore, be discussing psychoanalysis primarily in its Lacanian incarnation, the only one which has been of interest to *Screen*. And we shall further narrow our focus by dealing with Lacanian theory only in its manner of appropriation by *Screen*. Our interest is in the way in which this form of psychoanalysis has combined with semiotics and, particularly, Althusserian marxism to form an elegant, but quite unholy, Trinity. This striking theoretical synthesis has enabled *Screen* to develop a theory of ideology in articulation with a theory of the subject and a "materialist" theory of language: "a theory of the process and positions occupied by the the subject in relation to language and ideology."[69]

The idea that the "problematics" of historical materialism and semiotics could, and should, be supplemented by psychoanalysis was certainly not original to *Screen*. Julia Kristeva had already assimilated Lacan's work into her own semanalysis, claiming that "in respect of the subject and of signifying, it is the Freudian revolution which seems to me to have achieved the definitive displacement of the Western *episteme* from its presumed centrality".[70] And it is Althusser, of course, who created the theoretical space for the incorporation of Lacanian theory into marxism. This is most obviously the case with Althusser's theory of ideology, in which the conceptions of ideology as an "imaginary" relation, and as the "interpellation" of individuals as "subjects", are derived quite explicitly from Lacan, to supplement "lacunae" in Marx's work. Althusser has referred to Lacan's "intransigent and lucid — and for many years isolated — theoretical effort", acknowledging his "debt to an exemplary reading lesson". This latter phrase evokes the similarity between his own projected "return to Marx" and Lacan's "return to Freud". Both men have sought to sweep theoretical "deviations" out of their respective theoretical fields and to return to the "orthodoxy", the theoretical "purity" of the founders of their disciplines. Althusser was particularly impressed by Lacan's scientific pretensions, which were so close to his own. On the basis of Lacan's work he would claim that, like Marx, Freud had "opened a new [theoretical] continent, one which we are only just beginning to explore". And it is thus that he opened the way for a particularly *scientistic* appropriation of Freud. But, above all, the basis for the convergence of Althusser and Lacan lies in their common roots in structuralist theory and tradition, with its theoretical refusal of humanism, and, at a philosophical level, its attack on the cartesian *cogito*. For both theorists, Althusser's formulation, in "Freud and Lacan", is crucial:

> Freud has discovered for us that the real subject, the individual in his [*sic*] unique essence, has not the form of an ego, centred on the "ego", on "consciousness" or on "existence" — whether this is the existence of the for-itself, of the body-proper or of "behaviour" — that the human subject is de-centred, constituted by a structure which has no "centre" either, except in the imaginary misrecognition of the "ego", i.e. in the ideological formations in which it "recognises" itself.[71]

Following the examples of Kristeva and Althusser, and using the latter as the theoretical guarantor of its marxist "orthodoxy", *Screen* has constructed its own particular variant of post-structuralist theory. It has played an especially important role in establishing psychoanalysis within British cultural theory, and it has made this assimilation appear to be the culmination of an ineluctable and inexorable logic. Lacanian theory is seen as a master science that is able to rectify the faults and omissions of semiotics and historical materialism, before absorbing them into its own greater theoretical synthesis. Thus, *Screen* introduces Lacan to effect a theoretical *Aufhebung* that will "re-cast semiotics in a framework defined by psychoanalysis" (16, *1*, pp.5-6).

We can identify three important aspects of *Screen*'s appropriation of Lacan. Firstly, he is taken up as the basis for a "materialist" theory of language, and of symbolic forms in general, in that he elaborates the "radical", or diacritical, linguistic theory of Saussure. For Lacan, as for Saussure, "no meaning is sustained by anything other than reference to other meaning".[72] The second important aspect of Lacanian theory relates to the way in which it permits a sophistication of the Althusserian theory of ideology. For Lacan there is a "fundamental misunderstanding" involved in the successful use of language, "in which the subject is continually ignored as being caught up in a process of articulation to be taken as a fixed place founding the discourse". That is, the productivity or play of the signifiers is inhibited by the subject who "attempts to bring the signifying chain to an end" (15, *2*, p.18). *Screen*'s achievement is to relate Althusser's theory of the ideological interpellation of subjects to this theory of the placing of subject positions within language, the taking up of a place in regard to meaning. Althusser is criticised for not taking up the full implications of psychoanalysis, particularly in his conception of ideology. For example, his borrowing from Lacan of the term "imaginary" cannot rescue him "from the traditional subject of philosophy... As it stands, the term simply indicates the calling on the individual as agent, as a non-contradictory, homogeneous entity which is then the coherent support for ideological representations" (18, *1*, p.103). And finally, the third important aspect of Lacanian theory resides in the general philosophical critique of humanism — the dissolution of the *cogito* — to be found in all post-structuralist theory. Lacan "has read Freud as reformulating the cartesian *cogito* and destroying the subject as source and foundation — Lacan rewrites the *cogito,* in the light of Freud's discoveries as: I think where I am not and I am where I do not think" (15, *2*, pp. 17-18).

In these three aspects of Lacanian psychoanalysis we can see the impressive range of its theoretical repertoire. No longer is psychoanalysis of interest as a theory of neurosis or as a therapy. It is now understood as nothing less than "a science whose specific object is the unconscious and its formations, and which, as such, is a necessary component of historical materialism in the knowledge it produces of the construction of the subject". Moreover, "to refuse to pose the instance of the subject is to fall into idealism (the unity of consciousness as the founding disposition of the world) or its crude "materialist" counterpart (the subject-atom)" (16, *2*, p.86). Lacanian theory is, then, simultaneously a theory of ideology and — as the above quotations from Kristeva and from Althusser's "Lacan and Freud" essay attest — a critique of Western metaphysics. And it is able to assume this grand position, as the hammer of "crude" economistic marxism and of the idealist *cogito,* because it replaces the notion of the "ego" as the founding source of meaning, with the "problematic" of language. It is able to show how the (ideological or philosophical) "I" is positioned (genetically and structurally) in, and by, language and the symbolic realm. In the words of Lacan, "Man [sic] speaks therefore, but it is because the symbol has made him man [sic]". "It is the world of words which creates the world of things."[73]

In *Language and Materialism,* a book that presents and elaborates a position similar to that of *Screen,* Coward and Ellis point to the importance of Lacan's "materialist theory of language" for British cultural theory. Their somewhat immoderate defence of the semiotic-psychoanalytic "problematic" endorses the view that

"Man [*sic*] is constructed in the symbol, and is not pre-given or transcendent". For Coward and Ellis, "perhaps the most significant feature of twentieth-century intellectual development has been the way in which the study of language has opened the route to an understanding of mankind, social history and the laws of how a society functions". It is claimed that "all social practices can be understood as meanings, as signification and as circuits of exchange between subjects, and therefore can lean on linguistics as a model for the elaboration of their systematic reality". The "problematic" of language is taken to mark an "epistemological break" in the human sciences, the foundation of the era of the signifier, of materialism and anti-humanism. The basis for this "revolution" is the subsumption of all social practices into language, the reduction of social reality to its linguistic dimension. "Because all practices that make up a social totality take place in language, it becomes possible to consider language as the place in which the social individual is constructed."[74]

In this post-structuralist theory, in the words of Jean Hyppolite, it is "language which replaces the problem of God".[75] This amounts to the displacement of a Cartesian metaphysics of origin and essence, in favour of a metaphysics of language, of the Word. It has merely been the trading in of a centred metaphysics for a decentred one — reflecting the changed philosophical needs of the post-Einstein era, the era of an infinite, decentred and meaningless universe. The immediate social origin and basis for this new metaphysics is to be found in the way language has become fetishised in bourgeois society. Lacanian theory merely duplicates, partially and passively reflects — and thereby accepts — a situation in which language is no longer a tool for appropriating social reality, but an alienated and alienating system ("It is the world of words which creates the world of things"); a situation in which language has become separated from reference and denotation:

> Let me therefore say precisely what Language signifies in what it communicates: it is neither signal, nor sign, nor even sign of the thing in so far as the thing is an exterior reality. The relation between signifier and signified is entirely enclosed in the order of Language itself, which completely conditions its two terms.[76]

As this post-structural theory is taken up in British cultural theory, most notably by *Screen*, it becomes a philosophical anthropology, a theory of the "human condition". It is adopted as a theory of the constitution of the subject within the symbolic or cultural sphere. And at this theoretical juncture it absorbs the Althusserian theory of ideology, which, as we have already said, itself tends to assimilate the ideological into into the cultural. In our opinion the assimilation of Lacanian theory has turned social theory back to that philosophical or anthropological form from which Marx sought to release it. Our main criticism in this section is aimed at this ahistorical cultural anthropology, this "theory of the symbolic system as *imposed on the human animal* in its construction into a subject, and the dynamics and economics that imposition and construction imply" (16, *1,* p.6).

We want now to turn, however, to the question of the political and pedagogical style in which *Screen* has taken up psychoanalytic theory. Notably to the manner in which the problems of the relation between Freudian and marxist theory — and real problems there are — are obscured beneath a brusque rhetoric that declares psychoanalysis to be "appropriated as a political weapon". (16, *3,* p.6). That this appropriation of psychoanalysis raises important political and pedagogic questions became clear in 1976 with the resignation of four members of *Screen's* editorial board over just this issue. No lesson was learned. Criticised for the confusing and contradictory manner in which they had used Lacanian concepts, the remaining members replied by arguing that they were "engaging with the problem of describing the general terms of the cinematic experience not from the position of some already known and constituted knowledge but from within a process of understanding. The contradictions and differences produced are part of that process, of its possible advance" (16, *2,* p.113). The real problem is reduced to an internal theoretical hitch, proper to all sciences.

There are a number of obvious problems in relating psychoanalysis to marxism. They are faced by any attempt at a Freud-Marx synthesis, but they are particularly noticeable in the case of Lacan. Psychoanalysis tends to have no place for a theory of class, and to rely on a bourgeois conception of the "individual" versus "society". There is also a tendency for psychoanalysis to "neutralise" history. Luce Irigaray has, for example, criticised the "claim that the Oedipus complex is an *a priori* universal truth" as "ahistorical, and, indeed, naive."[77] It has been argued that psychoanalysis can only theorise social and historical relations within the terms of its own discourse, which is "but a huge metaphor for social relations". That is, it can think history only as it is represented, but cannot think that which founds this representation. On this basis, psychoanalysis only ever "sees in the real the effects of a symbolic whose figures (e.g. the Oedipus) are never themselves anything but empirical realities elevated to abstraction and fixed as structures of the unconscious".[78] In a defence of its adoption of psychoanalysis *Screen* has argued that

"Freud was quite capable of taking his patients' families and other social relations into account" (16, 2, p.85). There is, however, a difference between a framework which can be made to incorporate certain problems, and one which presents them as central. The neglect of concrete social relations and of historical specificity is a common thread which links Lacanian psychoanalysis with both Althusserianism and semiotics.

Another link is their scientism. Lacan presents his work as a return to a true conception of science and draws various comparisons with mathematics. *Screen*'s appropriation of psychoanalysis has been that of a ready made science which would fill a gap in marxism: the question of the subject in language "gives the necessity for the articulation within historical materialism of psychoanalytic theory (as science of the construction of the subject)" (15, 2, p.115). Until a very recent article by Stephen Heath, discussed below, *Screen*'s attitude towards Lacanian psychoanalysis was totally uncritical. The response to a polemic by Julia Lesage (of *Jump Cut*) against *Screen*'s use of Freud and Lacan, was to draw a strict distinction between the "social exploitation in ideology of 'vulgarised Freudian concepts'" and "Freud's scientific constructions" (16, 2, p.84), followed by a total defence of the latter (as read via Lacan).

We believe that Freudian theory is of very great importance for marxists, providing as it does an insight into the nature of subjectivity in bourgeois society, and, particularly, into the connection between neurosis and capitalist social relations.[79] The potential contribution of psychoanalytic theory cannot, however, be properly realised if marxists refuse to confront the problems it presents to them. Psychoanalysis has shown itself, in the past, to be a quite unreliable "political weapon". Our critique is not aimed, then, at Freudian theory as such. It is aimed rather at certain ways in which psychoanalysis has been appropriated, particularly at some of the attempts to establish a Freudo-marxist synthesis. *Screen*'s project is to develop a total social theory that can incorporate, and integrate, the theory of the subjective and objective aspects of social existence, a theory of the construction of the subject and the socio-historical articulation of that construction.

Whilst admiring *Screen*'s promethean ambitions, we feel that the fusion of marxist and Freudian theory presents certain problems that *Screen* has never confronted, let alone solved. We are in agreement with Joel Kovel when he says that "justice is done to Marx or Freud only by recognising the profound contradiction they pose for each other."[80] There is a real and constitutive contradiction within capitalist society between subject and object, between psyche and society. This contradiction can only be resolved through practice, by the abolition of capitalist social relations in favour of a socialist society. The unification of subjective and objective remains to be achieved; it is not to be decreed by theoretical fiat. The way in which historical materialism and psychoanalysis are at present external to each other therefore has its basis in reality. Fredric Jameson has pointed to the futility of prematurely amalgamating these two disciplines into "some unified anthropology":

> To say that both psychoanalysis and marxism are materialisms is simply to assert that each reveals an area in which human consciousness is not "master in its own house": only the areas decentred by each are the quite different ones of sexuality and of the class dynamics of social history. That these areas know local interrelationships — as when Reich shows how sexual repression is something like the cement which holds the authority fabric of society together — is undeniable; but none of these instinctual or ideological ion-exchanges in which a molecular element of one system is temporarily lent to the other for purposes of stabilisation, can properly furnish a model of the relationship of sexuality to class consciousness as a whole. Materialistic thinking, however, ought to have had enough practice of heterogeneity and discontinuity to entertain the possibility that human reality is fundamentally alienated in more than one way, and in ways which have little enough to do with each other.[81]

Moreover, whilst *Screen* talks of a psychoanalysis "established and exploited within historical materialism" (17, *4*, p.61), the reality of its practice is that historical materialism has in fact become constituted within a psychoanalytic ontology. It is here that we must qualify our description of *Screen*'s theory as a synthesis of Marx and Freud. Whilst *Screen* sets out to articulate Freudian and marxist theory, in practice the latter is totally subordinated and even extinguished by the imperialistic ambitions of psychoanalysis. And this psychoanalysis, bristling with the credentials that Althusser has given to it, then masquerades as the very latest thing in marxist theory. In the light of this development it is particularly important to point out that there are great dangers in psychoanalysis being applied beyond its sphere of competence. It is vital that when marxists use Freudian theory they do not allow it to blunt the edge of the marxist critique. Sherry Turkle has argued against psychoanalysis becoming a master science. In her view, other disciplines

> can truly contribute to psychoanalysis only by remaining in their own field of reference, by examining those aspects of the psychoanalytic *discours* that are not "visible" when one remains within the closed universe of psychoanalytic theory itself... "Multidisciplinarity" in the

context of psychoanalysis must mean a willingness to let other disciplines use their own methods to examine the analytic institution and analytic "ideology". It cannot mean subsuming these other *discours* into that of psychoanalysis, or in the case of Lacan, into the Lacanian hermeneutic.[82]

Within the pages of *Screen,* Freud is only ever viewed through the spectacles of Lacan — the important differences between them being entirely obscured. Other psychoanalytic theorists (Reich, Marcuse etc) are ignored or marginalised, being given the same treatment that Althusser deals out to the likes of Lukács and Korsch, whilst Lacan, with his excellent references from Althusser, is above suspicion, the defender of the faith. As was the case with Kristeva the influence on Lacan of Hegel and Heidegger is ignored. The exclusive and uncritical manner in which *Screen* has taken up Lacanian theory, and the dogmatic and unsubstantiated assertions as to the scientific and political importance of that theory, are far from helpful in the task of trying to understand the importance of Freudian theory for marxists. However, we invariably find ourselves faced with bold assertions like Coward and Ellis's claim that Lacan's interpretation of Freud "cannot ... contribute to that idealism which serves existing society".[83]

In dealing with the structuring of the subject within the system of language, Lacanian psychoanalysis provides the terrain on which semiotics converge with the Althusserian theory of ideology. In the rest of this section we shall look at the way *Screen* takes up the Lacanian concepts of the "imaginary" and the "symbolic" in its theory of ideology, and how this relates to its interest in realism.

For Lacan, the imaginary and the symbolic are both genetic and structural concepts. Genetically they refer to those stages of what Althusser, in his essay on "Freud and Lacan", has called "the long forced march which makes mammiferous larvae into human children, *masculine* or *feminine subjects",* or "the extraordinary adventure which from birth to the liquidation of the Oedipal phase transforms a small animal conceived by a man and a woman into a small human child". On this itinerary from nature to culture there are two important stages, the mirror-stage and the stage of the Oedipus complex, which are modalities of the imaginary and symbolic respectively. In the mirror-stage the child is "concerned with nothing but one alter ego, the mother", and "lives this dual intercourse in the mode of the imaginary fascination of the ego, being itself *that* other, *any* other, *every* other, all *the others* of primary narcissistic identification, never able to take up the objectfying distance of the third *vis à vis* either the other or itself".

This situation is terminated by the Oedipal phase, "in which a ternary structure emerges against the background of the dual structure" and "intrudes on the imaginary satisfaction of dual fascination", introducing the child to "the Symbolic Order, the order of objectifying language that will finally allow him [sic] to say: I, you, he, she or it, that will therefore allow the small child to situate itself as a *human* child in a world of adult thirds". Thereby is the child able to take up his/her place within the Symbolic, the Law of Order, which is "confounded in its *formal* essence with the order of language". In the Oedipal phase the child is born to language: "designated, assigned and localised within the law of language in which is established and presented all human order, i.e. every human role".[84]

These two stages of infancy can be taken as paradigms for all future imaginary and symbolic situations — the imaginary and symbolic being structural dimensions of all social reality and experience. The imaginary refers to that form of experience that takes the ego, the "I", as a unified phenomenon, to be the origin, the founding disposition of the world. "The subject is seen as the founding source of meanings — unproblematically standing outside an articulation in which it is, in fact, defined" (15, 2, p.17). Such a notion, it is maintained, can no longer be sustained in the face of Freud's discovery of the unconscious, which forces us to refuse any conception of consciousness as a unified and homogeneous phenomenon. Freud has pointed to "the lack of control of the conscious subject over his [sic] discourses", to "the distance between the subject of the act of signification and the conscious subject (the ego)" (15, 2, p.18). As we have seen, this imaginary form of perception is present in the cartesian *cogito*, which translates into philosophical form the fundamental misunderstanding by which the subject is taken to be the founding origin of discourse and meaning. The concept of the imaginary is taken up by Althusser to theorise ideology: ideology being the imaginary relation of individuals to their real conditions of existence. For Althusserians, ideology establishes individuals as coherent subjects within a contradictory world, each individual (mis)taking him/herself for the centre of the social process:

> The imaginary identity of ideology closes off the movement of contradictions, calling upon the subject as consistent. It puts the subject in the position of a homogeneous subject in relation to meaning, a subject who thinks him/herself to be the point of origin of ideas and of actions.[85]

The imaginary is characterised by unity, plenitude, oneness, totality. It is "characterised by the plentitude it confers on both subject and object, caught as they are outside any definition in terms of difference — given in a full substantial unity" (17, *3*, p.13).

The symbolic is the order of culture and language, of which the imaginary is an inflection. It is "an order that is intersected but not resumed by the ideological (ideology works *over* the symbolic *on* the subject for the imaginary)".[86] In contrast to the characteristics of homogeneity and resemblance that define the imaginary, the symbolic is the sphere of (sexual and linguistic) *difference*. It is "the whole cultural space which is structured like language through a set of differences and oppositions" (15, *2*, p.17). In this sense one can see that it is an elaboration and amplification of the diacritical, Saussurean conception of signification. "The introduction to the symbolic allows language to function as the grasping of opposition and difference" (16, *2*, p.11). The symbolic also entails a subject who is not homogeneous, who is excentric to him/herself: "Divided in the passage into and in language... the subject moves across the discursive play of consciousness and unconscious, image and letter" (16, *2*, p.88). Such a subject avoids "the imaginary world of projection in which the other is seen as the same and this sameness is in terms of the imaginary ideal ego — the complete self-mastery in which the movement of the symbolic would be reduced to the endless narcissistic identification of the mirror image" (16, *2*, p.12). He/she is able to accept a world that is other (or rather, Other) than him/herself, a world that is independent — the order of culture that is *imposed* on the human subject.

Clearly, the Lacanian concepts are imbricated with the semiotic concepts we have already looked at. The Lacanian and semiotic theoretical fields should not be seen as separate, but as existing in a close, symbiotic relationship. The difference between them is really one of emphasis: whilst semiotics is concerned primarily with language and the text, Lacanian psychoanalysis deals more thoroughly with the subject of ideology, the "reading" subject who confronts a given text.

Applying the concepts of the imaginary and the symbolic to the question of realism/non-realism, the realist text can be understood as characterised by the homogeneity of the imaginary. It is marked by "the conflation of the word and the thing — a necessary misrecognition (miscognition) which fails to place the meaning of the word in difference and opposition (in absence)" (16, *2*, p.11). Similarly, the reader or spectator of such a text is transfixed as a unified and cohesive ideological subject, placed in a "supra-positional omniscience, the full imaginary relation" (17, *3*, p.18). Primarily it is the narrative of the realist text that achieves this effect: "The time of (narrative) film is that of identity, centre, perspective, oneness, of the vision of the unified and unifying subject."[87]

If it is the homogeneity of the realist text that marks its "captation" by the imaginary of ideology and metaphysical essentialism, then the non-realist, or "deconstruction", text, which exposes difference and heterogeneity, can be seen as subversive of ideology. In such a text "language is understood in terms of lack and absence — the sign finds its definition diacritically through the absent syntagmatic and paradigmatic chains it enters into" (17, 3, p.14). Moreover, the non-realist text breaks the structured and unified security of the reader or spectator by fracturing the narrative that creates such an ideological positioning. It shifts from the imaginary of narrative to the symbolic of *discourse*. The latter term is intended to focus on "the dialectical relation between speaker and language in which language always already offers a position to the speaker and yet, at the same time, the act of speaking may itself displace those positions" (17, 3, p.12).

Screen has set up a binary opposition between texts that operate primarily in the imaginary mode and those that mobilise the symbolic; between those fixed within bourgeois ideology and those, revolutionary, texts that distance themselves from that ideology. There are those texts in which "subject and object [are] caught in an eternal paralysed fixity", and those that "investigate the very movement of articulation and difference" (15, 2, p.19). *Screen* shows little interest in the "content" of texts, and the significance of this as interventions in specific historical contexts: it is concerned only with the formal dialectic of imaginary and symbolic, homogeneity and heterogeneity. As a part of its arduous, and apparently interminable, task of refining its formalist theory of cinematic language and ideology, *Screen* has "appropriated" a number of Freudian and Lacanian concepts. These are, however, only a series of reformulations; each aims to express more precisely and rigorously the manner in which films are intersected by the symbolic and the imaginary.

There are three such concepts that are of particular importance. Following the example of Roland Barthes, *Screen* initially operationalised the Freudian concept of *fetishism*, referring to "the fetishistic position of the spectator — fixed in his [*sic*] position securely by the reality of the image" (15, *1*, p.9). Through the mechanics of fetishism "the subject is produced in a position of separation from which he [*sic*] is confirmed in an imaginary coherence...the condition of which is the ignorance of the structure of his production, of his setting in position" (15, 2, p.106). Again, we see the critique of homogeneity, with fetishism in representational, realist cinema being defined in terms of "the denial of work: that is, of heterogeneity and process" (16, *2*, p.87).

A second way of analysing the ideological fixation of the spectator, and one that permits the "articulation of film and ideology on the figure of the subject", is through the difficult concept of *suture,* derived from Lacan *via* Jacques-Alain Miller. Heath argues that, for Lacan, the suture is

> the situation in which the subject becomes an effect of the signifier: this situation in which he/she is stood in for. It thus relates to the relationship of the individual as subject to the chain of his/her discourse, and is a process which constantly attempts to close or bind up the gap between the subject and the signifier... It is... not possible to speak of a fully present (self-present) subject. He/she must be understood as essentially absent, and able to signify only because he/she produces him/herself in a position in relation to the signifier. Without the signifier there would be no subject. The suture constitutes an attempt to constantly fill up this gap between the subject and the signified in a situation in which it is doomed forever to be the effect of the signifier, represented or stood in for.

Ideology and the imaginary operate through the suture. In terms of the cinema, one can see that whilst the film text is a productivity, a movent, a process of which the (absent) subject is an effect, the suture operates to "stitch" or "tie" this subject into the text as the "I" for (and from) which it appears as an imaginary unity and coherence. "In its movement, its framings, its cuts, its intermittences, the film ceaselessly poses an absence, a lack, which is ceaselessly recaptured for... the film, that process binding the spectator as subject in the realisation of the film's space" (17, *3*, p.98). This is achieved, notably through "narrativisation", and through the perspective system ("the unity of place for vision").[88]

The third important concept is that of the mirror-stage, taken directly from Lacan. Laura Mulvey, for example talks of the mirror-stage in childhood being the "birth of the long love affair/despair between image and self-image which has found such intensity of expression in film and such joyous expression in the cinema audience". She goes on to describe how the cinema viewing experience creates "the sense of forgetting the world as the ego has subsequently come to know it", this being "reminiscent of that pre-subjective moment of image recognition". Furthermore the Hollywood star system can be explained in terms of the ego ideals associated with the imaginary experiences of the mirror stage (16, *3*, p.10).

The precise status of these various concepts is uncertain, to us at least. *Screen* has been criticised for using them in different ways and for different purposes, and has replied by arguing that discrepancies are inevitable in the process of scientific advance.

Yet this does not clarify whether these are scientific concepts — and if so, how is it possible to translate concepts from the field of psychoanalysis to that of film criticism —, whether they are metaphors, or whether they are analogies. To take the example of the mirror-stage, *Screen* is certainly aware that there are theoretical problems in taking this conception up analogically; from the point of view of its own theoretical "problematic", it could be criticised for lapsing into the imaginary register, by obscuring the difference between the terms compared. Heath has qualified *Screen*'s adoption of the mirror-stage, claiming that

> there is a relation between mirror-phase and cinematic institution that should be examined, yet the condition of such an examination is exactly the non-reduction of the *relation:* nothing is to be gained by describing cinema *as* the mirror-phase, the crux is the relation, that is, the difference, the supplacement — refiguration of a subject-spectator who has already completed the mirror-phase (16, *2,* p.87).

But still this does not escape the criticism that the concept is only an analogy. Nor does it explain what could be meant by "the difference, the supplacement".

It has been necessary to provide this long and difficult, but still simplified, outline, in order to give some idea of the complex array of Lacanian concepts upon which *Screen* draws to provide a (marxist) explication of the nature of cinematic ideology. How adequate has this theoretical machinery been to the task in hand? Has the marxist theory of ideology, of culture, or of language been advanced? Let us begin by saying that although *Screen* has produced a large body of work, this has all been confined to the same limited question of how film texts address their "readers". *Screen* has remained committed to the same narrow area of study, the same films, the same formalist method. has presented a series of formulations and reformulations, honing and polishing its concepts to find ever more satisfactory ways of describing the ideological effect of cinema. One way of situating *Screen*'s approach is to place it in the context of that form of criticism which has talked of Hollywood in terms of the "dream factory". It is not inapposite to compare its description of the viewing experience with that of Hugo Mauerhofer, writing in 1949, who describes

> the *boredom* lurking on the brink of the Cinema Situation, the increased readiness of the *imagination,* the uncritical voluntary *passivity,* and lastly, the *anonymity* which guides the spectator into his [*sic*] private sphere.[89]

Screen's theoretical formulation is far more complex and sophisticated, it goes without saying, and we do not want to belittle it by this comparison. But, we feel that it is possible to gain a useful insight into the nature of *Screen*'s contribution to film theory, by seeing it as a revivification — and a powerful one at that — of this theoretical current that has been so prominent in film studies.

For *Screen* ideology/subjectification in the cinema involves the "petrification of the spectator in a position of pseudo-dominance" (15, *2*, p.24). *Screen* is concerned with the "positioning of the subject" by a film, with the "kind of 'reader' and 'author' it constructs". Thus, representation is

> less immediately a matter of "what is represented" than of positioning; narrative in cinema is first and foremost the organisation of a point of view through the image-flow, the laying out of an intelligibility, the conversion of seen into scene as the direction of the viewing subject.[90]

This focus on the subjectification of the viewer by the realist text is the basis of most of *Screen*'s work. *Screen*'s concern with non-realist films can be understood in terms of the way they fracture the identity of the homogeneous, centred subject of ideology. The "revolutionary subject" is a decentred, heterogeneous phenomenon.[91]

Many points can be made in criticism of this formulation. Clearly it is unsatisfactory to argue that the viewer is (unilaterally) fixed in position by the film text, and we shall not pursue this criticism, which has been acknowledged in the pages of *Screen* (MacCabe, 17, *3*). In addition, within *Screen's* formulation the viewer-subject is reduced (like the text) to an incorporeal, anonymous and formal entity, the imaginary other that the film poses for itself. Such a conception is thoroughly ahistorical, the "reader" of all realist texts from the nineteenth century onwards being the same ossified, frozen subject. For *Screen,* ideology is produced by the *form* of realism. To escape, or rather disrupt, ideology it is necessary to have alternative films — of which there are, apparently, all too few — that will release viewers from ideological fixity and deliver them to the world of heterogeneity and difference. For some it is possible to distantiate themselves from ideology, by fracturing the unity of realist texts through the semiotic practice of decoding.

The emphasis on working on the deconstruction of texts leaves no room for pleasure. *Screen*'s assessment of films has no place for the discussion of humour, fascination, entertainment, the appreciation of beauty and grace. The only grounds it allows for involvement with film are purely intellectual ones. For *Screen,* most of the cinema audience seems to be comprised of "Gerald Fords", unable to both be entertained and to extract new knowledge from the film at the same time.

Screen's position is not quite so simple as we have presented it. While the above formulation *remains* a dominant moment in its theory, *Screen* has come to criticise the idea that texts unilaterally fix their "readers" as subjects, arguing that it is necessary to "understand the text's effectivity within the social process, which is to say we have to consider the relation between reader and text in its historical specificity" (17, *3*, p.24). In a critique of formalist aesthetics, Paul Willemen opposes "the suggestion that texts *construct* spectators" for "all its implications of subjugation, unilateral determination, not to say terrorism" (19, *1*, p.45).

Screen's response to the charge by the resigning members of the editorial board that it presented a picture of a "passive audience" which was "conceived as a monolith and never investigated" (16, *4*, p.129), was to accuse its critics of suggesting that the audience is simply active (outside contradiction) and film simply passive (its meanings unproblematically available to an audience without any activity on their part). *Screen* restates its position as an attempt "to explore the relation set up by the film (and by cinema itself) as subject positions binding individuals to the production of certain forms of totality, particularly images." It adds: "This does not mean that those individuals were passive but that both the contradictions sustained by the lived relationship of class positions in a confrontation with the meaning of film and the strategies of film to contain those contradictions should and could be analysed... Popular cinema (an ill-defined monolith?) can only be demonstrated as working-class value by showing its contradictions and the exploitation and use of them made by the working class in given situations" (17, *2*, p.115). As we have seen there are innumerable references in *Screen* to films binding individuals in subject positions, but no extended discussion, apart from brief remarks like these, of how contradiction may have its source in the audience. However, there is never any further indication of what the effects of different class positions in the audience are likely to be, and, more particularly, we are never shown how the reception of a film has been different amongst different audiences, in different periods.

When *Screen* recognises the existence of an empirical reader outside the text, and acknowledges that he/she is not simply constructed by that text, it is difficult to see how this second, subordinate, moment of *Screen*'s theory can be integrated with the first, although it is presented as a development of the earlier formulation, rather than as what it is, a (partial) break and an undermining. *Screen* is, apparently, fixed into an imaginary position, from which it can only see its body of work as homogeneous and unified. Although certain contributors to

Screen are aware of "the cumbersome extra-textual, the outside of the text" (19, *1*, p.43), this is invariably negated by a counter-tendency, influenced by the work of Hindess and Hirst, that deeply distrusts the category of the real, and in fact subsumes the extra-textual into the discursive. It is the concentration on texts, the principle of immanence, that continues to characterise *Screen*. Thus, in the very same article in which he stresses the importance of "analysing a film within a determinate social moment so that it is possible to determine what identifications will be made and by whom" (17, *3*, p.25), Colin MacCabe goes on to contrast two films *(Death by Hanging* and *The Lump),* making an *a priori* judgement on how each will be read on the basis of its formal structure alone.

It is difficult to see how *Screen*'s "problematic" could be made to incorporate an active, discriminating audience. The whole rationale of its theoretical project is based upon a resolute anti-humanism, which sees real, concrete individuals as "bearers" of social relations, and which, by positing the "primacy of the signifier", sees these individuals as effects of linguistic structures. *Screen* has no interest in "real" working-class people, who exist, for it, only as "stand-ins" within various discourses. It is only aware of the working class as an audience, as shadowy faces in the gloomy auditorium of a cinema effectively cut off from the rest of their lives. There is only the imaginary conception of an undifferentiated audience. Were it interested in the reality of that audience, *Screen* would see the importance of developing its understanding through empirical research.[92]

Screen has developed a theoretical position that sees only the passive aspect, the determined moment, of consumption. It has a fetishised conception of language as a reified entity that is imposed on individuals. This conception is naturalised, eternalised in the concept of the symbolic order. *Screen* is thereby unable to understand that the regressive aspect of film viewing is a historical product, the result of the imposition of the commodity form on the film as a use value. But this does not exhaust the film experience, for there is also the moment of active appropriation of meaning, the moment that refuses the fetishised, reified nature of the film as commodity. It is here that the work of Ernst Bloch is of such importance. Fredric Jameson has described how, for Bloch

> even a cultural product whose social function is that of *distracting* us can only realise that aim by fastening and harnessing our attention and our imaginative energies in some positive way and by some type of genuine, albeit disguised and distorted, content. Such content is for him what he calls "Hope", or in other words the permanent tension of human reality towards a radical transformation of itself and everything about it, towards a Utopian transfiguration of its own

existence as well as of its social context. To maintain that everything is a "figure of Hope" is to offer an analytical tool for detecting the presence of some Utopian contest even within the most degraded and degrading type of commercial product.[93]

As a coda to this section, we should add that very recently there has emerged within *Screen* a *tentative* distancing from Lacan. Stephen Heath has maintained that "to recognise the fundamental significance of Lacan's work, often built upon in *Screen,* is not to accept all its developments, positions, presentations". He has pointed to Lacan's "habitual self-presentation", his adoption of a position of assured knowledge, and, most importantly, his male style of discourse which may well be "a reflection of male domination". This is not, however, treated negatively as a defect of Lacanian theory. For Heath, "to criticise psychoanalysis in aspects of that theory is not, of course, to reject or refuse psychoanalysis, it is merely to treat the theory, and psychoanalysis with it, as non-homogeneous" (19, *3,* pp.51-3). Within Lacanian discourse this, of course, represents a positive virtue. *Vive la différence!* Heath's partial recognition that there are problems in Lacanian theory provides us with the familiar sight of *Screen* recognising something at long last — only to present it as an original discovery. Will this recognition of an inadequacy in its approach, and the similar ones *Screen* makes from time to time, lead to any fundamental change in the future? Unfortunately we have to agree with Andrew Britton[94]:

> The repeated claim that Lacanian structures are subject to particular historical reflections emerges as little more than a rhetorical device — a gesture towards dialectics which is instantly cancelled by the very terms of the system. The system is inherently resistant to the historically specific; it cannot acknowledge its possibility without disintegrating. Lacan deals with the givens of the human condition, explicitly unrelated to the social — like the "fall into the imaginary". One cannot then go on to say, "But of course, there is no subject outside the social formation", while the exclusion of the subject from the social formation is the major premise of the system.[95]

Screen*'s intervention in British culture*

Over the last few years *Screen* has produced a positive barrage of qualifications or self-criticisms of many of its fundamental positions: it has recognised that its definition of realism tends towards formalism, that films should not be seen as immutable structures determining the subject positions of viewers, that there is a need for conjunctural analysis, that Lacan's writings contain certain problems, and so on. These various statements can only appear as fundamental theoretical insights to those totally bound up in the straitjacket of *Screen*'s formalist aesthetics. Despite these various admissions, *Screen* has not seemed able to modify its practice by incorporating these qualifications into its subsequent analyses. They serve more as disclaimers to ward off possible criticism. We reject the claim that *Screen*'s theoretical problems are only the teething trouble associated with developing a theoretical area previously neglected by marxists. It is our belief that the direction taken by *Screen* is a cul-de-sac which can yield little useful knowledge about culture, or guide for cultural struggle. It becomes all the more important to say this as a whole generation of students take *Screen* to be their model for a marxist theory of film, and non-academic magazines like *Time Out* and *Spare Rib* are increasingly affected in their coverage of film by the theories first expounded in its pages.

In the criticisms we have made of *Screen* there is one question we have so far avoided: is it appropriate or not to describe *Screen* as marxist? Certainly there is little resemblance between the contents of *Screen* and the approach of Marx himself. The only basis on which a connection can be established is through *Screen*'s use of certain of Althusser's concepts — accepting Althusser's claim to be able to represent what Marx meant to say even if he never, or rarely, actually said it. As we have seen, *Screen* has now even begun to move on from Althusser. Does this mean we should deny its right to the label "marxist"? In a debate in the pages of *Screen* several members of the Centre for Contemporary Cultural Studies (CCCS) argued: "There may be many variants of marxism. But there must be limit positions which allow us to identify the terrain of the problematic, distinguishing it from others" (18, *4*, p.119). Ros Coward has responded to this position: "There is no such thing as 'limit positions'. Mao's and Lenin's writings would have been dismissed as outside their contemporary 'limit positions'" (18, *4*, p.122). Cutler, Hindess, Hirst and Hussain have echoed her point in a debate with Laurence Harris: "Harris attempts to counterpose a fruitful and coherent scientificity to a sterile and eclectic revisionism. In doing so he is forced to posit an 'orthodox' marxism secure in its truths... marxism has survived and can only survive by reconstruction. We are convinced that today this will have to be of the most radical kind, and involve the abandonment of a search for the 'essence' which gives its possessor scientificity. Marxists who deny others the name because they criticise Marx and change concepts take refuge from this uncertainty in an imaginary and sterile orthodoxy".[96]

We are not proposing a form of marxism "secure in its truths". By no means do we believe it necessary to accept everything Marx wrote. In particular, as Coward argues, the ideas on patriarchy and sexuality, which have originated in the women's movement, have shown the whole marxist tradition to be seriously inadequate. There is a constant need for questioning and rethinking, if marxism is not to retreat into dogma or is to provide new knowledge in a changing world. At the same time we agree with the CCCS writers that: "We cannot simply borrow and ditch and conflate at will, nominating the resulting porridge 'marxist' as we go" (18, *4,* p.119). There are crucial concepts — of totality, of social relations of production and so on — which seem to us to be the basis on which the most valuable work in the marxist tradition has been built. We do not find in the work of those who reject these concepts any comparable new knowledge. Until arguments are advanced which convince us that these concepts must be rejected, we will continue to accept them as defining marxism. If this provides us with a notion of limit positions then it must be said that *Screen* sorely tests those limits.

In 1974 an editorial in *Screen* acknowledged that "in the past *Screen*'s relation to British film culture and film making has been unclear to say the least" and promised more attention to "issues, events and films directly relevant to the present conjuncture of British film culture" (15, *3,* p.6). Two years later, in response to the charge that *Screen* ignored a whole series of crucial issues relating to the contemporary situation in British film and television, MacCabe justified this absence by arguing that there had been certain limitations imposed on the journal. But, he continued, "we are now in a position to start both [the] process of self-criticism and the undertaking of new projects" (17, *1,* p.101). Today, the number of articles devoted *only* to developing abstract theory still exceeds by far the number which relate in any discernable way to contemporary issues and struggles in Britain. While we recognise the need for theory, we believe this balance is wrong.

The type of intervention it is possible for *Screen* to make depends crucially on which films it decides to discuss. Looking back over copies of *Screen* for the past eight years it is striking how few films are discussed in detail. Those that are fall mainly into three categories — classical narrative cinema, and the political and aesthetic avant-gardes. The first category consists of those films *Screen* inherited from *auteur* criticism — Welles, Ford, Hitchcock, etc. and those lesser known directors discussed in a series of Edinburgh Film Festival monographs, to which many *Screen* writers contributed. Unlike the earlier form of criticism, which had looked to these films for the coherent vision of an artist, *Screen* was interested in gaps and dislocations which distinguished them from straight realist texts (i.e. from the model, or "ideal type" of a realist text). Prominent in the second category were those directors who for political reasons made a break with realist film making — Godard, Straub/Huillet and Oshima. The final category is the formalist avant-garde. This interest is of more recent origin than the other two, being signalled in a number of editorials in 1976: "there is no doubt that *Screen* has neglected the avant-garde film" (17, *1*, p.5); the "nearly exclusive concentration on narrative is no longer adequate" (17, *4*, p.6). Given *Screen*'s concern with films which break with realism all that is surprising is that it was so long before it started discussing films by Snow, Sharits, Brakhage, Gidal, etc.

As significant as what *Screen* includes is what it excludes from discussion. Agitprop, documentary films such as those of Cinema Action and the Newsreel Collective and naturalist political fiction like the television plays by Loach/Garnett have only been mentioned briefly, to be immediately dismissed on account of their realist form. These films have at least gained some attention in the pages of *Screen,* unlike the popular entertainment films of today (in contrast with those of twenty-five or more years ago). Terry Lovell argues elsewhere in this book that we should take the products of the mass entertainment industries seriously. As she says, a commodity may have several different use values, some of which may be in contradiction with its exhange value. These films may reinforce wants and aspirations inimical to capitalism. It is not possible to read off ideological effects simply from the manner of production, nor from the aesthetic form.

By ignoring these popular films, *Screen* has been unable to intervene in the everyday debates and controversies that go on amongst the vast majority of cinema goers. It should be a priority for marxists, attempting to intervene around film, to comment on films like *The Deer Hunter* and *The China Syndrome*. *Screen*'s attitude is the totally purist one, that will only deal with works considered worthy of its attention. This mandarin approach comes close to parody in Colin MacCabe's remarks about the medium of television. Responding to the argument that programmes which met *Screen*'s strict criteria would be turned down as "too difficult", he writes: "This may well be true but it raises the further question of whether the concept of 'audience' which is used for aesthetic judgements within television may render any political use of television fiction impossible".[97] It has become possible to suggest that a whole medium should be written off as an arena for intervention!

The practice of *Screen* has been to concentrate on established institutions and especially on ones connected with the state. *Screen* has concentrated its interventions on the BFI (with which it has many direct and indirect connections) and the Edinburgh Film

Festival. In a report on the 1976 festival it was stressed that, "the present institutions of which Edinburgh is one, provide the terrain on which ground has to be taken" (17, *4,* p.107). Similarly, John Ellis takes the position that it is "impossible to be puritanical in politics", and argues: "The BFI exists, like any other state institution, to include (which is not meant in the pejorative sense of 'contain' or 'recuperate') the competing ideologies which make up the space of its practice. It does not express a monolithic line, a single specifiable ideology or political position: it can only attempt to reproduce existing representations" (18, *1,* p.126). In the case of the BFI Production Board, which provides funds to make films, Ellis points out that it deals specifically with experimental film making: "This has the effect of turning it from being a lackey of the state to a body which is peculiarly open to oppositional/ independent/alternative forms; it takes them *a priori* as its brief" (18, *1,* p.125). But Ellis fails to recognise that there is more that has to be said about state institutions than that they include competing ideologies — even if this is also true. Nowhere in his article on the BFI Production Board does he suggest that there might be contradictions involved in accepting state funding.

The question of exactly when and how socialists should try to struggle *within* the apparatus of the capitalist state is an extremely complex one. One position which is gaining increasing acceptance on the left in Britain is Eurocommunism. The Communist Party has used Althusserian and neo-Gramscian theories to argue against positions which see the state as simply functional for the needs of capital and to stress the importance of struggle within the state apparatus. We believe that it is not possible to make a statement either one way or the other: yes, it is right to work within the state, or no it is wrong. It is all a matter of where you work and how, and even then there will be contradictions. We do agree with the criticisms of the view of the state as *only* functional for capital. Our positions on struggle within the state have been argued by the CSE State Group:

> The relationship between the capitalist nature of the state and the various struggles that take place around its activities becomes clearer if we make a distinction between state form and state apparatus. This is a distinction between the state as a bourgeois form of social relations and the state apparatus as an institution. Capital's survival depends on it being able to impose bourgeois forms of social relations not only in society at large but also within the state apparatus itself. There will always be a disjunction between the state apparatus and the state form. The state form is constantly being ruptured both within the state apparatus and in the daily contact between it and "citizens". The reproduction of capitalist relations constantly runs up against the

opposition (conscious and unconscious) which inevitably springs from the reality of a society based on exploitation: council tenants see bad housing conditions as an issue of class, community workers try to organise on the basis of a more meaningful category than "the community", socialists throughout the state apparatus seek ways of breaking out of the forms which constrict their daily lives. These correspond to the way the capitalist form is similarly threatened in the factory by actions such as absenteeism, sabotage and strikes. The fact that the state apparatus, like the factory, is the scene of a constant struggle to impose bourgeois forms upon activity within the state and upon relations between the state apparatus and society opens up the possibility of what might be called "oppositional space" within the state — of using the services provided by the state apparatus, or working within it, without *necessarily* accepting the state form.[98]

Thus, it is possible to struggle within the state apparatus, but only on the condition that we remember the overall capitalist *form* of the state. This is a contradiction which will continually be brought home in any struggle. The problem with Ellis's remarks quoted above it that he neglects the question of the state form.

Although Ellis states that his views should not be taken as those of *Screen,* there is one respect in which his article is typical of the journal: fundamental problems in strategy are never discussed openly in its pages. Nowhere do we find discussion of what might be the possible strategies for taking the ground on the terrain of existing institutions, or of why *Screen* adopts the one it does. Nowhere is it ever explained why film is such an important medium that *Screen* writers have chosen to concentrate their attentions on it. Nowhere are the implications of *Screen*'s relation to the BFI examined, or how this relation has changed over the years. It might be argued that *Screen*'s connection with the BFI prevents it from openly considering these questions. However, there was a period back in 1971 when *Screen* was prepared to be openly critical of the BFI. As the important contradictions and ambiguities of working through the state are never brought out we have no choice but to conclude that *Screen* regards the problems involved as slight.

The connections between theoretical positions and political ones is much more complex than is often portrayed. In Britain today it seems most common for Althusserians to adopt Eurocommunist politics. As Gideon Ben-Tovim notes, there has been a concerted effort by many Communist Party intellectuals to provide a theoretical underpinning for *The British Road to Socialism.* The theorist whose writings are most frequently used is Gramsci, but after him come various representatives of Althusserianism —

Althusser, Poulantzas, Hindess and Hirst, etc.[99] However, Althusseriansim has also been linked with currents to the left of the CP. The major form of left Althusserianism has been inspired by Maoism. For a brief period — around the time of the Cultural Revolution — Althusser himself "flirted" with this political current. Concepts from Mao's theoretical writings are taken up and asssimilated in *For Marx*. The Cultural Revolution seemed to vindicate Althusser's theory of the social "whole" and the role of "ideological struggle" within it. Althusser's followers in the French Communist Party's student organisation, the Union des Etudiants Communistes, split under the impact of the Cultural Revolution in 1966 to form their own Maoist group — the Union des Jeunes Communistes Marxistes-Leninistes (UJCML).[100] *Theoretical Practice,* the journal which played a key role in introducing Althusser to Britain, saw itself as "politically situated within the anti-revisionist movement" and for a time considered joining a small Maoist group, the CFB(ML).[101] One of the editors of *Screen* has linked his interest in Althusser/Lacan with invocations of Mao and the Cultural Revolution.[102] On the other hand Althusseriansim has led some in the opposite direction. Hindess and Hirst now argue for working in the Labour Party for gradual reforms from a position well to the right of Eurocommunism.[103] Finally in France the path for some former Althusserians has been to the *nouvelle philosophie.*[104]

However, while Althusserianism has been linked with a fairly wide spectrum of political positions the basic components of the theory, such as the fragmentation of the totality and the autonomy granted to intellectuals, lead to similar problems. Even when Althusserian theory is presented in a revolutionary guise the very nature of that theory still limits the resulting contribution to class struggle. We believe that with all forms of Althusserianism it is extremely difficult to escape from the impasse of "Western marxism", as described by Perry Anderson: isolation of intellectuals, stress on philosophy, separation from politics, etc.[105] Althusserian theory does not lead to one single political position but a number of aspects of that theory produce a *tendency* towards certain political consequences, bearing in mind that it is not necessarily the case that all varieties of Althusserianism will arrive at these consequences. We believe that Althusserian theory opens up a space for many — even polarised — political positions. It is the protean nature of Althusserianism, the fact that it can be all things to all persons, that makes it such a significant theoretical and political phenomenon.

There are serious difficulties in assigning *Screen* to any definite position on the political spectrum. In one sense it is deliberately apolitical, concentrating on theory and only very occasionally making any direct political statements. When those political statements are sifted out, through a careful reading of the journal, they correspond to more than one political position. Therefore, a political assessment of *Screen* has to be constructed, not from these explicit statements, but from reading between the lines and from the strategy (conscious or unconscious) contained in the way *Screen* intervenes in the BFI and British film culture. With respect to the latter we have the problem, as outsiders, of not having enough information to have a complete picture of *Screen's* activities. While the assessment is difficult, this much we are able to say: the theory of culture contained in *Screen* may not necessarily lead to Eurocommunist politics, but it does leave itself open to being easily appropriated by the Communist Party. This is irrespective of whether or not *Screen* wants its theory to be used in this way. If *Screen* and the Communist Party have converged over the last few years this may well be more because the CP, as part of its strategy of making friends with all "progressive" intellectuals, has moved towards *Screen,* rather than vice versa.

Another factor which complicates a political assessment of *Screen* is that it often combines an extremely radical and militant rhetoric with a somewhat less radical practice. For instance its advocacy only of films which break decisively with realism presents itself as an extremely daring position. John Ellis, in a discussion of the BFI Production Board, in the days before he became a member and it adopted a policy highly favourable to non-realist films, argued that the dangerous, subversive nature of these films was appreciated by members of the board: "There is no resistance to left-wing commitment, to the various trotskyist or workerist currents that predominate at the moment; because the films operate within the conventional documentary categories the Board finds little difficulty in funding them, and thus demonstrates its liberalism. Its resistance is to any form of deconstruction or interrogation of the cinema experience itself" (17, *1,* p.18). It seems an extremely radical position to sweep away all existing films, bar a few vaunted exceptions, as reactionary. This position displays all the violent rhetoric of those who pursue "the class struggle in theory".

At the same time as *Screen* displays this rhetoric, its practice (as far as we can gather from the information available to us) consists of working away gradually in the state and other established institutions, in a way which avoids open controversy or challenge. It also incorporates into its practice a whole series of conventions which characterise academicism. *Screen* by its very nature as a group of people focused around a journal, takes as its main concern the written word. Any journal finds it extremely difficult to break with the problem of the division between a group of active writers and a passive mass of consumers. In the case of *Screen* the level of "competence" expected of contributors seems likely to deter all but the boldest readers. *Screen* has a characteristically stern, academic appearance — page after page of uninterrupted text, with very few pictures or other visuals. Here is one instance where we would have no doubts about supporting a break with conventional forms. There are other crucial ways in which *Screen* reproduces taken-for-granted academic approaches. It accepts the strict divisions made between specific disciplines when it fails to connect film with other mass media. It implicitly accepts that division between high and mass culture which dismisses the latter, although of course it gives suitably sophisticated "materialist" reasons for promoting a particular group of films, which are accessible to very few people, as model texts. Thus there are innumerable reasons for concluding that *Screen* constitutes a much less radical break than it would like us to believe.

Displacing Althusser

We have tried to outline the development of what has become a new orthodoxy within marxist cultural theory. We have dealt with the proliferation, within Britain, of Althusserian marxism, and the way it has fused, in the case of *Screen,* with semiotic theory and Lacanian psychoanalysis. Whilst initially Althusserianism had a positive and stimulating effect — a "wind from the east", perhaps — it has since become an obstacle to further developments in cultural theory. Indeed, it has taken upon itself the task of ruling alternative positions out of order, thereby putting its veto on any debate other than that which is internal to the orthodoxy itself.

We have undertaken to criticise Althusserian theory from the point of view of a different conception of what a marxist cultural theory might be. In our opinion, Althusserians have weakened marxist theory by rejecting a whole dimension of Marx's work, the dimension represented by the theories of alienation and commodity fetishism. This dimension is not the be-all and end-all of marxist theory, but it is quite crucial, in that it theoretically appropriates a *central* phenomenon of bourgeois society. Such is the theoretical climate in cultural theory, that a taboo has been put on the use of these terms. It almost seems impertinent to take up these concepts, that Althusser has long since deposited in the theoretical dustbin; they have become irredeemably associated with the "deviations" of essentialism, economism, historicism, etc. Such is the absurdity of Althusserian theory, that because Althusserians consider fetishism to be *theoretically* unacceptable, they assume that the phenomena to which it refers cannot exist in *reality*.

There are two main objections commonly levelled at the position we are putting forward: (1) that it is economistic and reductionist because it talks of ideology/culture in the context of relations of production; and (2) following from this, that it reduces ideology to mere false consciousness. The first objection is based on a misunderstanding of the concept of "relations of production", one which reduces this concept to the "economic", in a narrow sense. Clearly, Marx uses the term "production" in a variety of senses, some of which can be taken for the "economic"; but within his work there is an overriding emphasis on production as the *totality* of the social process. "When we consider bourgeois society in the long view and as a whole, then the final result of the process of social production always appears as the society itself, i.e. the human being itself in its social relations... The direct production process itself here appears only as a moment".[106] The second objection fails to recognise that, in bourgeois society, fetishised social relation appear as *concrete* abstractions. Ideology is not *false* consciousness, because it duplicates a concrete *reality,* one that really does exist, one that imposes itself on the texture of everyday life. Or rather, it is a form of thought that is *true* in its perception of bourgeois social reality, but false in taking a mediated (historical) reality as immediate. Nor is ideology, in this conception, immaterial, a mere epiphenomenon; it is an illusion, but one that is the "most efficacious reality, the spell that holds the world bewitched" (Adorno).

In the context of this article, the usefulness of the theory of alienation/fetishism can be established by the light it throws on the nature of Althusserian theory itself. Thus, we can see the Althusserian theory of a fragmented "social formation" as an alienated conception. It merely duplicates the fractured totality of bourgeois society, reproduces acritically the illusory forms, the surface appearances of that society. As such it is a positivistic social theory which takes what is a mediated product, achieved through the long process of bourgeois class rule, as an immediate and eternal truth. In the face of such a static, one-dimensional conception of society, a critical marxist social theory must "dissolve the rigidity of an object frozen in the here-and-now into a field of tensions between the possible and the actual".[107]

In like manner, the Lacano-Althusserian theory of language is a thoroughly alienated conception, which replicates, at the level of theory, that alienation of language and meaning which has increasingly come to characterise late bourgeois societies, which seek to extend the domination of capital to the subjective sphere itself. The notion, put forward by Marx, in *The German Ideology,* of language as "practical, real consciousness", the medium through which men and women appropriate the real world, is dismissed as "ideological". For the Althusserians of *Screen,* language — eternalised as the symbolic — is a reified entity, detached from real people (taken out of their mouths, as it were). It has become a hypostatised "Law" that, like capital, imposes itself on subjects, "bearers", who are now playthings not of the Gods, but of the Signifier(s).

The fetishism of theory (as "theoretical practice") provides a third example of the alienated nature of Althusserian marxism. Theory is no longer related to social reality, but hovers in its own asocial realm, a spectre haunting the academy. The concept of "theoretical practice" represents a grotesque rationalisation, within marxist theory, of the separation of mental from manual labour in the real world. Marx commented on this form of alienated reasoning when he said of Proudhon: "[The] moment we cease to pursue the historical movement of production relations, of which the categories, are but the theoretical expression, the moment we want to see in these categories no more than ideas, spontaneous thoughts independent of real relations, we are forced to attribute the origin of these thoughts to the movement of pure reason." For Proudhon, "all that exists, all that lives on land and under water can be reduced by abstraction to a logical category — ...the whole real world can be drowned...in a world of abstractions, in the world of logical categories." Proudhon is criticised for not realising that categories are only the theoretical expressions or abstractions of real social relations. "M. Proudhon, holding things upside down like a true philospher, sees in actual relations nothing but the incarnation of these principles, of these categories."[108] The resemblance between Proudhon and Althusser is remarkable, to say the least.

In this article we have taken up the concepts of fetishism and alienation not as a systematic alternative to the Althusserian position we criticise, but as a mode of critique, a tool for displacing the solidity and reified immediacy of bourgeois society. To present our point of view as a ready-made synthesis would be to succumb to a fetishised conception of theory. And this must be the fate of any *a priori* theoretical structure — such as the Althusserian "theoretical practice" — which develops in isolation from (political) practice. It is because our critique is aimed at this form of theorising that we have not confined ourselves purely to Althusserian marxism as a theoretical phenomenon, but have put forward comments upon its political nature and implications. Because our own theoretical position is not immune to this fault which so characterises Althusserianism, because of the immense difficulties in integrating theoretical and political activity, these comments are put forward as tentative and exploratory. They are offered only as one contribution to the necessary debate on the politics of culture.

Postscript

Just as we were correcting the proofs of this essay a new issue of *Screen* was published (20, 3/4, Winter 1979/80). The editorial claimed there had been a "reassessment of the role and intention of the magazine" which had led to "a revised project and a new format" (p.7). In particular it said that *Screen* would in future be more concerned with "cultural practices" other than film and television and with current debates over institutional structures and policies (p.9). The contents of this issue show some movement along those lines. We would welcome such changes — indeed they are ones we call for in our paper — although this welcome has to be a cautious one in the light of similar promises in the past. *Screen*'s self-analysis does not extend to any adequate explanation of why it has taken a decade to begin to make these changes. Has it simply been an inexplicable oversight or has it been connected in some way with the journal's theory?

Screen's redesign is disappointingly similar to its old one. We find it amazing that a journal concerned with culture has paid so little attention to its appearance. *Screen* typically draws a simple polarity between itself and the "redundant illustrations" of most film magazines (p.13). Any alternative involving the creative use of visual material is not considered.

Another issue the editorial takes up is the difficulty of the writing in *Screen*. By providing an obscure and unhelpful definition of "academic" (which seems to mean something which is not self-reflective), *Screen* is by definition not academic. However, it is admitted that the journal has been vulnerable to the pressures exerted by "academia" (p.8). Again *Screen* attempts to defend itself with a ridiculous polarity: between its contents and "forms of 'easy' writing" (which apparently establish an imaginary relation between reader and text; pp. 10-11).

Finally *Screen* makes the allegation that while its theory is flexible, its critics are dogmatic. Kevin Robbins [*sic*] and Andrew Britton are accused of "an obstinate foreclosure of understanding for which *Screen* need bear no responsibility" (p.12). The claim that the journal has changed is used to make it immune from criticism. Indeed the only criticism *Screen* is ever prepared to accept is its own self-criticism, even when this recognises some of the points previously made by outsiders. We believe that *Screen* has had to be "flexible" because on so many occasions it has got itself trapped in theoretical dead-ends. We also deny that we are dogmatists and accept the need to constantly reassess the marxist tradition, but we don't accept, for example, that the only way to have a "dialogue with feminist currents" is from a Lacanian position. It is a pity if the attempt to open out *Screen* to a wider range of contents is accompanied by an unchanged attitude which portrays all external criticism as unworthy of attention.

Notes

1. This is a revised version of a paper written early in 1978 for the conference of the British Sociological Association on the Sociology of Culture. We would like to thank the other contributors to this book as well as Les Levidow and Bob Young for comments on the earlier draft. Special thanks to Sharon Fryer and, especially, Sharon Williams for deciphering the manuscript and typing it. In this rewrite we have taken into account some of the recent developments in *Screen*, up to the current issue (Spring 1979), although we don't believe these changes significantly affect our evaluation of *Screen*. We have modified and restructured much of the paper, but not as extensively as we would have liked if we had more time and energy to devote to the Sisyphean task of keeping up with all the twists and turns of *Screen*. Kevin Robins has published a short article, "Althusserian Marxism and Media Studies: the case of *Screen*", in *Media, Culture and Society*, 1, *4*, 1979, which covers some of the points raised in this essay.
2. To keep footnotes to a manageable number we will give references to *Screen* in this form in the text.
3. L. Althusser, *Reading Capital* (London, NLB, 1970) p. 97.
4. Cf. L. Althusser, *Lenin and Philosophy and Other Essays* (London, NLB, 1971) pp. 129-31.
5. M. Wirth, "Towards a Critique of the Theory of State Monopoly Capitalism", *Economy and Society*, 6, *3*, 1977, p. 313n.
6. L. Colletti, "Marxism and the Dialectic", *New Left Review*, 93, 1975, p. 28.
7. G. Lukács, *History and Class Consciousness* (London, Merlin, 1971), p. 27.
8. L. Colletti, *From Rousseau to Lenin* (London, NLB, 1972), p. 65.
9. G. Lukács, op. cit., p. 28.
10. E. P. Thompson, *The Poverty of Theory* (London, Merlin, 1978), p. 288. Some Althusserians concede the enormous difficulties involved in viewing societies as a series of levels. Laurence Harris has made the astonishing admission that a decade after Althusser formulated the concepts of "determination in the last instance" and "relative autonomy": "it is clear that no writers have actually been able to use the concepts in such a way as to adequately theorise the links between different spheres." Yet he is only able to suggest that we should "carry on the required work on the development of the

concepts." L. Harris, "The Science of the Economy", *Economy and Society*, 7, *3*, 1978, p. 296.
11. L. Colletti, op. cit., p. 78.
12. Cf. I. I. Rubin, *Essays on Marx's Theory of Value* (Detroit, Black and Red, 1972), esp. pp. 37 ff.
13. K. Marx, *Capital,* vol. 1 (Harmondsworth, Penguin, 1976), p. 168, 164, 165 (our emphasis).
14. K. Marx, ibid, p. 494n (our emphasis).
15. K. Marx, *Capital*, vol. 3 (London, Lawrence and Wishart, 1972), p. 86, p. 138; K. Marx, *Grundrisse* (Harmondsworth, Penguin, 1973), p. 247; K. Marx, *Capital*, vol. 1 (Harmondsworth, Penguin, 1976), p. 165.
16. F. Dröge, "Medien und Gesellschaftliches Bewusstsein", in D. Baake (ed.), *Kritische Medientheorien* (Munich, Juventa, 1974), p. 89.
17. Althusser's approach to class has been convincingly criticised in E. P. Thompson, op. cit., pp. 295ff.
18. H. Gerstenberger, "Fetish and Control", *CSE 1977 Conference: Papers and Abstracts* (London, CSE, 1977) p. 5. This is of course based on the argument put forward by Marx in his critique of the Hegelian theory of the state.
19. F. Dröge, op. cit., p. 91. On this theme cf. P. Bächlin, *Film als Ware* (Basel, Burg Verlag, 1945).
20. J. Hirsch, op cit., pp. 203-04.
21. M. Postone, "Necessity, Labour and Time: A Reinterpretation of the Marxian Critique of Capitalism", *Social Research,* 45, *4*, 1978, pp. 764-65.
22. This has been effectively argued at length in E. P. Thompson, op. cit. The need to examine specific historical forms has also been strongly maintained by J. Holloway and S. Picciotto, "Capital, Crisis and the State", *Capital and Class 2*, 1977, p. 85; I. I. Rubin, op. cit., pp. 32-4, p. 37, p. 91; H. Gerstenberger, "The Formation of the Bourgeois State", *Bulletin of the Conference of Socialist Economists,* 13, 1976; J. Hirsch, "Elemente einer materialistischen Staatstheorie" in C. von Braunmühl et al., *Probleme einer materialistischen Staatstheorie* (Frankfurt, Suhrkamp, 1973).
23. L. Althusser, *Lenin and Philosophy and Other Essays* (London, NLB, 1971), pp. 123-73, from which the quotations are taken.
24. A. Badiou and F. Balmès, *De l'Idéologie* (Paris, Maspéro, 1976), p. 30.
25. J. Rancière, *La Leçon d'Althusser* (Paris, Gallimard, 1974), pp. 231-32.
26. L. Colletti, "Introduction" in K. Marx, *Early Writings* (Harmondsworth, Penguin, 1975), p. 38; A. Sohn-Rethel, "Intellectual and Manual Labour", *Radical Philosophy,* 6, 1973, p. 31.
27. K. Marx, *Theories of Surplus Value,* vol. 3 (London, Lawrence and Wishart, 1972), p. 296 (our emphasis).
28. J-M. Vincent, "Introduction" in J-M. Vincent et al., *L'Etat Contemporain et le Marxisme* (Paris, Maspéro, 1975), p. 20.

29. For example, B. Hindess and P. Q. Hirst, "Letter to *Economy and Society*", *Economy and Society*, 4, 2, 1975, p. 240.
30. B. Hindess and P. Q. Hirst, op. cit., p. 234; G. Burchell, "Discourse: Terminable and Interminable", *Radical Philosophy*, 18, 1977, pp. 29-30.
31. P. Q. Hirst "Althusser and the Theory of Ideology", *Economy and Society*, 5, 4, 1976, p. 396, 410.
32. Given the space we have available in this essay, it is impossible to do full justice to *Screen*. We will not deal with its use of Russian formalism nor (in any detail) of Brecht, nor with the translations it has published from *Cahiers du Cinéma* and *Cinéthique*. We will concentrate on articles by members of the editorial board, or those close to them, which have been published in *Screen* or a few related publications such as the Edinburgh Film Festival monographs. Of course *Screen* doesn't contain a single homogeneous position (in particular the four members of the editorial board who resigned in 1976 had a significantly different position from the others). However, from our external vantage point, the differences within the present editorial board don't loom so large.
33. L. Althusser, *For Marx* (Harmondsworth, Penguin, 1969), p. 24n; L. Althusser, *Lenin and Philosophy and Other Essays* (London, NLB, 1971), p. 24.
34. J. Rancière, op. cit., p. 139.
35. C. MacCabe, "Memory, Phantasy, Identity: *Days of Hope* and the Politics of the Past", *Edinburgh Magazine*, 2, 1977, p. 16.
36. L. Althusser, *For Marx* (Harmondsworth, Penguin, 1969), p. 24; L. Althusser, *Reading Capital* (London, NLB, 1970), p. 141.
37. In particular all of the left still has much to learn from some of the ideas on forms of organisation which have developed within the women's movement, as has been convincingly argued in S. Rowbotham, L. Segal and H. Wainwright, *Beyond the Fragments* (London and Newcastle, Newcastle Socialist Centre and Islington Community Press, 1979).
38. Lotta Continua, "Who We Are" (mimeo), 1972, p. 3.
39. G. Nowell-Smith, "On the Writing of the History of the Cinema: Some Problems", *Edinburgh Magazine*, 2, 1977, p. 8.
40. The depth of MacCabe's commitment to the work of Hindess and Hirst is shown by his vehement defence of it against their critics: "The attacks on that work have generally limited themselves to accusations of academicism and idealism from a position of pious marxism which stinks of the university." C. MacCabe, "On discourse", *Economy and Society*, 8, 3, 1979, p. 304n. 1.
41. On the theory of state monopoly capitalism see M. Wirth, op. cit., and H. Gerstenberger "Theory of the State: Special Features of the Discussion in the FRG," *German Political Studies*, vol. 2 (Beverley Hills, Sage, 1976).
42. On the state as a form of the capital relation, see J. Holloway and S. Picciotto, op. cit.; and CSE State Group, *Struggle over the State* (London, CSE Books, 1979).

43. Cf. S. Heath, "Contexts", *Edinburgh Magazine* 2, 1977, pp. 38-9.
44. G. Burchell, op. cit., p. 30.
45. A. Britton, "The Ideology of *Screen*", *Movie* 26, 1979, p. 13.
46. P. Wollen, *Signs and Meanings in the Cinema* (London, Secker and Warburg/BF1, 3rd edition, 1972), p. 78. See also A. Tudor, *Theories of Film* (London, Secker and Warburg/BF1, 1974), ch. 5.
47. P. Wollen, op. cit., p. 116.
48. J. Culler, *Structuralist Poetics* (London, Routledge and Kegan Paul, 1975), p. 4, 5.
49. R. Barthes, *Mythologies* (St Albans, Paladin, 1973), p. 135.
50. G. Nowell-Smith, "Moving on from Metz", *Jump Cut* 12/13, 1976, p. 40.
51. See N. Burch, *Theory of Film Practice* (London, Secker and Warburg, 1973); N. Burch and J. Dana, "Propositions", *Afterimage* 5, 1974; and note the presence in *Screen* of the formalist writers, based at the University of Wisconsin, who have been influenced by Burch.
52. C. Kleinhans, "Swinging on Burch's Theory", *Jump Cut* 10/11, 1976, p. 64.
53. J. Kristeva, quoted by P. Lewis, "Revolutionary Semiotics", *Diacritics*, Fall 1974, p. 31.
54. Also cf. G. Nowell-Smith, op. cit., p. 41; MacCabe in *Screen*, 17, 3, p. 21; C. Johnston, "Towards a Feminist Film Practice: Some Theses", *Edinburgh Magazine*, 1, 1976, p. 58. The most sympathetic member of the *Screen* editorial board to Kristeva has been John Ellis. See "Ideology and Subjectivity", *Working Papers in Cultural Studies*, 9, 1976.
55. J. Kristeva, *Semeiotikè* (Paris, Seuil, 1969), p. 30.
56. J. Kristeva, ibid., p. 32.
57. R. Barthes, *Image-Music-Text* (Glasgow, Fontana/Collins, 1977), p. 166, 167.
58. J. Culler, op. cit., p. 19.
59. S. Heath, *Vertige du Déplacement* (Paris, Fayard, 1974), p. 73.
60. J. Culler, op. cit., p. 245.
61. E. Balibar and P. Macherey, "Sur la Littérature comme forme idéologique. Quelques hypothèses marxistes", *Littérature*, 13, 1974, p. 42.
62. S. Heath, op. cit., p. 77.
63. Indeed, as Andrew Britton points out, *Screen* is a perfect example of the way in which "once an untenable definition has been established, an inordinate and distorted significance is attached for good or ill, to instances which show the definition to be incorrect." A. Britton, op. cit., p. 21. In this way the original classification is made to appear even more valid and useful.
64. cf. G. Nowell-Smith, op. cit., p. 41.
65. B. Sichère, "Le Faux Matérialisme 'Tel Quel'", in *Marxisme-Léninisme et psychanalyse,* Cahiers Yenan 1 (Paris, Maspéro, 1975), p. 111-12.
66. S. Heath, "Film Performance", *Cine-tracts*, 2, 1977, p. 16.
67. cf. S. Heath, ibid., p. 14, "Screen Images, Film Memory",

Edinburgh Magazine, 1, 1976, p. 41; and *Screen*, 14, *3*, p. 23.

68. One example of an approach which seems to us to be extremely interesting from the (admittedly limited) knowledge we have of it is, the "practical semiotics" developed by the political radio stations in Italy, notably Radio Alice in Bologna. They have been concerned with the manipulation of the codes of language, but also with making radio into a means of communication by turning listeners into contributors, passing information on to those on demonstrations, etc. Cf. M. Morris "Eurocommunism vs Semiological Delinquency", in P. Foss and M. Morris (eds.), *Language, Sexuality and Subversion* (Darlingson, Australia, Feral, 1978). See also Collectif A/Traverso, *Radio Alice, Radio Libre* (Paris, LSC, J-P. Delarge, 1977); Franco Berardi "Bifo", *Le Ciel est enfin tombé sur la terre* (Paris, Seuil, 1978).

69. R. Coward and J. Ellis, *Language and Materialism* (London, Routledge and Kegan Paul, 1977), p. 7.

70. J. Kristeva, "The System and the Speaking Subject", *Times Literary Supplement*, 12 October 1973, p. 1249.

71. Quotations from L. Althusser, *Reading Capital* (London, NLB, 1970), p. 16n; L. Althusser, *Lenin and Philosophy and other Essays* (London, NLB, 1971), p. 42, p. 201.

72. J. Lacan, "The Insistence of the Letter in the Unconscious", in J. Ehrmann (ed.), *Structuralism* (New York, Doubleday Anchor, 1970), p. 106.

73. J. Lacan, "The Function of Language in Psychoanalysis", in A. Wilden (ed.), *The Language of The Self* (Baltimore and London: John Hopkins), 1968, p. 39.

74. R. Coward and J. Ellis, op. cit., p. 23, p. 1.

75. J. Hyppolite, "Hegel's Phenomenology and Psychoanalysis", in W. E. Steinkraus (ed.), *New Studies in Hegel's Philosophy* (New York, Holt, Rhinehart and Winston), 1971, p. 58.

76. J. Lacan, "Discours de Jacques Lacan (26 Septembre, 1953)," in *Actes du Congrès de Rome, La Psychanalyse* I, 1956, quoted from A. Wilden (ed.), op. cit., p. 123.

77. Luce Irigaray, "Women's exile", *Ideology and Consciousness* 1, 1977, p. 70.

78. *Marxisme-Léninisme et psychanalyse,* Cahier-Yenan I (Paris, Maspéro, 1975), p. 61 (B. Sichère), p. 15 (introduction).

79. It is clearly not possible to illuminate this point. It must suffice to refer readers to the following important works: Joel Kovel, "Therapy in Late Capitalism," *Telos,* 30, Winter 1976/1977; Joel Kovel, "The Marxist View of Man and Psychoanalysis", *Social Research,* 43, *2,* Summer 1976; Michael Schneider, *Neurosis and Civilisation* [in the German original this is "Neurosis and Class Struggle"!] (New York, Seabury Press, 1975); Kovel's review of Schneider, *Telos,* 27, Spring 1976.

80. Joel Kovel, "The Marxist View of Man and Psychoanalysis", *Social Research,* 43, *2,* Summer 1976, p. 221.

81. F. Jameson, "Imaginary and Symbolic in Lacan", *Yale French Studies* 55/56, 1977, pp. 385-386.

82. S. Turkle, "Contemporary French Psychoanalysis", *The Human Context,* 7, *2,* 1975, p. 339.
83. R. Coward and J. Ellis, op. cit., p. 95.
84. L. Althusser, *Lenin and Philosophy and Other Essays* (London, NLB, 1971), pp. 190, 189, 193.
85. R. Coward and J. Ellis, op. cit., p. 77.
86. S. Heath, "On Screen, In Frame: Film and Ideology", *Quarterly Review of Film Studies,* 1, *3,* August 1976, p. 255.
87. S. Heath, "Screen Images, Film Memory", *Edinburgh Magazine,* 1, 1976, p. 35.
88. Quotations in this paragraph are from S. Heath, "On Screen, In Frame: Film and Ideology," *Quarterly Review of Film Studies,* 1, *3,* August 1976, p. 261; C. Johnston, op. cit., p. 52. On the concept of suture, see also the articles by Heath, Miller and Oudart in *Screen,* 18, *4.*
89. H. Mauerhofer, "Psychology of Film Experience", *Penguin Film Review,* 8, 1949.
90. S. Heath, "*Jaws,* ideology and film theory," *Times Higher Education Supplement,* 26 March 1976, p. 11.
91. For a critique of this position, see Nicholas Garnham's article on *Screen,* in *Screen,* 20, *1.*
92. Through reception aesthetics, for example. See P. U. Hohendahl, "Introduction to Reception Aesthetics", *New German Critique,* 7, Winter 1976; and Andreas Huyssen's review of Terry Eagleton, *Clio,* 7, *2,* Winter 1978, which criticises Eagleton for seeing the question of how a reader experiences a work of art as an *a priori* matter.
93. F. Jameson, "Introduction/Prospectus: To reconsider the relationship of Marxism to utopian thought," *The Minnesota Review,* 6, Spring 1976, pp. 57-58.
94. A. Britton, op. cit., p. 6.
95. In this article we have not dealt with perhaps the most important argument that has been advanced to defend Lacanian psychoanalysis: that it helps to understand the nature of women's oppression. In Britain, it has, indeed, played an important part in theorising patriarchal society and culture. Against this, it should be borne in mind that because Lacanian theory is abstract and formal and provides a cultural anthropology, it has difficulty in intervening in everyday cultural and political issues. Any discussion of Lacanian psychoanalysis should also bear in mind that very strong arguments have been advanced against it for the way it *upholds* patriarchal values and *rationalises* women's oppression. See C. Baliteau, "La fin d'une parade misogyne: la psychanalyse lacanienne", *Les Temps Modernes,* July 1975; L. Irigarary, "Misère de la psychanalyse: de quelques considérations trop actuelles," *Critique,* 365, October 1977. We cannot accept Ros Coward's use of the connection between her Lacanian-Althusserian theory and the women's movement as a hammer to crush all possible criticism (18, *1,* p. 122).
96. A. Cutler, B. Hindess, P. Hirst and A. Hussain, "An Imaginary

Orthodoxy — A Reply to Laurence Harris", *Economy and Society,* 8, *3,* 1979, p. 341.
97. C. MacCabe, "Memory, Phantasy, Identity", op. cit., p. 16.
98. CSE State Group, op. cit., p. 19.
99. G. Ben-Tovim, "The Struggle Against Racism: Theoretical and Strategic Perspectives", *Marxism Today,* July 1978, p. 203. For an explicit statement on the connections between the *British Road* and a neo-Gramscian theory, see G. Bridges "The Communist Party and the Struggle for Hegemony," *The Socialist Register,* 1977 (London, Merlin, 1977, pp. 27-8.
100. On the relationship between Althusser and Maoism and the nature of the UJC (ML) see J. Rancière, op. cit.
101. For its political stance see Editorial, *Theoretical Practice*, 1, 1971, p. 3; on its relationship with the CFB (ML), see D. Macey and J. Taylor, *The Theoreticism of "Theoretical Practice"* (London, 1974), pp. 42-43, 58. It is also interesting to note that Ben Brewster, one of those most responsible for forming *Theoretical Practice,* resigned from the editorial board of *NLR* in 1971 because it printed an article critical of Chinese Foreign Policy over the uprising in Sri Lanka: an article which diverged from "what I regard as a marxist-leninist political and theoretical position", B. Brewster, "Communication", *NLR* 70, 1971, pp. 110-11.
102. For example see J. Ellis, op. cit., p. 207, 208, or R. Coward and J. Ellis, op. cit., p. 70.
103. For Hindess and Hirst's current position see A. Cutler, B. Hindess, P. Hirst and A. Hussain, *Marx's* Capital *and Capitalism Today* (London, Routledge and Kegan Paul, 1977-8, conclusion.)
104. For a convincing argument that the *nouvelle philosophie* has much in common with the Althusserian past of many of its principal exponents, especially with regard to the role of intellectuals and the struggle in theory, see J. Rancière, "Reply to Lévy", *Telos* 33, 1977, pp. 120-21.
105. P. Anderson, *Considerations on Western Marxism* (London, NLB, 1976).
106. K. Marx, *Grundrisse* (Harmondsworth, Penguin, 1973), p. 712. On the concept of production, see W. Suchting, "Marx on the Dialectics of Production and Consumption in the *Grundrisse*", *Social Praxis,* 3, *3/4,* 1975.
107. T. W. Adorno, "Sociology and Empirical Research", in P. Connerton (ed.), *Critical Sociology* (Harmondsworth, Penguin 1976), p. 238.
108. K. Marx, *The Poverty of Philosophy,* in K. Marx and F. Engels, *Collected Works,* vol. 6, (London, Lawrence and Wishart, 1976), pp. 164-5.

TERRY LOVELL

The Social Relations of Cultural Production:
Absent Centre of a New Discourse[1]

The influence of Althusserian and post-Althusserian marxism has been uneven throughout the social sciences and the humanities, but nowhere has its impact been greater than on the area of cultural studies, especially film and literature. The need for more systematic approaches in this interdisciplinary area had long been felt, and marxism was recognised as a potential resource. The complex of theories — Lacanian psychoanalysis, semiology, and Althusserian marxism — which were brought to bear on cultural studies in the late sixties and early seventies achieved an effective identification between itself, "theory" *per se,* and marxism. This was not done without a certain amount of intellectual intimidation, which Althusser's hostility to "empiricism" "humanism" and "historicism" encouraged. Since these terms of abuse could be applied to such a broad spectrum of approaches, *any* opposition to or questioning of the new orthodoxy could be branded as empiricist, anti-theoretical or even as anti-intellectual. Many people came to believe that if you were "for" theory and intellectual rigour, and "for" marxism, you were *therefore* "for" Althusserianism. Intellectual battle lines were drawn in simple black and white terms.

This paper was written at what looks retrospectively like the high point of the Althusserian tide in marxist cultural studies. It was written out of a sense that before any intervention could be made in marxist cultural studies from a different perspective, accounts had to be settled with the new orthodoxy. It also came from the belief that marxist theory did indeed have something to offer cultural studies which was in danger of being lost in the premature sweeping aside of almost all previous marxist interventions in this area as "humanist", "empiricist" or "historicist". In disposing so completely of earlier traditions valuable lessons were lost; for many of the errors of Lukács, the Frankfurt School, etc. were not, or not only, those identified and carefully guarded against as instances of these three cardinal sins, but errors to which the new theorists were blind and which they frequently shared with those that they dismissed. It is striking, for instance, that the new orthodoxy, in all its variants, shared with Frankfurt marxism and with Lukács a deep distrust of popular forms: and with the former, hostility to realism and the identification of the avant-garde as the chief hope for progressive or revolutionary art. Brecht had made it clear that the relationship between the popular, the realistic and the avant-garde was no simple matter. Yet Brecht was mobilised behind the new tendency in a manner which simplified that relationship and disguised the extent to which Brecht shared common ground with his adversaries, including Lukács.

Since this paper was first written, the tide has begun to turn. There is evidence of a greater diversity within the ranks of marxist cultural studies, of a willingness to put in question or even discard things that a year or two ago would have been held to be axiomatic; a willingness to explore new (and old) avenues. This being so, it might be asked why a paper written in response to an earlier, harder intellectual climate should now be published. The strongest justification is that the new openness is eclectic, hesitant and *ad hoc,* and still moves within the parameters set by the new orthodoxy. There is an even greater urgency now that accounts be settled; that the whole history of marxist cultural studies, including the Althusserian intervention, be rethought, and a viable marxist aesthetics and politics be developed. The need for systematic and rigorous work in cultural studies which lead to the upsurge of Althusserianism is no less now than it was then. *Ad hoc* eclecticism is no substitute.

Althusser's theory of ideology, together with Jacques Lacan's reinterpretation of Freud, and "semiotics" or "semiology", have, in the past decade, inspired a resurgence of work within marxist cultural studies. This complex of theories, in various permutations, combinations and varieties, has been applied to film, literature, television, education, and the whole broad spectrum of what Althusser names "the ideological state apparatus". Not surprisingly, the results of this spate of intellectual activity have been uneven in quality. At worst, a new and ill-digested vocabulary has been applied with scant regard to consistency of usage, to its appropriateness in a given context, or to clarity of expression. Such abuses are the penalty which is always and necessarily paid for any important new intellectual developments. More seriously, even the more impressive and substantial contributions to cultural studies from these sources are characterised by difficulties and ambiguities of a fundamental kind. This tendency, or rather, complex of tendencies, has dominated the field of marxist cultural studies now for a considerable period of time, without having made significant progress towards resolving, or even seriously confronting, these problems. The aim of this paper is to trace these problems to their source in the conceptual, theoretical and epistemological underpinnings of Althusser's theory of ideology.

What do we ask and expect of a marxist approach to cultural studies? First, a theory which is able to locate "cultural production" within the broader social formation of which it is a part. In particular, this requires the situating of film, literature, etc. in their relationship to and within a particular "mode of production". We should not be intimidated by fear of accusations of economic reductionism from insisting firmly that it is this socio-economic situating of cultural production which defines and is specific to the marxist approach. Althusser's principle of the relative autonomy of levels of the social formation carries with it the danger of a loss of the specificity of marxism.

Secondly, the conceptual and theoretical framework of marxist cultural studies must leave space for a characterisation of its object which recognises and gives due place to the specificity of that object. Here we need to exercise some caution. For the plea for specificity has covered the imposition of requirements upon marxist cultural studies which cannot be met without abandoning marxism. Due place must be given to the differences in materials, in manner of meaning, construction, etc. which characterise the different forms of cultural production. And in giving this due place, marxist theorists will be constrained to draw upon the results of more specialised disciplines such as psychoanalysis and linguistics. But there are two points which must be made here. First, this drawing upon the results of other disciplines is to be conducted critically and with caution. They will usually be transformed in the process. This is not because marxism claims universal applicability in every sphere of enquiry. Rather, because the disciplines concerned are usually social sciences and as such, have built into them substantive assumptions about the nature of social reality and social action, and methodological assumptions about the proper conduct of social science. Where these assumptions are fundamentally incompatible with the substantive and methodological assumptions on which marxism is predicated, then the two cannot be cobbled together, or used side by side and without modification of either. The compatibility of marxism and psychoanalysis has often been questioned. While I believe that it is necessary for marxists to come to terms with psychoanalysis, I do not think that the Lacanian variant of that theory is compatible with marxism, and likewise I believe that certain variations of modern linguistics are also premised on radically different assumptions to those of marxism. Secondly, we should be clear as to what the principle of respect for the specificity of cultural production does and does not license. In particular it does not allow us to choose between the alternatives offered us by Althusser, between "expressive totalities" and "structured totalities". Lukács and others are said to have retained a Hegelian type of "totality" which Marx himself had moved beyond. In this "expressive totality" the contradictions of the economic infrastructure, principally those which arise from the antagonistic relationship between labour and capital, are reflected in the various levels of the superstructure. In a "structured totality" the levels of the social formation are held to have "relative autonomy", so that each has its own specific contradictions and its own contribution to make to the outcome of any given historical conjuncture. But the notion of "specificity" used here is not the same as that used above in relation to film and literature. It is not my intention to defend the concepts of "reflection" and "expressive totality". But it is clear that literature, film, etc. *could* be held to be "expressions" of the contradictions of the social relations of production without necessarily denying their specificity. Their specificity *might* lie in the particular form in which these contradictions were expressed, and the particular materials and processes of meaning construction which they utilise. The argument against reflection theories confuses two things; the question of what cultural products express, and the question of their causative power in the social formation. There are four possibilities here, not two. Cultural products may be expressions of contradictions of the infrastructure *and* have causative power in the social formation; they may be independent expressions and have no causative power, etc. What film, literature, etc. express, and how their production relates to the remainder of the social formation, can only be determined by analysis. It is also possible, indeed likely, that the relationship is a variable one, different at different periods of history and according to the type of cultural production concerned.

Thirdly, marxist cultural studies must achieve the goal of all sciences, that of the production of explanatory theories, in this case of cultural production and consumption. And finally, it must go beyond explanation to provide a basis for political intervention at the points of production, consumption and distribution.

I will argue that several of these requirements of marxist cultural studies are not and cannot be met within the confines of Althusser's theory of ideology.

In developing his theories of knowledge and ideology, Althusser wanted to shift away from the model of a real world of social relations reflected in a mirror world of knowledge and ideology.

Therefore he redefined the latter as *part* of the social world, practices in their own right with definite products and definite effects on the rest of the social formation. However, to draw attention to the mode of existence of knowledge and ideology as practices with real effects is not to dispose of the question of the epistemological status of the products of those practices vis-à-vis their objects of reference. "Reflection" and "production" are not mutually exclusive alternatives. The question whether ideas are adequate in relation to their objects of reference is independent of the question of their material effects. And indeed Althusser never abandons the question of adequacy in relation to the practice of knowledge production. A large part of *For Marx* and *Reading Capital* is addressed to the question of the relationship between knowledge and its object. The fact that he fails to provide an adequate account of this relationship, and that he cannot do so within the terms of his theory of knowledge,[2] need not concern us here. In the case of "ideological practice" Althusser makes a more persistent attempt to transform ideology from a body of ideas which stand in some relationship of (in)adequacy to their objects, into a material practice with real effects. Yet the connection which links ideology to epistemological inadequacy dies hard, and traces of the concept of "false consciousness" remain perhaps in Althusser's "misrecognition". Ideology is, for Althusser, closely bound to the concept of the "subject" and of "consciousness". But his theory of the constitution of the subject in and through ideology, entails that any "recognition" by a subject of his/her position within, or relationship to, the social relations of the social formation, is necessarily *mis*-recognition. It is difficult to avoid the implication here of some kind of epistemological inadequacy, something very like false consciousness.

Paul Hirst, in his critiques of Althusser, attempts a more consistent development of Althusser's theory of ideology, by interpreting it as neither true nor false — not an epistemological category at all. He argues that "Ideology is not illusory... it's not falsity, because how can something which has effects be false? It would be like saying a black pudding or a steamroller is false".[3] Hirst uses the manifest absurdity of calling black pudding false to imply that to call *anything* false which, like black pudding, has real effects, would be to commit a comparable solecism. But black pudding is inappropriately labelled "false" not because it has real effects (like causing indigestion), but because it is not a proposition and does not entail any propositions. Ideology is indeed embodied in practice, and it is, in its most effective forms, "lived". But even where it is most deeply embedded in real social relations, it retains a close relationship to its own propositional forms. In whatever other manner ideology exists, it also exists as a body of ideas, and the question of the adequacy or inadequacy of those ideas to their objects is the major line of demarcation, the justification for, the distinction between ideology and science. Ideology has traditionally designated socially motivated falsity. I would contend that this tradition is useful, and that moreover both Althusser and the post-Althusserians continue to draw, covertly, upon this traditional meaning. But to do so covertly rather than overtly is to escape, in any given instance, the necessity to provide any justification or criterion for the designation of ideas as ideological. It also makes it very much easier to protect the concept of "theoretical practice" from too close scrutiny. None of the criteria offered by Althusser to characterise the theoretical practice of science is adequate to distinguish that practice from that of the production of theoretical ideologies.

It is in his attempt to specify the nature of "ideological practice" that Althusser has had most influence on cultural studies. He distinguishes between "particular ideologies" and "ideology in general". Particular ideologies are expressions of class positions, which "depend in the last resort on the history of social formations and thus of the modes of production combined in social formations, and of the class struggles which develop in them".[4] Ideology in general is, by contrast, free of historical determination. Like the unconscious which structures it, ideology is eternal, ahistorical. Somewhat cryptically, Althusser defines ideology in general as "a 'representation' of the imaginary relationship of individuals to their real conditions of existence".[5] It is in respect of his concept of ideology in general that Althusser's work on ideology departs most radically from previous marxist traditions, and hence is most original. It is also, unfortunately, most problematic.

Althusser identifies Marx's "break" with humanism as the turning point in the development of the marxist problematic. He sees pre-marxist humanism (including that of the early Marx) as rooted in the subject-object dialectic which has dominated western thought since Descartes. This takes its given point of departure in the constituting individual subject, the cartesian ego which creates the social world and reconstitutes it in knowledge. One of Althusser's chief concerns is to place this ego in question, to make it problematic, and to transform it from a constituting subject to a constituted object. For Althusser, the subject is the product of a particular practice. The production of subjects is the work of ideology. The ego, being thus transformed into an object or product, cannot go on performing its role of guarantor of knowledge. The individuals who people Althusser's social world are subject *to* it rather than constitutive *of* it. They do not make history. Subjects are merely the necessary "supports" for a world they had no hand in making. The social role of ideology is the constitution of subject-supports of the right kind, in the space allotted them in a pre-given structure of social relations.

This work of constitution takes place first of all within the family. It is here that Althusser draws upon the work of Lacan. In the course of this borrowing he simplifies and distorts Lacan, but there is no need to document that process here.[6] What Althusserian marxism shares with Lacanian psychoanalysis and with semiology is its displacement of the subject from the centre of the human sciences. Hence the significance of Althusser's claim that Marx broke decisively with humanism. Freud, it is claimed, revealed in his study of the unconscious the fractured, multifaceted and contradictory nature of the self, in stark contrast to the controlled and controlling ego of rationalism and empiricism and of everyday experience. Lacan drew upon Freud's account of the oedipal drama, identifying its processes as the condition of the human infant's entry into language and into society. This process is also that which constitutes the child as subject. The experiencing subject is formed in the "imaginary" mode. It recognises itself in the image of another. Or rather, misrecognises itself. For the other through which the self is identified is an idealised other, unified and in command of itself and its environment. This necessary misrecognition through which the child becomes his or her self, is the bedrock of ideology, consciousness, action and experience. It is because of this suspect origin of experience in ideological misrecognition that it can have no part to play in knowledge construction. Hence Althusser's implacable hostility to all forms of empiricism, and hence also his attempt to provide an account of knowledge production in which the subject has no part. This creates problems not only for Althusser's theory of science, but also for his account of political practice, as we shall see.

Before returning to these problems, I want briefly to indicate some ways in which Althusser's theory of ideology has informed recent developments in cultural studies. While Althusser himself equivocates about the place of "authentic art"[7] in the structure of the social formation — he recognises that it is not knowledge, but can't quite bring himself to place it within ideological practice either — it is within the framework of the theory of ideology that Althusser has been influential in cultural studies. The most striking result of this influence has been the hostility of marxist cultural studies to all forms of realism. This follows directly from

Althusser's analysis of ideological production. For if the role of ideology is to produce (mis)recognition of the individual's relationship to the social relations in which he/she participates, then any cultural artefact which stakes its claim to significance upon its ability to reveal that relationship in a recognisable form, is by that token actually revealing *itself* as ideology in action. Just as all self-recognition by the experiencing subject is based on the misrecognition of the imaginary, so all representation of the real necessarily misrepresents. But this is the whole point of realist art. Its product is, precisely, the "recognition" by the subject it (re)constitutes, its readers and viewers, that this is indeed the way things are, this is indeed me, and this is indeed my relationship to the way that things are. The scope of the concept of realism as it is used here should be emphasised. Colin MacCabe[8] identifies "realism" in certain mechanisms which generate this "recognition effect", which is the effect of ideological production. These mechanisms are, first, certain "discursive practices" common to all "realist texts". Such texts, we are told, contain a hierarchy of "discourses" at the apex of which is one which is privileged, and which purports "adequacy to the real". Against this touchstone we are invited to judge the remaining "discourses" of the hierarchy. The text produces the ideological effect when its reader, or, in the case of film, the viewer, recognises and assents to the "truth" which is represented. Through this misrecognition the dominant social relations of production are naturalised and validated as necessary and inevitable. Secondly, as part of "ideological practice" cultural production is engaged in the process of constituting subjects. Of course, viewers and audiences do not come to the text as Lacanian "hommelettes" but as already constituted individual subjects. However the process of constituting subjects is not a once and for all process, completed when the oedipal complex is successfully resolved. The fragmentary and contradictory self is always in question, always available for temporary or permenant reconstitution. The literary or filmic text plays its part in constituting the subject by inscribing the viewer/reader within the text itself. The "classic realist text" provides a place which the viewer/reader must occupy if he/she is to enter into the fiction, and be entertained. And it is from this proffered position that (mis)recognition takes place and the ideological effect is produced.

The Althusserian approach to cultural production generates a dilemma for producers of film, literature, etc. He/she is constrained, on penalty of non-communication, to use the available repertoire of "signifying practices" which is familiar to the audience/reader. But these are the very signifying practices which generate "the ideological effect". The producer who wishes to engage in revolutionary struggle on the front of cultural production must find some way of escaping this dilemma. One way to do this is by displaying the text as *work*, instead of as mirror to reality. This is done by drawing attention within the text to the text's signifying practices. Where the "classic realist text" disguises its processes of production, the "revolutionary" text displays them, and demonstrates the production of the ideological effect, thus alerting the reader/viewer to the ways in which they are manipulated. This has the curious effect that the "revolutionary text" is always in a sense about itself, about the process of signification. Indeed it seems that the reality of signification is the one privileged exception to the rule that the structures of the imagination cannot reveal the real. Texts can tell the truth about their own construction where all other revelations are closed to them. Where the "classic realist text" is closed, allowing to the reader only the position within which he/she is inscribed, the "revolutionary text" is open. The reader is forced from passivity as a consumer of pre-given meanings, into being active co-producer, for there is no longer a privileged discourse to guide them.

The concept of realism which is in play here is, as I have said, extremely broad — so broad, I would argue, as to be useless. *All* texts, more or less, belong within it. For no text is authorless, however scrupulous we are in remembering to place its author's name in inverted commas. And all texts place limits upon the position from which they may be read. Conversely, no text ever succeeds in achieving complete closure, so that it can be read in one and only one way, as MacCabe himself now acknowledges.[9] A truly "open" text in the sense used here would, however, be a text which said nothing; an achievement which might reasonably be considered as harmless rather than revolutionary. As any course in elementary logic will show, a condition of saying anything is that you don't say everything, i.e. some possibilities are excluded.

In fact, the difference between text and text is not the difference between openness and closure, but between those which yield up their "dominant discourse" and their manner of inscribing the subject more or less readily. Certainly the texts of neither Brecht nor Godard are open.[10] But while a category which is so comprehensively inclusive is of no analytical value, it does have certain distinct effects. The texts which are relatively less yielding of their "dominant discourse" are those which are experimental. Those which are more yielding are those with whose conventions we are more familiar, and which are therefore easier to read. This category necessarily includes all popular forms. The most damaging effect of Althusserianism on marxist cultural studies has been a negative attitude towards all art which is easy to read and demands little work, because its form is familiar. The avant-garde, not notable, despite Brecht's cautious optimism, for its working-class appeal,[11] is identified as the most promising source of "progressive" or "revolutionary" art. If only what is familiar is popular, and if what is familiar falls almost by definition under the category of "realism", i.e. the category of bourgeois ideological forms, then it follows that popular forms will be automatically discounted for purposes of ideological resistance.

The dilemma which Althusser's theory of ideology has led to in cultural studies and cultural politics lies in the two equally problematic strategies which it licenses. On the one hand a defensive "unmasking" of the materials enjoyed by and accessible to the working class. This dismissal is qualified only to the extent that the text is marred by disruptions, "cracks" and "fissures" through which the text exposes itself for what it really is — ideological production. On the other hand, a positive reappraisal is made of the avant-garde, exclusive preserve of an intellectual and privileged élite, thoroughly encapsulated within existing social relations. For if popular forms reproduce social relations by naturalising them, the avant-garde serves the same function through different means. As the Althusserians Macherey and Balibar write, "The production of the literary ideological effect in the discourse of *literature* (not the debased language of the dominated) reaffirms their inferiority. Therefore the effects are felt not only by those who effectively practise literature but also among those who ignore it."[12] How is it possible to produce "revolutionary texts" within a language and discourse in which only the dominant have any facility? If these two strategies between them map out the boundaries of the class struggle in cultural production, that struggle is already lost. It must be conducted on more favourable terrain.

Introducing the concept of "class struggle" raises a further question which must be addressed to Althusserian marxism. A class in struggle is a class *subject,* a "we" who struggle. While Althusser theorises a constitut*ed* individual subject, his theory leaves no more room for a constitut*ing* collective subject than it does for the constituting ego. The work of ideology was seen to be that of producing a subject "who freely accepts his [sic] subjection."[13] The constituting ideological production is itself authorless, specifically not the product of subjects. Who or what, then, is to struggle in this class struggle which is so freely evoked? Again, Hirst performs his valuable *reductio ad absurdum*. "The subject lives 'as if' it were a subject, and through the 'as if', it really does have a determinate effect."[14] The real effects, it should be noted, cannot be those which the subjects intend, for in that case they would be real subjects and not just "as if" subjects. The absurdity is most readily apparent when this proposition is put in the form of an imperative, addressed to the working class. "My analysis shows you that you are not real, but only 'as if' subjects. Nevertheless you must participate to the full in the class struggle, as though the 'as if' were real, and you really could hope to be the authors of history. Rest assured that your struggles will have real effects, although not the effects for which you are struggling." A less compelling call to arms can scarcely be imagined. Moreover it is not just the working class who are duped by the "as if". Althusser, and Hirst and Hindess, are compelled to make an exception for themselves — the educators who after all, it seems, stand in no need of education, and who are privileged through theoretically informed political practice to bring the blind, directionless processes of history under control and direction. Either there are *no* constituting subjects, individual or collective, and we may as well let history and the class struggle take their course. Or there are real possibilities of conscious intervention through organised political action. If the latter is the case, as it must be for marxists, then this action and its actors must be *theorised,* rather than invoked in rhetoric in service of a theory in which they have no place.

For Marx the subject of history is the class struggle, and the subjects of that struggle are organised social classes. Political activity is activity whose goal is to bring class power under conscious direction, so that class interests and political goals are served. Such activity makes no sense unless subjects exist which are constituting as well as constituted. It cannot be conducted by the subject-puppets of the "as if". For Marx, these class subjects are a function of the dominant social relations of production, in this case, the relationship between labour and capital. It is true that Marx gives us no adequate account of the manner of the constitution of the individual human subject. It has been argued[15] that this is for the good and simple reason that he does not need one for the purposes of his theory. But if this is an "absence" in Marx, then any attempt to fill it must at least meet the requirement that it be compatible with Marx's own account of the constitution of the *class* subject, and its role in struggle, The account proposed by Althusser, adapted from Lacan, does not meet this minimal requirement. The constitution of the individual subject as described by Lacan is achieved with no reference from start to finish to social class. It is quasi-universal, identical for all individuals within capitalism and indeed beyond capitalism. It has no history. It is differentiated only along lines of sex. This sexual differentiation is, it is true, crucially important, and is one very good reason for the interest which feminists have taken in Lacan, and the sense that we have that Marx's theory of the class subject leaves out something which cannot be ignored, nor inserted within space of his theory through minor adjustments. But to trade a constituted and constituting class subject which has no sex, for a constituted individual subject which is sexed but has neither class nor constituting power, yields a very dubious gain. On the one hand, recognition by marxists of the family as problematic, and careful scrutiny of its processes, is long overdue. On the other, an account of sexed identity which locates the constitution of women in processes so massively concentrated in the first few years of life, more or less completed with the resolution of the oedipus complex, is to place women and their politics under a crippling burden of determination in an epoch of their lives in which they have the least possibility of control and change. Lacan's theory of the subject is in my view a deeply pessimistic one for the women's movement. It leaves women struggling within the "I" of individual sexed identity, and is as unable to give an account of the generation of the "we" of the women's movement as it is of the "we" of the class struggle.

Marx's theory of social formations requires and posits a class subject, then, subject of the class struggle and not just subject *to* the determinations of the social formation. If the very constitution of the class subject were to take place in and by the dominant ideology (for "ideology in general" — the constitution of subjects — takes place only through particular ideologies), then the subject's very experience of the world would occur within terms and identities which undermine its struggles at source. *Ad hoc* attempts have been made to escape this monistic view of ideological determination. Althusser in some of his later writings, from *Lenin and Philosophy* onwards, attempts to give more adequate space to class struggle, class experience, and "competing ideologies". Yet it should be noted that it is in this same work that he spells out his theory of "ideology in general",[16] in which the problem is most acute. As long as ideology in general is specified in terms which have no reference to or place for the struggle between labour and capital, then that struggle cannot structure the relationship between particular ideologies either. It will always appear as secondary, superimposed on more fundamental, timeless struggles between sexes and generations, in the course of which the human infant becomes a person. If there is to be room later for the class struggle between competing ideologies, then that struggle must already be "present in its effects" at the moment of constitution of the subject, later destined to participate in those struggles. And indeed those effects *are* present in the arena in which those processes occur — the family. The family is not a separate level of an articulated social formation existing outside of but in relationship to the dominant mode of production. The individual is not constituted as a subject within a timeless and classless oedipal conflict, nor does the individual acquire his/her class identity only upon entry to the labour market and economic production. The antagonistic relation between labour and capital is already present in *capitalist* family forms. Within the family the chief differentia are those of sex and generation. But the family within which these differentials are so constituted by the processes which Freud tried to describe, is always a historically specific form of the family, fundamentally affected already by its place within a particular mode of production. Family members acquire a class identity which they share across the antagonisms of sex and generation. Their sex certainly places them in different relationships to their class, and this difference has been unpardonably neglected in marxist theory. Just as sex differences and antagonisms carry on into class relations and class struggles, so class antagonisms and differences inform sexual differences and antagonisms. Yet this class difference is entirely absent from the Lacanian analysis of the family which Althusser has so uncritically appropriated. When we speak of "the family", "the state", "ideology", etc. we are not speaking of semi-autonomous or fully autonomous[17] "levels" of a social formation of which the mode of production is simply another, rather more privileged level. To do so is, paradoxically, to engage in an economistic reduction of the mode of production. Rather, the familial political and ideological forms of capitalism are forms of the social relations of the capitalist mode of production.[18] They are part of the mode of production, not something external to, but articulated with it. The fact that those social relations are antagonistic means that the class struggle does not have to be sneaked in through the back door, or superimposed upon more fundamental antagonisms. It is present in its own right throughout.

The consequences of this theory of "ideology in general" for cultural analysis can be seen in a narrowing down of the meanings and effects of films and literature to psychoanalytic concepts and processes. Now films, novels, etc. are polysemic, and in most cultural products the processes of the unconscious will constitute one important layer of meaning. But to appropriate cultural production *per se* to a mirror image of those processes, using identical mechanisms such as displacement and condensation, is to deny the fundamental importance of class antagonisms and class identities, which surely find their own layers of meaning in cultural products. They are not simply avatars of the primary processes. The gaze of Lincoln cannot be *reduced* to the castrating stare of the patriarch.[19] These kinds of interpretations are the inevitable outcome of an apolitical and asocial theory of the constitution of the subject and his/her entry into society. The relationship between labour and capital is not a re-enactment of the relationship between father and son. This kind of reductionism is no better than the economic reductionism it hopes to displace.

The above can be construed as a plea for a theory of the constitution of the subject which does not thereby reduce that subject to an object and incapacitate it for any constituting role through political struggle. I now want to return to Althusser's discussion of one particular kind of practice, whose product is knowledge, to show how his account of this practice is vitiated by the evacuation of the concept of the subject.

For Althusser, the empiricist fallacy lies in the belief that knowledge is "inscribed" in the world, and can therefore be extracted from that world through a process of abstraction from the experiences of a subject. To avoid this "fallacy" he produces, as we have seen, a theory of knowledge which eliminates experience altogether from the practice of knowledge construction, relegating it to the inferior realm of ideology. Experience becomes the product of ideological practice, rather than of social reality. It cannot therefore provide any guide to social reality. Practical activity in and on the world is also firmly relegated in the same manner. "There is no practice," states Althusser, "except by and in an ideology."[20] Yet the belief that knowledge is a function of the unity of theory and practice is fundamental to marxism. Marxism relates theory to the world not through the distanced and "objective" contemplation of empiricism, but through the practical activity of the partisan activity in and on the world, which changes it. The kind of practical activity in which people engage will depend upon their position within the structure of social relations, the manner and extent of political mobilisation, and the level of consciousness. It is in this sense that marxism generates a "sociology of knowledge" in which experience and consciousness, as well as theory, have a vital role to play. This is not to claim that marxism is a form of empiricism, or that Marx saw experience as anything but an equivocal and treacherous guide to social reality. The "truths" which are (mis)recognised in ideology depend upon what "everyone knows" — certain common experiences to which those truths draw attention for their validation, and from which they draw "obvious" conclusions. Those which interested Marx were the "truths" of the market place — "this sphere... a very Eden of the innate rights of man. There alone rule freedom, Equality, Property and Bentham."[21] The "truths" denied or ignored by political economy are not generated by theory alone, but are those which find their validation, the necessary answering recognition, in yet other experiences and practical activities. Many of the truths of the market place make very little sense of the experiences of production, and common sense is as full of truisms which are in contradiction with the dominant ideology as those which confirm it. Gramsci, to whom Althusser's theory of particular ideologies owes a great deal, is careful to avoid either a populist celebration of common sense, or an elitist condemnation. He distinguishes between "common sense" and "good sense", and recognises the characteristic disunity and contradictoriness of the former. The latter he describes as "the healthy nucleus that exists in 'common sense'... and which deserves to be made more unitary and coherent."[22] The fact that the nature of production, and of sexuality and sexual domination, is obscured by political economy and patriarchal ideology respectively, does not mean that those relations are "lived" and experienced only within the terms of those ideologies. They are also lived in the terms of "good sense" — in contradictory and sometimes incoherent ways which escape the categories of the dominant ideology. They are expressed in the wordless recognition of a glance or laugh exchanged, for instance between women in occasional acknowledgement of the disparity between ideology and experience. These other terms in which social relations are "lived" outside of the dominant ideology can be brought to the status of knowledge, "given the unity and coherence they deserve", only when they inform and are transformed by, systematic theory. The development of such theory in turn depends on collective organisation and political activity around the practices which originally gave rise to that "good sense".

It might be thought that since Althusser conceives of knowledge as a practice, then he is explicitly giving practical activity a vital role in knowledge production. So he is. But the "practical activity" which he finds relevant to knowledge construction is not what most marxists have in mind when they speak of the union of theory and practice. They include only those practices traditionally recognised as part of the knowledge process — theory construction (which itself becomes a specific practice), the development and testing of concepts, etc. The practices of other levels of the social formation are excluded, *even where the theory in question is a theory of those levels*. It is no exaggeration to say that Althusser's theory of knowledge production entails that the experiences of practical political activity are quite irrelevant to the task of constructing an adequate theory of the political. It is true that Althusser draws back from this implication in *Lenin and Philosophy,* and returns to orthodoxy through repeated eulogies of the wisdom of the working class in its struggles. But these revisions are nowhere worked back into the body of his theory, and the theory as it stands has no place for them.

The "truths" of marxism might just as well be falsities if they find no answering recognition in experience, and a theory of knowledge which eliminates experience altogether deprives theory of any political role. A close relationship to practical activity and experience is an absolute condition of any theory "coming into its own in action."[23]

A fundamental premise, then, of any marxist theory has to be that there are key areas of experience generating activity which are and have to be suppressed or distorted within the dominant ideology. While that suppression makes it difficult to give a name to those experiences and to understand their significance, yet they are essential to the production of knowledge. The point may be underlined by a different example. Female sexuality is largely subsumed, in ideological representation, under male orgiastic pleasure, in intercourse and simultaneous orgasm. This myth is incredibly persistent, in the face of a large weight of empirical evidence that many women never experience orgasm in intercourse; in the face of the plain facts of female anatomy which make it pretty obvious why this is so, and in the face of knowledge of female masturbation and its importance in the development of female sexuality. The myth is continued in much of the literature of "liberated" women, as well as in more reactionary sources. School textbooks on sex education are, perhaps not surprisingly, the worst offenders. The clitoris is literally missing from a number of those which are still in use today, and it is staggering how many young girls do not know that they have one.[24] More surprisingly, genuine attempts to produce more adequate sexual knowledge, which are frank and open about masturbation, slip back into the comfortable myth when it comes to describing "real" sex — thus in an otherwise excellent booklet we are told, "If it is a boy and girl making love, the boy can put his erect penis into the girl's vagina. One or both of the lovers move so that the penis slides backwards and forwards in the vagina. Strong feelings of physical pleasure build up until orgasm is reached."[25] One might ask "whose orgasm?", and set this idyllic scene against a "reality" which large numbers of women must recognise with a smile: "Yes, I always fake orgasms. It just seems polite. Why be rude?"[26] These women for whom experience does not quite live up to promise are, of course, offered an implicit fallback position which explains this failure. They are frigid (even if they have multiple orgasms through masturbation). And as long as they are trapped within the "I" of individual experience they are unable to give this label the lie. It is only with other women, and with the development of the "we" that this mismatch between experience and theory may be exposed, and a more adequate theory developed.

A radical theory which challenges existing orthodoxy must involve the process of recognition, or recovery of experience. If recognition is spurned as the mark of ideology, then science is stripped of its effectiveness. The importance of ideological struggle is threefold. It is a struggle to prevent the appropriation of the experience of the oppressed to the categories of bourgeois ideology; to articulate and draw attention to those experiences, wishes, hopes and aspirations which are generated in social relations but cannot be accommodated to the categories of bourgeois ideology or met by capitalism; and above all, to keep alive the hope and belief that social relations can be changed so that those aspirations can be met. In the course of ideological struggle, powerful emotional and aesthetic pleasures and commitments may be mobilised. This is why bourgeois ideology is not best opposed by "marxist science" alone, and why the mass media are such an important site of struggle.

The problem which Althusser and his followers are attempting to solve in their development of the theory of ideology is one which has plagued marxism since its inception. It has oscillated between allowing the realm of ideology too much and too little autonomy. Too much, when it is theorised as a separate realm, an independent level of the social formation with its own history, in some kind of articulation with an equally independent "mode of production" identified as "the economic" level, too little when it is reduced to an epiphenomenal reflex of some contradiction within the economy. The first error consists of treating the phenomenal forms of capitalism as though they were what they appeared to be — independent and autonomous practices each with their own "conditions of existence" in the other practices of the social formation, and each with its own specific "effectivity" in relation to the others, in the manner of Weberian sociology.[27] The second sees these phenomenal forms as *mere* appearances. Yet in his discussion of commodity fetishism Marx argues that under capitalism social relations do not merely take on the *appearance* of a social relationship between things, *they actually exist in that fetishised form*. Those theories which take the forms at face value, see the forms, but do not explain what it is that they are forms *of,* and why the social relations of production should take those particular forms that they have under capitalism. The

Althusserian tendency, especially as further developed by Hindess and Hirst, falls headlong into the first error in its anxiety to avoid the second. Both errors are real, and both must be avoided. It might be thought that the argument that the family, ideology, the state, etc, are not independent levels, but are familial, ideological and political *forms* of the social relations of capitalist production, is simply a more sophisticated formulation of the old reductionism. Certainly, in itself it solves no problems and offers no explanations; general formulations never do. But they redirect substantive work differently, have different heuristic value. Stress must be placed on the fact that the forms are forms of the *social* relations of production, not the epiphenomena of some narrowly defined economic practice.

Ideas and ideologies are generated in practical activity, as well as through theoretical elaborations. With the division of labour between mental and manual forms, the elaboration of ideas and ideologies becomes the work of specialists, and they may become relatively detached from their origin in practical activity. Not all ideas are equally involved on a day to day basis in ideological struggle. Ideas are fully ideological in the sense used here when they are distortions which are motivated in relation to class structure and class interest, and when they are *mobilised in the class struggle*. As they become (relatively) detached from their source, they may, like Gramsci's traditional intellectuals, become in appearance and to some extent in fact, "relatively autonomous". But unlike Althusser's relative autonomy, this is an autonomy which is relative to their ineffectiveness, their lack of engagement in, lack of effect upon, the class struggle. This formulation allows theology for instance its own history, articulated significantly with the history of social relations of production only at certain key points. We are not compelled to engage in the search for "real" economic motives behind every theological dispute, in the manner which has brought "vulgar marxism" into disrepute. Yet such disputes cannot be dismissed either as of mere scholastic interest. For they are potent sources of an "ideological reserve army" which may be drawn into combat when the troops in the front line have exhausted their usefulness. This "mobilisation effect" is of critical importance. It is the reason why Brecht refused to *dismiss* the avant-garde, and recognised its importance for the development of socialist art. He argued that we must be tolerant of experiments which seem of no immediate interest from a class perspective, and whose unfamiliarity may be alienating to a mass audience.[28] Yet it goes without saying that the bourgeoisie will have its avant-garde also. Novelty alone does not guarantee ideological credentials, and the monopoly of the intellectual elite of the bourgeoisie of higher education and of intellectual and artistic production makes experimental art more the property of the bourgeoisie than of the masses.

How and whether political mobilisation of cultural innovations takes place depends partly on the origins of those innovations. At the very least, their use is constrained by their source. Thus Christianity had greater potential for political mobilisation in popular millennial movements than other world religions because of its origin as a "religion of the oppressed", and elements of its subversive radicalism survived its transformation into an imperial religion, to fuel the bourgeoisie in its moment of revolution, as well as the uprisings of peasants and workers in innumerable millennial movements in medieval Europe.

We have seen that Althusser's theory of ideology aimed at a decisive shift from the concept of reflection to that of production. Ideology was no longer to be seen as the reflection in some non-material realm of the real social relations of the economic infrastructure, but as a real, material practice, with a real product and a real effectivity. All of which is unexceptionable, with the reservations noted above, that "reflection" and "production" in this context are not necessarily contraries, and that epistemological questions to do with the relationship between ideology and its referents still remain. But it is now necessary to interrogate more closely the concept of "production" which is in play. For Althusser and his followers in cultural studies use "production" as a metaphor only, while "material" ceases to qualify "practice" or "production" once the two terms have become coextensive. Althusser uses "production" almost interchangeably with "practice". He defines "practice in general" as

> any *transformation* of a determinate given raw material into a determinate *product,* a transformation effected by determinate human labour, using determinate means (of production). In any practice thus conceived, the *determinate* moment (or element) is neither the raw materials, nor the product, but the practice in the narrow sense, the moment of *labour of transformation* itself.[29]

Ideology is one such practice, and its material base, claims Althusser, is not some other practice belonging to the social infrastructure, but its own "material" processes of production — its own "labour of transformation" of its raw materials. This shift of emphasis from reflection to production might be expected to lead to analyses of texts within the context of the forces and relations of production within which they are created. On the whole it has done nothing of the kind, but has reinforced quite traditional textual analysis. The "production" referred to is the production of "the ideological effect" within the text, and this is read off from the text alone. This narrow textualism has been complemented in the case of film by an even narrower technologism, which locates the production of the "ideological effect" in the relationship between viewer, screen and projector.[30] This technological approach short-circuits even the necessity for textual analysis, and its logical implication is that film, by virtue of its very apparatus of production and consumption, is captured irrevocably for bourgeois ideology.

The inadequacies of both of these approaches stem from the metaphorical definition of production, quoted above. For *the* key term of Marx's concept is missing — the "social relations of production". If the social relations of production exist outside of production rather than defining it, then production is reduced to "the work process".[31] The social relations of literary and film production cannot be "read off" from the text, nor from the apparatus of production and consumption, any more than the social relations of capitalism can be read off from the motor car. Investigation of production requires more than the analysis of "the labour process". Yet the particular social relations within which the production of film and literature takes place have definite consequences for their ability to generate "the ideological effect".

With the penetration of capital into cultural production, the product is transformed into a commodity. As such, literary and film production do not constitute, as Terry Eagleton would have it, distinct "modes of production".[32] They differ from capitalist production of other commodities only in the manner and extent of the penetration of capital, and in the differences between the commodities produced. Not all ideology is generated through the production and consumption of commodities. Major sectors of "ideological production" exist outside of market relations altogether, such as the school. Here I am concerned only with the transformation of cultural production into commodity production, and with the limits and constraints which that transformation places upon the use of such commodities to produce the "ideological effect".

Like all commodities, film and literature, television programmes, etc. have both use-value and value. It is because they have value (a definite quantity of "homogeneous human labour" has been expended in their production, so that they can be exchanged proportionately with other commodities of equal value) that their production can be used to create surplus-value and contribute to the accumulation of capital. The "use-value" of a commodity is a function of the uses to which it is put in consumption, and clearly the same commodity may have a number of different use-values for the same consumer, and for different consumers. Marx, in his analysis of capitalist commodity production, makes no attempt to theorise the use-values of commodities. He differentiates them only in so far as they belong to "Department 1" or "Department 2"[33] — for individual or for productive consumption. The reason for his lack of interest in commodities as use-values is similar to his lack of concern with individual human beings. Capitalist commodity production discounts the particular qualities of things and people, which give them their usefulness, because it is *per se* engaged in the production of surplus-value rather than utilities. It is indifferent to the use-value of the commodity produced, just so long as it *has* a use-value which can meet effective demand. The single commodity whose use-value Marx does analyse is the commodity labour-power. Its use-value to its capitalist purchaser is its capacity to produce more value than it itself contains. It is the contradiction between the use-value and the value of this unique commodity which provides Marx with the key to the mystery of the production of surplus-value and profits. Using this example, then, we can assume that the use-value and the value of the commodities of cultural production may also be contradictory.

Marx analyses both the dynamics and contradictions of "individual capitals", and of capitalism as a social totality. For instance there are no mechanisms at the level of individual capitals to ensure that individual capitalist commodity production matches up to social necessity, or social possibility. For instance, Marx analyses the relationship between production in Departments 1 and 2, and shows how these may be in equilibrium. But Mandel has argued that this is a limit case, and that disequilibrium is quite normal.[34] There is no guarantee that what is socially necessary for capitalism will actually be produced, nor that what is produced will be socially necessary. In other words, the social usefulness of a commodity for capitalism may be in contradiction with its value.

This argument is of direct relevance to cultural production. Frequently marxist analysis of cultural production as ideology falls into a form of functionalism. Capitalism is identified as having certain ideological "needs", and cultural production is analysed for the manner in which it meets these needs. This functionalist argument often draws tacitly upon another argument, that this function of cultural production is facilitated by the commodity form of cultural production. The penetration of cultural production by capital aids the subordination of that production to the ideological needs of capitalism. But the analysis developed above of the disjunction between social need and the commodity form indicates that this argument is invalid.

Sometimes this gap between social need and commodity production can be closed, for instance by state intervention in the commodity market, or in production. Thus the needs for armaments are met by government contracts to the arms industry. But in the case of ideology, this is not possible, for the simple reason that the ideological needs of capitalism in relation to cultural commodites are met through individual consumption. We may, however, take it as axiomatic that people do not read novels and go to the movies *in order to* consume (bourgeois) ideology and thereby meet the ideological requirements of capitalism. As with other commodities which belong to the "department" of individual consumption, they are bought and consumed for the sake of their use-value for the individual who purchases them (with occasional exceptions, such as the purchase of government war bonds out of patriotism). We have absolutely no grounds to suppose that the use-value of cultural products will be readily commensurable with the ideological needs of capitalism, and should view with great suspicion a theory which claims that, to capitalism's great good fortune, what gives the audience pleasure is the same thing which produces "the ideological effect".

It follows that in the sphere of ideological production, there is a divergence between the interests of "particular capitals" in maximising surplus-value production by producing *any* commodity, no matter how subversive, for which there is an effective demand; and the collective interests of "many capitals" to secure the ideological well-being of capitalism. Capitalism as a whole cannot remain indifferent to the use-value of commodities produced by individual capitals. But it also follows that the securing of "ideological production" becomes problematic when it is left to the agency of capitalist producers. The question of whether or not the consumption of cultural products will or will not produce "the ideological effect" cannot be determined *a priori* on the basis that those products are produced capitalistically. What is required here, and what Marx's own writing nowhere supplies, is a marxist theory of capitalist consumption. Within any such theory, use-value would have to be a central concept.

It is for these reasons that the question of "the pleasure of the text" is such an important one. The Althusserians have, it is true, raised this question, and deserve credit for having done so.[35] But they have reduced the use-value of the text to its pleasure in the narrow Freudian sense. There is no doubt that pleasures which derive from the processes which Freud analysed are at play within literary and film texts. But it would be a grave error to assume that the polysemic text can be reduced to this one layer of meaning, or that "Freudian pleasures" play neatly into the ideological requirements of capitalism. It is just as possible that they might act to cut open ideology; more likely that there are contradictory tensions here. Secondly, other sources and types of pleasure may be identified as contributing to the use-value of the text for different audiences/readers. In his important work on utopianism in entertainment,[36] Richard Dyer has begun the work of mapping out some of these. Some stem from the promises of capitalism itself, which it cannot meet. Others no doubt stem from interests and concerns which transcend capitalism, such as those discussed by Timpanaro in relation to the natural limits of human society — concern with birth, death, ageing — problems which take different forms in different social formations, but which not even the most exemplary socialism could hope to resolve.[37] The work of mapping the pleasures, use-values and functions of texts is still to be done, and what has been done already has generally been outside of marxist cultural studies.

The paradoxical effects for capitalism of the penetration of cultural production by capital are a matter of conscious concern for certain groups of people within capitalist society, outside of the point of production itself; for the ideologues and guardians of "moral standards" who swell the ranks of Gramsci's "traditional intellectuals". Every successive capitalist penetration of this kind has been followed by an outburst of "moral panic". In the eighteenth century the rise of the novel provoked widespread dismay. It was attacked for its alleged pernicious effects on weak-minded women and servants. It was universally slammed, from pulpit to review. This spectacle was repeated twice in the twentieth century over film, and then television, with regard to their feared effects upon equally weak-minded children and adolescents. (Men, it seems, safely past puberty, stand in no need of moral protection). "Effects studies" have been the meat and drink of countless media specialists in various disciplines ever since. But there has been relatively little interest in the question of how the "anarchy of capitalist production", and the various contradictions noted above attendant upon the penetration of capital in cultural production, are actually negotiated. The history of censorship within the different media should be examined from this point of view, as well as the increasing role of the state, for instance in support through such bodies as the Arts Council. The whole area of the organisation and control (or absence of control) of cultural consumption needs to be made problematic. The approach from the point of view of production has been no more able to raise such questions than was the older reflection theory.

Finally it should be reiterated that marxism yields no *a priori* or theoretical grounds for anticipating the results of ideological analysis of capitalist commodities, from films to motor cars, in the absence of a theory of the capitalist mode of consumption. The marxist theory of production indicates that capitalist commodity production cannot fail to leave space for counter-ideologies, as well as for the expression of wants and aspirations which cannot be fully articulated within bourgeois ideology, nor met by capitalism. It leaves space therefore for strategies of ideological and cultural struggle based upon workers within the mass entertainment industries and not just upon minority producers of alternative forms outside of the mainstream and outside of capitalist channels of production and consumption. Brecht, who has been widely invoked to legitimate the anti-realist thrust of the Althusserians in cultural studies, may be given the last word:

> Realistic means: discovering the causal complexes of society/ unmasking the prevailing view of things as the view of those who rule it/writing from the standpoint of the class which offers the broadest solutions for the pressing difficulties in which human society is caught/emphasising the element of development/making possible the concrete, and making possible abstraction from it. . . .
>
> It is in the interests of the people, of the broad working masses to get a faithful image of life from literature... unconditionally comprehensible and helpful to them — in other words, popular.[38]

Notes

1. This paper was written before I had the benefit of reading E. P. Thompson's essay on Althusser. It was presented in an earlier version to a film study group in Berkeley in Spring 1978, and at the Conference of Socialist Economists in the Summer. Subsequently I have been working on a much longer exploration of many of the issues of marxist aesthetics and politics which are raised here. This is due to be published as a monograph entitled *Realism and Ideology* by the British Film Institute. Because of their common origins and concerns, there is a certain amount of overlap between them.
2. For a clear account of why this is so, see Ted Benton, *Philosophical Foundations of the Three Sociologies* (London, 1977), ch. 9.
3. P. Hirst, *Problems and Advances in the Theory of Ideology* (London, Communist University, 1976), p. 16.
4. L. Althusser, *Lenin and Philosophy* (London, 1971), p. 159.
5. Ibid, p. 162.
6. For an introduction to Lacan's theory of the subject, see R. Coward and J. Ellis, *Language and Materialism* (London, 1977), ch. 6.
7. L. Althusser, op. cit.
8. C. MacCabe, "Realism and the Cinema", *Screen*, 15, 2, 1974.
9. C. MacCabe, "Principles of Realism and Pleasure", *Screen*, 17, 3, 1976.

10. A. Lovell, "A Short Organum for Epic Theatre and Counter-Cinema" (unpublished), 1979.
11. B. Brecht, "Against Georg Lukács", *New Left Review,* 84, 1974.
12. E. Balibar and P. Macherey, "Sur la Littérature Common Forme Ideologique", *Littérature* no. 13, 1974 (my translation).
13. L. Althusser, *Lenin and Philosophy*, p. 182.
14. P. Hirst, op. cit., p. 13.
15. V. Molina, "Notes on Marx and the problem of individuality", *Cultural Studies* no. 10, 1977.
16. I.e. in the essay cited above, in *Lenin and Philosophy,* "Ideology and Ideological State Apparatuses".
17. In their auto-critique, B. Hindess and P. Hirst, *Modes of Production and Social Formations* (London, Macmillan, 1976).
18. This account of the "developed forms of the social relations of production" is discussed in this volume by Simon Clarke.
19. See the interpretation offered in "John Ford's *Young Mr Lincoln*", a collective text by the editors of *Cahiers du Cinéma*, in *Screen*, 13, *3*, 1972.
20. Althusser, op. cit., p. 170.
21. K. Marx *Capital,* vol. 1 (London, 1970), p. 176.
22. A. Gramsci, *Prison Notebooks* (London, 1971), p. 328.
23. W. Benjamin.
24. *Spare Rib,* no. 75, Oct. 1978, comments "It is staggering how many teenage girls are unaware of the existence of the clitoris, or the possibility of female orgasm", p. 15.
25. George Green Community Education Project, Social Education Unit 3, 1979.
26. S. Hite,*The Hite Report* (London, Talmy Franklin Ltd, 1976).
27. Weber's massive work *Economy and Society* consists entirely of typologies. Of each type, whether of economic action, political legitimation, religion, etc., he asks two questions: "What are its conditions of existence, and what are its consequences, particularly with respect to the development of capitalism?" The similarity to the formulations of Hindess and Hirst is striking, despite their very different theories of knowledge.
28. B. Brecht, op. cit.
29. L. Althusser, *For Marx,* (London, Penguin Books, 1969), p. 166/7.
30. J-L. Baudry, "The Apparatus", *Camera Obscura,* no. 1, 1976.
31. Again, see Simon Clarke's excellent discussion of this reduction of the economic to the work process, op. cit.
32. T. Eagleton, *Criticism and Ideology* (London, 1976).
33. K. Marx, *Capital,* vol. 2, ch. 20.
34. E. Mandel, *Late Capitalism* (London, New Left Books, 1972).
35. For example, see Laura Mulvey, "Visual Pleasure and Narrative Cinema", *Screen,* 16, *3*.
36. Richard Dyer, "Entertainment and Utopia", *Movie,* 27, 1977.
37. S. Timpanaro, *On Materialism* (London, New Left Books, 1976).
38. Brecht, op. cit.